New Riders' Guide to
NetWare Certification

Dorothy Cady

New Riders Publishing, Indianapolis, Indiana

New Riders' Guide to NetWare Certification

By Dorothy Cady

Published by:
New Riders Publishing
201 West 103rd St.
Indianapolis, IN 46290 USA

Printed in the United States of America   2 3 4 5 6 7 8 9 0

Library of Congress Cataloging-in-Publication Data

```
Cady, Dorothy L., 1953-
   New Riders' guide to NetWare certification / Dorothy Cady.
      p.    cm.
   Includes index.
   ISBN 1-56205-311-6 : $19.95
   1. Operating systems (Computers)—Study and teaching.  2. NetWare
(Computer file)—Study and teaching.  3. Electronic data processing
personnel—Certification.   I. Title.  II. Title: Guide to NetWare
Certification.
QA76.76.O63C34  1994
005.7'1369—dc20                                        94-10088
                                                            CIP
```

Warning and Disclaimer

This book is designed to provide information about NetWare certification. Every effort has been made to make this book as complete and as accurate as possible, but no warranty or fitness is implied.

The information is provided on an "as is" basis. The author and New Riders Publishing shall have neither liability or responsibility to any person or entity with respect to loss or damages arising from the information contained in this book or the use of the disks or programs that may accompany it.

Publisher	Lloyd J. Short
Associate Publisher	Tim Huddleston
Managing Editor	Matthew Morrill
Acquisitions Manager	Cheri Robinson
Product Development Manager	Rob Tidrow
Marketing Manager	Ray Robinson
Acquisitions Editor	Alicia Krakovitz
Product Director	Drew Heywood
Senior Editor	Tad Ringo

Copy Editors

Sarah Kearns	Cliff Shubs
John Sleeva	Suzanne Snyder

Technical Editor	Kim Green
Acquisitions Coordinator	Stacey Beheler
Editorial Assistant	Karen Opal
Publisher's Assistant	Melissa Lynch
Imprint Manager	Juli Cook
Book Designer	Roger Morgan
Production Analysts	Dennis Clay Hager
	Mary Beth Wakefield

Production Team

Carol Bowers	Ayrika Bryant
Juli Cook	Karen Dodson
Terri Edwards	Rich Evers
Kimberly K. Hannel	Angela P. Judy
Debbie Kincaid	Stephanie J. McComb
Casey Price	Michelle M. Self
Susan Shepard	Ann Sippel

Indexer	Greg Eldred

About the Author

Dorothy Cady has more than 20 years in the computer science field, with many of those years dedicated to designing and documenting computer applications software. She started in the computer field when application programs were loaded into mainframes using punched card decks.

Ms. Cady has since moved into working with PCs and networking software. Employed by Novell, Inc. as a Senior Technical Writer, she has spent the past four years developing her expertise in Novell NetWare products. Ms. Cady is a Certified NetWare Engineer (CNE) and a Certified NetWare Instructor (CNI).

In addition to her full-time employment for Novell, Ms. Cady teaches computer science and networking classes at Utah Valley State College. She juggles her remaining time between her two children (a six-year-old son named Ray and a ten-year-old daughter named Shana), her husband, Raymond, and freelance writing projects. She is the author of *Inside Personal NetWare*, also published by New Riders Publishing.

Acknowledgments

I wish to give my thanks and voice my appreciation to three groups of people who should be acknowledged for the successful completion and delivery of this book.

Thanks go first to the hard-working and dedicated Novell education division employees who answered all of my questions whenever I called.

Second, thanks and congratulations go to the staff at New Riders Publishing whose diligence and fortitude helped to ensure that I successfully completed this book. A special thanks is owed to Drew Heywood (a dedicated and tireless friend), Tad Ringo (who makes my writing look good), and Alicia Krakovitz (who keeps me on target and on schedule).

Third, I want to add a special thanks and give my love to my husband, Raymond Cady, D.C., my son, Raymond Michael Cady III, and my daughter, Shana Michelle Cady. Without them, I am but dust in the wind.

Trademark Acknowledgments

All terms mentioned in this book that are known to be trademarks or service marks have been appropriately capitalized. New Riders Publishing cannot attest to the accuracy of this information. Use of a term in this book should not be regarded as affecting the validity of any trademark or service mark. NetWare is a registered trademark of Novell, Inc.

Contents at a Glance

Introduction   **1**

  1 Introducing the Novell Certification Programs   13

  2 Preparing To Become NetWare Certified   51

  3 Training To Become NetWare Certified   79

  4 Testing   121

  5 Becoming a Certified NetWare Instructor   153

  6 Choosing Your Certification Courses   233

    Glossary of Terms and Acronyms   293

  A Choosing Courses/Tests   305

  B Important Addresses and Numbers   309

Index   **313**

Table of Contents

Introduction   **1**

    Who Should Read This Book   2

    Why You Should Read This Book   3

    Overview   4

    What This Book Covers   5

    About Novell and Its Support Certification Programs   7

    Conventions Used in This Book   9

    Learning More about Novell NetWare   10

    Publisher's Note   11

1   Introducing the Novell Certification Programs   **13**

    The Certified NetWare Administrator (CNA) Program   14

      What Is the CNA Program?   *14*

      Why Become a CNA?   *16*

      What You Will Learn   *16*

      What Are the Certification Requirements?   *18*

      How To Begin   *18*

    The Certified NetWare Engineer (CNE) Program   20

      What Is the CNE Program?   *20*

      Why Become a CNE?   *23*

      What You Will Learn   *25*

      What Are the Certification Requirements?   *25*

      How To Begin   *27*

    The Enterprise CNE (ECNE) Program   30

      What Is the ECNE Program?   *30*

      Why Become an ECNE?   *32*

      What You Will Learn   *32*

      What Are the Certification Requirements?   *33*

      How To Begin   *34*

    The Certified NetWare Instructor (CNI) Program   35

      What Is the CNI Program?   *35*

      Why Become a CNI?   *36*

      What You Will Learn   *36*

      What Are the Certification Requirements?   *36*

      How To Begin   *37*

Using What You Learn 42
Where To Look for Employment Opportunities 44
Where To Get Networking Experience 47
Summary 49

2 Preparing To Become NetWare Certified 51

Prerequisites for Each Certification Program 51
Prerequisites for the CNA Program 52
Prerequisites for the CNE Program 55
Prerequisites for the ECNE Program 58
Prerequisites for the CNI Program 59
The Certification Process 61
For CNAs 62
For CNEs 64
For ECNEs 68
For CNIs 74
Summary 77

3 Training to Become NetWare Certified 79

Making the Most of Hands-On and Self-Study Options 80
Ways To Make the Most of Hands-On Learning 81
Techniques and Tips for Making the Most of Self Study 83
Hands-On Learning and Test Taking 88
Using CBTs and Tutorials for Maximum Effectiveness 92
An Overview of the Novell CBTs 92
An Overview of Novell Tutorials 96
What Is Available 96
Where To Find the CBTs and Tutorial 97
How the CBTs and Tutorial Work 98
Novell Certification Assessment Disk 99
Techniques and Tips for Getting
  the Most Out of CBTs and Tutorials 103
Choosing and Taking the Right Courses To
  Meet Your Certification Needs 105
Taking Courses from NAECs versus NEAPs 105
What Courses Are Available? 108
What It Costs To Take a Course 111

How Taking a Course Can Help You 112
Hints and Tips for Getting the Most Out of a Course 113
Getting More Information on Novell Courses 114
Calling Novell for Information 114
Using FaxBack 116
Summary 119

4 Testing **121**

Understanding the Testing Process 122
How the Testing Process Works 122
What Do the Tests Cost? 124
Where Are the Tests Administered? 124
Taking the Different Types of Tests 125
CNE Assessment Test 126
Adaptive Testing 130
Form (or Standard) Testing 131
Hints and Tips for Doing Your Best on the Tests 133
Answering Typical Test Questions 134
Who Prepares Test Questions? 134
How Are Test Questions Checked for Validity? 135
How Do Course Objectives and Test Questions Relate? 136
What Are Typical Test Questions Like? 137
Pretesting Yourself 139
Why and How To Create Your Own Test Questions 140
Using Your Own Test Questions To Review and Prepare 150
Where To Obtain Information on Taking the Tests 151
Summary 152

5 Becoming a Certified NetWare Instructor **153**

Preparing To Become a CNI 154
Attending a Presentation Skills Course 155
Getting Experience 156
*Completing and Submitting
Your Application and Related Documents* 163

Increasing Your Chances of Getting Accepted
  into the CNI Program   170
    Program Prerequisites   172
    Certification Requirements   173
    The Application Process   174
Understanding the IPE   176
    How the IPE Is Scored   178
    Hints from Successful CNI Candidates   179
Developing IPE-Relevant Teaching Skills   180
    Presentation Characteristics   180
    Presentation Mechanics   188
Deciding Where To Go from Here   230
Summary   230

6 Choosing Your Certification Courses   233

Selecting the Right Courses for Certification   234
    Course Options for CNAs   234
    Course Options for CNEs   237
    Course Options for ECNEs   242
    Course Options for CNIs   246
    Core/OS Product Group   249
    Advanced Product Courses Group   250
    Development Product Courses Group   252
Understanding the Course Descriptions
  and Objectives for Ten Common Certification Tests   253
    DOS/Microcomputer Concepts for NetWare Users   254
    NetWare 2.2: System Manager   258
    NetWare 2.2: Advanced System Manager   261
    NetWare 3.1x Administration   264
    NetWare 3.1x Advanced Administration   268
    NetWare 4.0 Administration   271
    NetWare 3.11 to 4.0 Update   276
    NetWare 4.0 Installation and Configuration   278
    Networking Technologies   281
    NetWare Service and Support   285

Considering Other Available NetWare Tests
and Their Descriptions   288
    Fundamentals of Internetwork and Management Design   288
    UNIX OS Fundamentals for NetWare Users   289
    NetWare 4.0 Advanced Administration   289
    NetWare Dial-in/Dial-out Connectivity   290
    LAN Workplace for DOS 4.1 Administration   290
    NetWare TCP/IP Transport   290
    NetWare NFS   291
    LANalyzer for Windows   291
Summary   292

Glossary of Terms and Acronyms   **293**

A   Choosing Courses/Tests   **305**

B   Important Addresses and Numbers   **309**

Telephone Numbers   309
Fax Numbers   310
Addresses   310

Index   **313**

Introduction

Twenty-plus years ago, few people had ever heard of the personal computer (PC). Today, small and large businesses alike use PCs to accomplish many varied tasks. In addition, many home offices and classrooms from kindergarten through professional sport PCs. PCs have become an integral part of everyday life.

It is more than just the PC itself that matters in our daily lives. It is what each of us does with the PC that really counts. People have found many ways to effectively use their PCs. Networking their PCs (connecting one or more PCs together to combine their resources) is one way many individuals and companies use their PCs to get the most out of their computers.

To share computer resources, the computers must be physically connected to each other. In addition, once the PCs are connected, they require some type of instruction on just how to go about sharing those resources. These instructions are provided by special computer programs called *networking software*.

Although there are several companies that provide networking software, Novell, Inc. is the largest of these companies, providing 70 percent or more of the networking software available throughout the United States and many other parts of the world. Novell calls its different versions of networking software *NetWare*.

Along with the benefits provided by new technology comes the need for competent, well-trained individuals to take responsibility for and properly apply this technology. Networking and NetWare are no exception. As sales of NetWare began to increase, Novell recognized the need to educate users who support NetWare. Businesses using NetWare also recognized their need to identify and hire competent NetWare networking individuals.

To fill that need, Novell has developed a series of programs known as Novell's *NetWare Certification* programs. The intent of these programs is to train and certify qualified individuals in the use and administration of Novell NetWare. There are four programs:

- ◆ Certified NetWare Administrator (CNA)
- ◆ Certified NetWare Engineer (CNE)
- ◆ Enterprise Certified NetWare Engineer (ECNE)
- ◆ Certified NetWare Instructor (CNI)

This book guides you through the process of obtaining certification in each of Novell's four certification programs. It shows you how to apply for certification, how to get the training you need, where and how to take and successfully pass the exams required for certification, and much more.

Who Should Read This Book

New Riders' Guide to NetWare Certification is intended for anyone who works with or desires to work with any of Novell's NetWare operating systems.

This book is for you if you want to upgrade your skills and your résumé with a certification from Novell, or if your job responsibilities include working with any of Novell's NetWare products as either a user or an administrator.

You should read this book if you simply want to know more about NetWare, but also if you want to pass the certification exams to show that you have become a more knowledgeable NetWare user or administrator.

This book is for you if you are already a CNE who wants to go on to become an ECNE.

In addition, you should read this book if you are or want to be an instructor or trainer—you can add the CNI certification and consequently the certified NetWare courses to your list of training skills.

Why You Should Read This Book

There are many third-party reference books, including New Riders' line of technical references, available to you that help you learn what you need to know about NetWare to pass the certification exams and be prepared to work with a Novell NetWare network. But what is commonly lacking in most reference works is detailed information about what it means to you to become NetWare certified, as well as how to go about the process and be successful at it with the least amount of effort.

New Riders' Guide to NetWare Certification tells you what it takes to become NetWare certified in any of the four available NetWare certifications. You should also read this book to become better prepared to pass your exams the first time you take them. In addition, if you want to know what you can expect to learn and do during the entire certification process, then you should read this book.

If you want to become a NetWare Certified Instructor, you should also read this book. Although many individuals seek Novell's CNA, CNE, and ECNE certifications, there are fewer individuals looking to become CNIs. Therefore, those few available books that do discuss the NetWare certification programs do not go into a great deal of information about the CNI program. This book covers the CNI program in depth, ranging from explaining the basics of the program itself to teaching you the presentation skills Novell expects you to have mastered as a CNI candidate.

Should you read this book even if you are not seeking a CNI certification? The answer is "yes." Even if you do not want to become a CNI yourself, you should read this book including the CNI portion of this book because it teaches you the following:

◆ What you can expect from those CNIs who are teaching certified NetWare courses, if and when you choose to take them

◆ How a typical Novell authorized course approaches teaching various NetWare and networking-related topics, so that if you choose not to take a course, you still have a feel for the importance of the material within a given course

◆ Aspects of courses that Novell considers important enough to have CNIs stress, so that you can give special study attention to these items as well

◆ Presentation skills that you can adapt to use as study skills to increase your own retention of information

◆ Skills you can use when you have to make management or other presentations, whether your presentations are NetWare-related or not

Overview

In this book you find answers to your questions about Novell and its certification programs. You also find out exactly what you need to know in order to pass the exams required for NetWare certification. In addition, this book gives you study hints and detailed information on taking and passing the tests on your first try. (At $85 per exam, you do not want to have to take an exam more than one time.) The book also provides detailed information about each of the certification programs so you can choose the one that is right for you.

Unlike the computer-based training (CBT) products, courses, third-party books, and Novell education books that teach people about Novell's various products and how to manage and use them, this book shows you how to obtain one or more Novell certifications. It does not teach you about NetWare. Instead, it teaches you how to learn about NetWare and how to pass the exams, earning NetWare certification in the process.

After reading this book you will know whether or not any of the Novell certification programs are right for you. You will also discover which certification program interests you the most, and how to successfully pursue that particular certification.

What This Book Covers

New Riders' Guide to NetWare Certification is divided into six chapters to give you the information you need to successfully choose, enroll in, and complete one or more of Novell's certification programs.

Chapter 1, "Introducing the Novell Certification Programs," provides you with the following:

◆ An overview of each of the certification programs

◆ Answers to the questions most commonly asked by NetWare certification candidates

Chapter 2, "Preparing To Become NetWare Certified," shows you:

◆ What you must do to obtain one or more of the NetWare certifications

◆ The prerequisites you must meet for each of the certification programs

◆ The process involved in obtaining each of the certifications

◆ The paths to certification available to you, and which paths require you to take the fewest number of exams

Chapter 3, "Training To Become NetWare Certified," shows you:

◆ The types of training available for certification (self-study, on-the-job training, CBTs or tutorials, and certified courses available from Novell Authorized Education Centers (NAECs) and Novell Education Academic Partners (NEAPs)

◆ How to obtain additional information about any of these training options

◆ Where to get the training you need

◆ How to use the FaxBack program that Novell provides to obtain the most current certification program information

◆ Tips and techniques for studying the information you need to learn so that you can successfully pass the required examinations and perform the duties of a NetWare user or administrator

Chapter 4, "Testing," shows you:

◆ What you need to know in order to pass the various certification tests

◆ How the testing process works so you will know what to expect when you take a certification test

◆ Samples of typical test questions and how those test questions relate to the course objectives, helping you to focus your studies where you need them the most

◆ How you can create your own test questions that resemble the types of questions you can expect to see on the certification exams, letting you take your own customized pretests

◆ Where you can take certification tests

◆ Basic test-taking techniques that, when applied to any test, can help you respond to those questions about which you are a little unsure

Chapter 5, "Becoming a Certified NetWare Instructor," shows you:

◆ The specific teaching skills you must acquire in order to pass the Instructor Performance Evaluation (IPE) examination that each CNI candidate must take

◆ What you can expect when you take an IPE

◆ How to get the most out of taking an IPE

◆ Some hints and tips for taking an IPE

Chapter 6, "Choosing Your Certification Courses," shows you:

◆ Which courses are currently available through Novell education outlets

◆ A brief description of each available course

◆ Which courses are most commonly taken for certification as a CNA, CNE, or ECNE

◆ The course objectives for the seven most commonly taken certification courses and/or exams

About Novell and Its Support Certification Programs

When you are responsible for supporting millions of LANs and LAN administrators, you cannot affordably hire enough staff to provide that support effectively. You can, however, do the next best thing: you can see to it that LAN administrators, major LAN users, and third-party companies are well trained to help provide some of that support. Setting up an educational organization and certification programs that ensure people are well-trained in networking is a way to accomplish this goal. This is just what Novell has done in order to meet their support needs.

Because Novell networks can be found worldwide, this support must also be provided worldwide. Therefore, Novell developed a training support network that consists of approximately 1,000 NAECs and NEAPs worldwide.

The goal of this training support network is twofold: first, to provide a high-quality education to those who want knowledge and skill with Novell's NetWare products, and second, to support Novell's mission, "to accelerate the growth of network computing."

To accomplish these goals, NAECs and NEAPs provide more than 30 different NetWare networking-related courses to approximately 200,000 students per year.

To ensure the quality of these courses and ultimately the quality of a student's NetWare networking knowledge and skills, NAECs and NEAPs must meet Novell's stringent requirements before they are allowed to teach certified NetWare courses using certified NetWare training materials.

One of the requirements that they must meet includes having qualified instructors to teach these courses. Not only must the facility, course, and course materials be certified by Novell, but so too must the instructor. Thus, Novell created the Certified NetWare Instructor (CNI) training and certification programs.

In addition, Novell makes available, to those who prefer self-study over attending standardized instructor-led courses, other alternative methods of learning NetWare such as CBT materials, reference books (published by Novell Press), workbooks designed specifically for self-study, and video-based training. In addition, Novell sponsors or supports various conferences (such as Comdex and BrainShare) and user groups such as NetWare Users International (NUI) and the Certified NetWare Engineer Professional Association (CNEPA).

For individuals who obtain most of their NetWare knowledge by working in a company that uses NetWare, Novell also provides access to NetWire on CompuServe. NetWire is an online 24-hour NetWare information service providing access to information such as Novell product descriptions and press releases, technical support, and patches and upgrades to NetWare products.

However you decide to go about obtaining your Novell NetWare knowledge, the fact that you have successfully mastered at least the minimum skills and information required to successfully work with and/or support a NetWare network is a major accomplishment. Novell recognizes the importance of that accomplishment as well. That is one reason why Novell developed its certification programs. It is not the only reason, however. The other main reason for the development of Novell's certification programs was to provide the industry as a whole with a method of recognizing individuals who are qualified to administer NetWare networks.

Novell strongly supports NetWare certification. This book supports Novell's efforts at industry standardization, recognition, and growth by showing individuals such as yourself just how to go about becoming NetWare certified.

Conventions Used in This Book

As you read through this book, you find that special formatting has been used throughout the text to help you get the most out of this book. To simplify the book's discussions when these special notes or special formatting are used, several conventions have been established.

Where appropriate, special typefaces are used as well. *Italics* are used to define terms introduced for the first time, as well as to specify names of files and directories. **Boldface** identifies user input such as information or commands you are being instructed to type at the system prompt.

Notes of interest are distinguished with a special margin icon. There are two types of notes used in this book.

The first type is a general interest note.

General interest notes provide information that is of value to you, but which may not fit comfortably into the context of the current discussion.

The second type of note is an Author's Note.

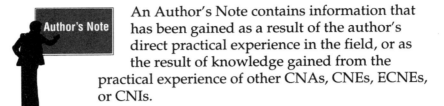 An Author's Note contains information that has been gained as a result of the author's direct practical experience in the field, or as the result of knowledge gained from the practical experience of other CNAs, CNEs, ECNEs, or CNIs.

Other items of interest are distinguished with special margin icons as well. These items include tips and warnings.

 Tips provide additional helpful information to help you do your best when working with NetWare or when working on obtaining one or more of Novell's certifications.

 Warnings provide information that points out when a potential problem exists that you should be aware of. Warnings may also provide proposed solutions to the potential problem.

Learning More about Novell NetWare

New Riders Publishing has a complete line of reference books that can help you gain the NetWare knowledge that you need in order to obtain one or more of Novell's certifications, as well as to gain a thorough understanding of networking with NetWare.

New Riders' reference books cover all of Novell's current NetWare operating systems including NetWare 2, 3, and 4, as well as Personal NetWare, Novell's peer-to-peer operating system.

Available New Riders' reference books include the following:

◆ *NetWare Training Guide: Managing NetWare Systems*

◆ *NetWare Training Guide: NetWare 4 Update*

◆ *NetWare Training Guide: NetWare 4.0 Administration*

◆ *Inside NetWare 3.12*

◆ *NetWare: The Professional Reference*

To purchase any of these books, contact your local book seller. If you are unable to find any of these books, you can order them by calling 1-800-428-5331.

Publisher's Note

The staff of New Riders Publishing is committed to bringing you the very best in computer reference material. Each New Riders book is the result of months of work by authors and staff, who research and refine the information contained within its covers.

As part of this commitment to you, the NRP reader, New Riders invites your input. Please let us know if you enjoy this book, if you have trouble with the information and examples presented, or if you have a suggestion for the next edition.

If you have a question or comment about any New Riders book, please write to NRP at the following address:

New Riders Publishing
Attn: Associate Publisher
201 W. 103rd Street
Indianapolis, IN 46290

If you prefer, you can fax New Riders Publishing at (317) 571-4670.

New Riders also maintains a CompuServe forum. We welcome your participation in this forum (**GO NEWRIDERS**). Please feel free to post a public message there if you have a question or comment about this or any other New Riders product. If you prefer, however, you can send a private message directly to this book's product director at (73164,2773).

We will respond to as many readers as we can. Please note that New Riders cannot serve as a technical resource for NetWare-related questions, including hardware- or software-related problems. Refer to the documentation that accompanies your hardware or software package for help with specific problems.

Thank you for selecting *New Riders' Guide to NetWare Certification.*

Introducing the Novell Certification Programs

1 CHAPTER

Do you work for a company that has installed Novell NetWare? Are you a college student studying computer science and looking for a niche in which to specialize? Are you a small-business owner running NetWare who needs to know how to get the most out of your network? Do you want to earn more money or simply gain the respect of your peers? Are you so interested in computers that you just want to learn everything you possibly can? Do you want to update your resume with the skills that prospective employers need and look for?

If you answered yes to any of these questions, you are a potential candidate for one or more of Novell's four NetWare certification programs.

Each of these four certification programs is designed to fulfill your need to learn more about the NetWare LAN you work with and to be recognized as a professional in your field. Each program instills knowledge that employers look to identify and hire; they want individuals who are competent in using, administering, trouble-shooting, or teaching NetWare.

If you are not sure whether or not Novell certification is right for you, or which certification you should pursue, reading this chapter will help you make those decisions. After reading this chapter, you will understand the following about each of the four certification programs:

◆   What each certification program is all about

◆   Why you should obtain a particular NetWare certification

◆   What you will learn while going through each of the certification programs

◆   What the requirements are for each certification program

◆   How to get started in each of the four certification programs

In addition, once you have read the information on each of the four certification programs, you will learn what you can do with the knowledge you gain from each. You also learn where to find more information about the industry in general, and where to look for potential career opportunities.

The Certified NetWare Administrator (CNA) Program

This section discusses the CNA program and is designed to help you determine if this is the right Novell certification program for you.

What Is the CNA Program?

The CNA program is Novell's entry-level program, designed for people who want to know more about a specific Novell NetWare operating system. At present, the CNA certification program is offered for specialization in any one of three NetWare operating systems, with a fourth one scheduled to be added in the first half of 1994. These operating systems include the following:

◆ NetWare 2—Novell's network operating system for personal computers (PCs) with an Intel 80286 microprocessor. (Although NetWare 2 works fine with 80386, 80486, and Pentium processors, either NetWare 3 or 4 is required to utilize the full power of those more advanced microprocessors.) NetWare 2 is the only NetWare operating system (OS) that runs in either dedicated mode (with the file server functioning only as a file server) or nondedicated mode (with the file server capable of running as either a file server or a workstation-PC that can access a NetWare network).

◆ NetWare 3—Novell's network operating system designed to take advantage of the more advanced capabilities of PCs with an Intel 80386, 80486, or Pentium microprocessor. NetWare 3 runs only in dedicated mode.

◆ NetWare 4—Novell's most advanced network operating system designed to take advantage of Intel 80386, 80486, or Pentium microprocessors, as well as to provide users with access to network resources in a manner similar to the way an organization is structured. This feature is known as NetWare Directory Services.

◆ UnixWare—Novell's network operating system designed for UNIX-based computers.

The purpose of the CNA program is to train people to administer NetWare 2, 3, 4, and UnixWare local area networks (LANs). LANs connect personal computers together to share electronic resources such as printing, file storage, and applications software.

Administering a NetWare network is no easy task, especially if you truly want to get the most out of your network. Novell's CNA certification program can help you, but it is not the only reason to become a CNA. The next section discusses other reasons to become a CNA.

Why Become a CNA?

If you presently work in a NetWare environment, becoming a Certified NetWare Administrator provides several benefits, including the following:

◆ Increased on-the-job knowledge and skill

◆ Greater potential for job advancement

◆ Addition of variety and challenge to your current job

◆ The respect of your peers

◆ Increased interaction with people

If you are already the administrator for a Novell NetWare network, whether for a small business or a Fortune 500 company, some of the other benefits of becoming certified as an administrator include the following:

◆ Improved reputation among your peers and employers

◆ Better ability to support your Novell NetWare network

◆ Establishment of a special working relationship with Novell and other organizations in the industry

◆ Personal networking that enables you to interact with and learn from the experiences of other Novell NetWare administrators

Whether you work in a NetWare environment or plan to soon, the CNA program greatly enhances your knowledge of and experience with Novell's NetWare and/or UnixWare products.

The CNA program teaches you many things about the version of NetWare or UnixWare that you are interested in. Much of the information you will learn will prove to be useful in your networking career as well as in your daily job.

What You Will Learn

When you decide to become a Certified NetWare Administrator, your first decision will be to determine in which version of

Novell's operating system (OS) you want to become certified. If you presently work in a company that uses a particular NetWare OS, your choice may be easy. If you are still deciding in which OS version to become certified, you will need to consider the advantages and disadvantages of each before you settle on one.

While going through the process of becoming NetWare certified, your knowledge of the NetWare OS version that you chose for certification grows substantially. Depending on the OS version in which you choose to pursue certification, you will soon learn a great deal of information about networking with Novell's NetWare and UnixWare products, including the following:

◆ The responsibilities of a network administrator

◆ Basics of hardware (equipment) and software (programs)

◆ How to design, create, and monitor network directories

◆ The process of setting up and accessing network drives

◆ Responsibilities and details of securing your network

◆ How to use NetWare menus to accomplish networking tasks

◆ Various Supervisor and console commands and functions

◆ What it takes to set-up, monitor, and customize printing

◆ Things to consider when adding application software

◆ Ways to simplify network access using login scripts and menus

◆ Responsibilities and procedures for backing up your network

◆ How NetWare and workstations are installed

◆ The importance and process of controlling your network

◆ How to implement and use NetWare accounting features

◆ Ways to increase the performance of your network

◆ Remote management of your network

◆ Problem prevention and troubleshooting

◆ NetWare Name Service basics

17

Now that you know what types of information you can learn, you need to know the certification requirements.

What Are the Certification Requirements?

Because the CNA program is Novell's entry-level certification program, it is also the easiest certification to obtain. However, it is not without its own prerequisites.

Before you can become certified, you need some minimum knowledge of computer hardware and software. In particular, you need a working knowledge of DOS (Disk Operating System). DOS is the software that gets a computer up and running when you first turn it on. It allows the computer to communicate with you, responding to your requests.

Therefore, the first requirement of CNA certification is a basic knowledge and understanding of microhardware (hardware for personal computers, or PCs) and microcomputer (PC) concepts, as well as a working knowledge of DOS.

The next prerequisite for certification is that you know for which of the Novell operating systems you want your certification issued. As stated earlier, you can become certified in NetWare 2, 3, or 4, or in UnixWare.

Once you make that decision, all you have to do is study for, register for, take, and pass a single test, which must be taken at an authorized testing location.

How To Begin

To obtain your certification as a Novell Certified NetWare Administrator, complete the steps shown in the following list.

1. Familiarize yourself with microcomputers and DOS.

2. Choose the Novell operating system that you want to learn about (NetWare 2, 3, or 4, or UnixWare).

3. Study the student course material and/or any third-party books you have for your chosen operating sytem.

Be sure to study all the information related to the course objectives. The course objectives for the most common Novell courses are included in this book. To obtain course objectives for other courses, call Novell Education at 1-800-233-EDUC (if calling from within the United States or Canada), or 1-801-429-5508, Monday through Friday, 7 AM to 5 PM MST.

4. Telephone Drake Training and Technologies and schedule a time and place to take your test. From within the United States or Canada, call 1-800-RED-EXAM, 7 AM to 6 PM Central. From outside the United States or Canada, call 1-612-921-4127, Mon-Fri. When you call, be prepared to give the following information:

   ◆ Your social security number or Novell testing number

   ◆ Your complete mailing address

   ◆ The number of the test you want to take

   ◆ The date you want to take the test

   ◆ The method you are using to pay for the test

5. Pay for the test.

You are required to pay for the examination before you take it. The price of a single examination at the time of the printing of this book was $85. The Drake Testing Center can tell you if this amount has changed. You can pay for your test over the phone using a credit card. This is convenient if you want to take the test within just a couple of days. Otherwise, you can mail a check or money order to:

Drake Training and Technologies
8800 Queen Avenue South
Bloomington, MN 55431

6. Take two forms of identification with you to the testing center. At least one of these must be a photo ID, such as a driver's license, an employer-issued ID badge, or a state-issued ID card. Arrive at least 15 minutes before your scheduled test time so that you can sign in and start the test on time.

7. Take and pass the CNA examination.

You and Novell are both notified of your test results within five working days. If you passed the test, Novell sends your certification papers plus any additional Novell-related information you need to have.

If you did not pass the test, you must retake the test, and Novell recommends that you take the related courses.

The Certified NetWare Engineer (CNE) Program

This section will help you decide whether you should pursue a CNE certification after obtaining your CNA, skip the CNA program and work only toward a CNE, or obtain your CNE primarily as a stepping stone toward obtaining your Enterprise Certified Netware Engineer certification (ECNE).

What Is the CNE Program?

Certification as a NetWare Engineer was the least difficult of Novell's certification programs before the CNA program was introduced. NetWare administrators are focused on the tasks required to administor a NetWare network on a daily basis. The skills of a NetWare engineer must also include the installation and maintenance of network hardware, including cabling systems, servers, and workstations. NetWare engineers must be able to install NetWare and to configure it for the needs of each specific network. Candidates for Certified NetWare Engineer status include technicians at authorized Novell resellers, consultants, corporate network administrators, and others.

Once you complete the CNE requirements, you have obtained an extended amount of knowledge about at least one of the NetWare operating systems, but usually you will have learned about two. In addition, as a CNE you have gained knowledge about networking in general, as well as information to help you troubleshoot problems on and maintain a NetWare network.

Today's CNE certification program not only lets you become certified in NetWare 2 and NetWare 3 operating systems, but also has been expanded to allow you to become certified in NetWare 4 and UnixWare operating systems.

As with the CNA program, there are many reasons why you might want to consider expanding your certification to that of CNE, or why you might want to skip the CNA certification and go right into the CNE program.

Unlike the CNA program, which requires only that you take and pass one test, Novell's CNE and ECNE certification programs are designed much like that of the certification programs found at your local community college.

The design of a community college certification program is such that it is easy to understand the requirements. Also, the programs are designed specifically to educate individuals who need that information as quickly as possible. Novell's certification program design works much like that of the community college certification programs in that it specifies the following courses:

◆ Prerequisites (DOS/Microcomputer Concepts or UNIX OS Fundamentals), as well as a signed CNE agreement filed with Novell

◆ Basic requirements (System Manager or Administration, and Advanced System Manager or Advanced Administration courses and/or tests for the operating system that you choose)

21

- ◆ Core requirements (NetWare Service and Support and Networking Technologies)
- ◆ Electives (a full range from which to choose)

In addition, Novell's certification program assigns credits to each related test that you pass. This is similar to a community college, where you receive a set number of college credits for taking and successfully completing specific college courses. (The main difference between Novell's certification program and going to a community college is that Novell does not require you to take the course, only that you pass the test to prove your proficiency.) A minimum number of credits taken in each of the categories in the preceding list are required for certification.

Taking and passing Novell's required CNE courses does not give you college credit, however. If you want college credit for the related Novell courses, you must take the equivalent of these courses from a Novell Education Academic Partner (NEAP), a college or university that teaches Novell courses as part of its regular curriculum.

If you take the equivalent Novell course from a NEAP, you follow all the same course guidelines that you would for any other college-level course. In other words, you must enroll in the course, attend regularly scheduled classes, attend for a full semester or quarter, take at least a final exam (usually also a mid-term and other exams), and complete the course with a passing grade.

If you take the actual Novell course from a Novell Authorized Education Center (NAEC), the course is usually taught for eight consecutive hours per day, anywhere from two to five days, depending on the course. Although you receive a certificate for completing the course, you do not have to take mid-term or final exams (although some courses do have something reasonably equivalent, but without the grade).

To prove your proficiency in a given Novell course or topic, you must take and pass the official Novell test, taken through a Drake Training and Technologies Authorized Testing Center (DATC). You must take and pass the required tests through a DATC, whether or not you ever take a related NEAP or NAEC course.

The tests that you take to obtain a CNE are determined for you by the operating system emphasis that you choose, except for the electives, which you select from a list.

Before you can become a CNE, you must have passed the tests to obtain two credits of prerequisites, five credits of operating system requirements, eight credits of core requirements, and four credits of CNE electives. Figure 1.1 shows the route that you must navigate to become a CNE.

Why Become a CNE?

You may choose to become a NetWare CNE to expand your current NetWare-related job knowledge and skills, improve your potential for job advancement, add variety and challenge to your current job, gain the respect of your peers, or just to increase your interaction with other people.

Becoming a CNE has other benefits, including the following:

◆ Industry-wide recognition of your accomplishment, due in part to the increased level of difficulty it takes to obtain this certification

◆ An increase in your overall networking knowledge, as well as in your knowledge of NetWare operating systems

◆ The ability to troubleshoot network problems, and the knowledge necessary to correct those problems

◆ Potential for obtaining a position with a Novell-authorized reseller, or as an independent industry consultant.

◆ Priority attention from Novell technical support (NTS) if you call them for assistance. This includes two free calls for support to NTS, good for one year from the date you become certified.

◆ The ability to receive a 50% discount on subsequent NTS support calls.

◆ A free issue of Novell's *Network Support Encyclopedia* (NSE) Professional Volume.

◆ Permission from Novell to use the CNE logo on you letter-head, business cards, directory advertisements, and other business literature. (Copies of the logo are included in your *Welcome Aboard* kit.)

Figure 1.1

Novell CNE test chart.

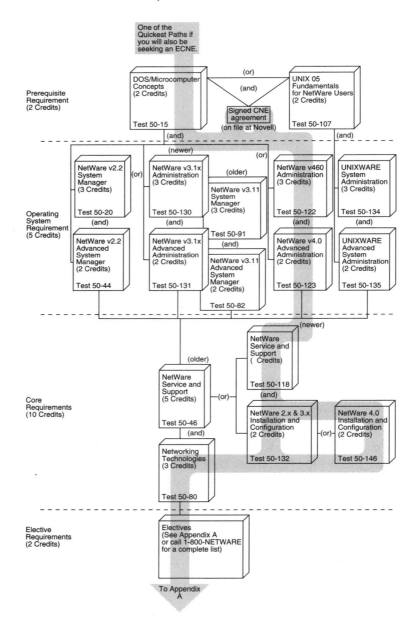

Some of the benefits of becoming a Novell CNE are also directly related to what you learn as you go through the CNE certification program. For example, the more you learn about Novell's operating systems, the easier it becomes to troubleshoot network problems when you encounter them. Therefore, going through the CNE program and learning about NetWare also benefits you because of what you learn.

What You Will Learn

If you obtained your CNA before obtaining your CNE—even though this is not a requirement—you will have already learned many things about Novell's networking products. As a CNE, you also learn the following:

- ◆ The same information you learned as a CNA, but for two of Novell's operating systems, not just for one.

- ◆ Details about how information and requests are transferred across a network

- ◆ How to install a NetWare or UnixWare network

- ◆ How to troubleshoot and solve problems on your network

- ◆ Additional information related to networking, depending on the elective tests you chose to take

As you can probably tell by the increased amount of information that you learn through the CNE program, there is a corresponding increase in certification requirements.

What Are the Certification Requirements?

A CNE must learn all the same information as the CNA, but this is just a beginning. A CNE must become proficient in the following:

- ◆ Microcomputer concepts and DOS (or UNIX operating system fundamentals, if you are certifying in UnixWare instead of NetWare)

- ◆ One of Novell's operating systems, such as NetWare 2, 3, or 4, or UnixWare

◆ A second Novell operating system or any of Novell's available elective courses to meet the minimum elective requirements of four credits

To become a CNE, you must pass all the required tests as previously outlined in figure 1.1. You must also complete Novell's required paperwork, signing and returning the ECNE/CNE Agreement signature card. Then, you must continue to fulfill your agreement with Novell.

Once you sign and return the ECNE/CNE Agreement signature card, you agree to abide by Novell's requirements for a CNE or an ECNE; Novell has a complete certification agreement to which you commit.

 For a copy of the Novell certification agreement, call Novell at 1-800-NETWARE (in the United States and Canada), or 1-801-429-5588, and ask for a copy of the *CNE & ECNE Programs Novell Support Certification* booklet.

As a CNE, you should also know that you may have continuing certification requirements to meet. Novell makes these requirements to help you keep up with technological advancements in network computing and in NetWare specifically. Novell wants to make sure that all of its CNEs can continue to provide quality support to the NetWare products for which they are responsible. Therefore, all CNEs are notified when a continuing education requirement must be met.

Once notified of a continuing education requirement, you usually have six months within which to complete it. If you do not meet that requirement, Novell revokes your certification. To regain your certification, you have to start over and meet all of the current Novell certification requirements.

Because of this stringent policy, Novell continues to have highly-qualified individuals as CNEs. To make certain that you do not miss being notified of a continuing education requirement, be sure to keep Novell notified of any change of address. Mail address changes to Novell at the following address:

> Novell CNE/ECNE Administration
> 122 East 1700 South, MS E-31-1
> Provo, Utah 84606

How To Begin

To obtain your certification as a Novell Certified NetWare Administrator, complete the steps shown in the following list:

1. Familiarize yourself with microcomputers and DOS, or with UNIX operating system fundamentals.

2. Choose the Novell operating system that you want to learn about in order to meet the operating system requirements of five credits.

3. Study the student course material and/or any third-party books you have for your chosen operating sytem.

 The course objectives for the most common Novell courses are included in this book. To obtain course objectives for other courses call Novell Education at 1-800-233-EDUC (if calling from within the United States or Canada), or 1-801-429-5508, Monday through Friday, 7 AM to 5 PM MST.

4. Study the information to meet the core requirements (NetWare Service and Support and Networking Technologies), and to take and pass the related tests.

5. Choose your electives (you are required to have an additional four credits of electives), and study to take the related tests.

6. Call the Drake Training and Technologies number and schedule a time and place to take your tests. You can call them and take each test after you have studied the material, or you can arrange to take the tests one after the other.

There are a minimum of seven tests that you must take. Therefore, taking them all at once is not recommended. Novell suggests taking related tests within six weeks of your studies or related coursework.

7. The number to call to register for a test if you are calling from within the United States or Canada is 1-800-RED-EXAM, Monday through Friday, 7 AM to 6 PM CST. If you are calling from outside the United States or Canada, call 1-612-921-4127, Monday through Friday.

 When you call to register for your first test, you are enrolled in the CNE program. Once you take your first test, pass or fail, you have one year in which to complete all requirements for your CNE certification.

8. When you call, be prepared to give them some information, including the following:

   ◆ Your Social Security number or Novell testing number

   ◆ Your complete mailing address

   ◆ The number of the test you want to take

   ◆ The date and time you want to take the test

   ◆ The method you are using to pay for the test

 The fee for a single test is $85. However, because fees can change, ask about their current fee when you call Drake. Also, ask about their program that lets you take the seventh test free. As of the printing of this book, Drake lets you register for and take your seventh CNE test at no charge. However, as that is subject to change, you should ask Drake about the current status of this program when you call them.

9. Pay for the test.

Note

You are required to pay for the examination before you take it. The price of a single examination at the time of the printing of this book is $85. (The Drake Testing Center can tell you if this amount has changed.) You can pay for your test over the telephone using a credit card. This is convenient if you want to take the test within just a couple of days. Otherwise, you can mail a check or money order to:

> Drake Training and Technologies
> 8800 Queen Avenue South
> Bloomington, MN 55431

10. Take two forms of identification with you to the testing center. At least one of those must be a photo ID, such as a driver's license, an employer-issued ID badge, or a state-issued ID card. Arrive a minimum of 15 minutes before your scheduled test time, so that you can sign in and start the test on time.

11. Take and pass the test. As mentioned previously, you must pass a minimum of seven tests to become a CNE. Therefore, you must repeat this process for each test you take.

Note

Both you and Novell are notified of your test results, within five working days. Novell tracks the results of each of your tests for you. Once you have passed all of the required tests, Novell sends you their official *Welcome Aboard* kit. This kit contains: your letter stating that you are a CNE, your official CNE certification, your CNE ID number (used when calling Novell technical support), and a request for a passport-size photo. Within five weeks of returning your photo, Novell creates and sends to you your official Novell CNE ID badge.

During the process of becoming a CNE, Novell requires that you agree to abide by legal guidelines that it has established for CNEs. These legal guidelines are set forth in the *CNE & ECNE Programs Novell Support Certification* booklet available from Novell. Your signature on the ECNE/CNE Agreement signature card is required, and must be on file at Novell.

You may receive a copy of this information by calling Novell's FaxBack line and having it faxed to you, or by contacting Novell directly at 1-800-NETWARE.

To reach the FaxBack line, call 1-800-233-3382 (from within the United States or Canada) or 1-801-429-5363.

The Enterprise CNE (ECNE) Program

Though it may not have been obvious from the information that you have read so far, the CNA and CNE certifications are useful primarily for individuals working in local NetWare networking environments. The ECNE program is geared towards people who must or want to work with geographically bigger networks, known as Enterprise networks.

A local area network is usually geographically restricted. That is, it often consists of a small geographic location, such as the computers of a given company within a city or a state. An enterprise network is geographically more expansive and may include the international offices of a large corporation, or those of a country's entire governmental structure.

As you may have guessed, an ECNE certification is also more encompassing.

What Is the ECNE Program?

The ECNE program is one in which you show your extended Novell networking knowledge, particularly in one or more of Novell's operating systems designed for enterprise-wide networks.

The ECNE program requires you to choose either the NetWare 3 or 4 operating system track, as these are the two operating systems most commonly used in an enterprise-wide network.

In addition, you must demonstrate additional competence by obtaining elective credits in more areas. The total elective credits required depend on exactly which operating system track you choose. However, the minimum requirement is nine credits of electives. Figure 1.2 shows the route that you must navigate in order to become an ECNE.

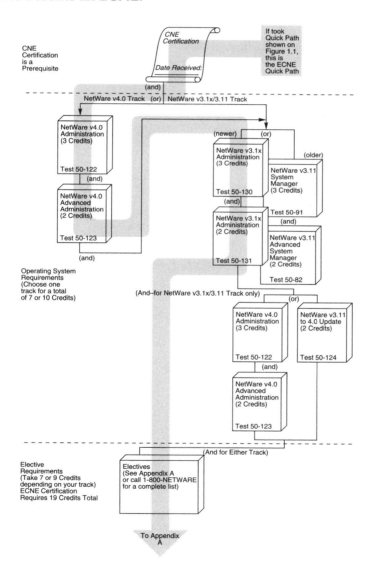

Figure 1.2

Navigating the Novell ECNE tests.

Why Become an ECNE?

All of the same reasons for becoming a CNE apply to the ECNE certification program. There are two main differences, however.

- ◆ First, your industry recognition is enhanced by your Enterprise certification. You are recognized as having knowledge and competence beyond that of the CNE.

- ◆ Second, you are allowed to use the ECNE logo. If you are also a CNE, you may continue to use that logo as well.

What You Will Learn

Several of the ECNE certification requirements can be summed up by telling you that, before you can become an ECNE, you must first become certified as a CNE. Therefore, all of the CNE certification requirements also apply to the ECNE program.

For example, you learn the following:

- ◆ The responsibilities of a Network administrator
- ◆ Basics of microcomputer hardware and software
- ◆ How to design, create, and monitor network directories
- ◆ The process of setting up and accessing network drives
- ◆ Responsibilities and details of securing your network
- ◆ How to use NetWare menus to accomplish networking tasks
- ◆ How to use various Supervisor and console commands and functions
- ◆ The same information you learned as a CNA, but for two of Novell's operating systems, not just for one.
- ◆ Details about how information and requests are transferred across a network
- ◆ How to install a NetWare or UnixWare network
- ◆ How to troubleshoot and solve problems on your network

◆ Additional information related to networking, depending on the elective tests you chose to take

From your additional electives you may also learn about the following:

◆ Novell's other product offerings

◆ Internetwork and network management design

◆ In-depth information about printing in a NetWare environment

◆ UnixWare, if it was not your choice for the operating system track

◆ NetWare for NFS Gateways or SAA

◆ NetWare Global MHS

There are many other topics from which you can choose your elective credits, therefore there are many other items of interest that you can learn while studying to become an ECNE. These are just some of them.

As with Novell's other certification programs, there are specific certification requirements for the ECNE program.

What Are the Certification Requirements?

In addition, ECNEs must have a minimum of nine elective credits, rather than the four required for CNEs. Also, the four elective credits received for your CNE can apply toward the nine required for the ECNE.

ECNEs are also required to have NetWare 3 or NetWare 4 as their operating system track. Therefore, if you selected NetWare 2 as your operating system track for your CNE, you must take either NetWare 3 or 4 for your ECNE operating system track. The NetWare 2 or UnixWare tests are applied as elective credits, if you took either for your CNE Track.

There is a major difference between the CNE and ECNE programs, however. Once you begin the CNE program, you have one year from the time you take the first test to complete your requirements for CNE certification. There is no time limit for ECNE.

However, you should be aware that Novell reserves the right to change its ECNE certification requirements (as is also true for the CNE program) whenever it feels the need to do so. If you have not completed the ECNE requirements before Novell makes a change to them, you may be required to meet the changed certification requirements in order to become an ECNE. In addition, you might also be required to meet additional continuing certification requirements.

In addition, you do not have to pre-register for ECNE certification as you do for CNE certification. When you call to sign up to take your first CNE test, you are registered for the CNE program. Reregistering is not necessary.

How To Begin

To become a Novell Enterprise Certified NetWare Engineer (ECNE), complete the steps shown in the following list:

1. Complete all requirements for and obtain your CNE certification.

2. Choose the Novell operating system that you want to learn about in order to meet the NetWare operating system track requirements (NetWare 3 or 4).

3. Take the related operating system courses or study the information yourself.

4. Take and pass the related operating system course tests for the ECNE NetWare operating system track that you chose.

5. Study for, take, and pass the tests for the elective courses that you selected in order to meet the requirements for a minimum of nine elective course credits.

Once you have taken and passed all of the proficiency tests required for ECNE certification, you receive Novell's *Welcome*

Aboard kit for ECNEs. This kit contains your letter stating that you are now an ECNE, your official ECNE certification, and a request for a passport-size photo. It takes approximately three weeks for your kit to arrive and five weeks to get the photo ID.

The Certified NetWare Instructor (CNI) Program

The CNI program is designed to ensure that people who take Novell courses from certified locations are taking these courses from individuals who are qualified to teach them.

The CNI program ensures that these Novell-certified instructors know what they are talking about when they teach you about Novell products. As a student, you are assured that you are learning from qualified instructors.

As a Novell Certified NetWare Instructor, you know that you have reached a level of Novell networking knowledge that is recognized and respected in the industry.

What Is the CNI Program?

The CNI program is designed, not just to certify people to teach Novell courses, but to ensure that a sufficient level of knowledge is available to NetWare users, resellers, administrators, and others who need that information.

The networking industry as a whole is becoming more and more complex. Networking technology and products are also becoming more sophisticated. Novell is the recognized leader in networking technology, therefore, most of Novell's networking products are also quite sophisticated. The use and administration of such a technical environment requires knowledgeable people. Novell networking is enhanced and supported through the CNI program and its trained staff.

Why Become a CNI?

Besides the knowledge you gain by obtaining certification as a CNI, there are other benefits to becoming certified.

As a CNI candidate, you will be learning about and teaching cutting-edge networking technology. Once you achieve your CNI certification, you'll also have the full support of Novell behind you.

As a CNI, you can teach certified Novell courses at either NAECs or NEAPs. You will have a certain amount of independence because you can often set your own hours and days. You may establish a relationship with a NAEC or a NEAP and work full-time, part-time, or even on a per-contract basis.

You can have your name added to a list of independent or self-employed contract CNIs. This list is then used by NAECs and NEAPs to find a substitute instructor when their regular CNI is unavailable to teach a course.

If you have ever wanted to be self-employed, just love to teach, or really enjoy learning about NetWare, the CNI program provides you with many personal benefits in addition to the professional ones.

What You Will Learn

As with the CNA, CNE, and ECNE certification programs, you learn about networking with Novell products. Unlike these programs however, you do not have to learn about many of the Novell products that you do not wish to teach. There are still some prerequisites to certification, however.

What Are the Certification Requirements?

To become a CNI, you must meet several prerequisite requirements, including the following:

- ◆ A working knowledge of microcomputers and operating systems such as DOS or UNIX fundamentals

- ◆ A minimum of one year of experience as an instructor in the area in which you want to specialize

- ◆ Presentation skills that are strong and effective, often gained by having a year or more of experience teaching adults

- ◆ Skill in communicating technical information both clearly and accurately

- ◆ The ability to effectively manage a classroom of students

- ◆ A positive and enthusiastic attitude

These prerequisites are considered minimums. You must also apply to become a CNI and be approved before you are allowed to enter the program.

How To Begin

To become a CNI, you must first be accepted into the CNI program. Acceptance depends first upon your meeting the minimum requirements, submitting an application, and telling Novell which course you want to use as your target certification course—the course you intend to use in order to demonstrate your teaching proficiency and technical knowledge through Novell's Instructor Performance Evaluation (IPE) class.

In addition to submitting your application, you must submit the necessary certification IPE fee.

Note   Presently, the IPE fee is $500. Only one IPE is required for certification in each of the three available certification groups. In addition, you do not have to become certified in anything other than the core operating system product group if you prefer not to.

Certification Options

You can certify to teach courses in one or all of Novell's three certification categories. Those categories include the following:

◆ Core operating system product courses

◆ Advanced product courses

◆ Development product courses

Before you can be certified to teach any of the courses in the second and third categories, you first must become certified in the core operating system product category.

Certification in the core operating system product category lets you teach the Novell courses shown in the following list. Note that the courses shown in bold type are eligible IPE courses.

105	Introduction to Networking
200	**Networking Technologies**
501	NetWare 2.2: System Manager
502	NetWare 2.2: Advanced System Manager
506	NetWare 3.11: OS Features Review
507	NetWare 3.11 to 3.12 Update Seminar
508	**NetWare 3.1x Administration**
518	**NetWare 3.1x Advanced Administration**
520	**NetWare 4.0 Administration**
525	**NetWare 4.0 Advanced Administration**
526	NetWare 3.11 to 4.0 Update
530	**NetWare 4.0 Design and Implementation**
535	**Printing with NetWare**
801	**NetWare Service and Support**
802	NetWare 2.x/3.x Installation and Configuration Workshop
804	NetWare 4.0 Installation and Configuration Workshop

Certification in the Advanced Product Courses category lets you teach the Novell courses shown in the following list. Again, the courses shown in bold are eligible IPE courses. The courses shown in bold and italic are eligible UNIX IPE courses.

205	Fundamentals of Internetwork Management and Design
220	UNIX OS Fundamentals for NetWare Users
601	LAN Workplace for DOS Administration (UNIX)
605	*NetWare TCP/IP Transport*
610	*NetWare NFS*
611	NetWare FLeX/IP (UNIX)
615	NetWare for Macintosh Connectivity
625	NetWare NFS Gateway (UNIX)
678	UnixWare Installation and Configuration
680	*UnixWare System Administration*
685	*UnixWare Advanced System Administration*
718	**NetWare Connect**
720	**NetWare for SAA: Installation and Troubleshooting**
740	**NetWare Internetworking Products**
750	NetWare Global MHS
851	UnixWare Service and Support

Certification in the Development Product Courses category lets you teach the Novell courses shown in the following list. Note that the courses shown in bold are eligible IPE courses.

904	Btrieve: An Overview
905	**Programming with Btrieve**
907	Xtrieve PLUS
911	**NetWare Database Administrator**

912	**Programming with NetWare SQL**
930	**NetWare Programming: NLM Development**
940	NetWare Programming: Basic Services
941	**NetWare Programming Directory Services**
945	NetWare Programming: Protocol Support

These course lists are updated periodically. You can obtain the most current copy of the list by calling FaxBack at 1-800-233-3392 or 1-801-429-5363. You can also obtain a current list from you Novell Technology Institute (NTI) manager or Area Education Manager (AEM).

Certification Steps To Follow

To obtain your certification as a Novell Certified NetWare Instructor, complete the steps shown in the following list:

If you are submitting your application in the United States or Canada, submit it to your NTI manager. In all other areas, submit your application to your AEM.

To find out the current cost of your chosen IPE, contact your NTI manager or AEM. To find out who your NTI manager or AEM is, or to receive a copy of the latest version of Novell's *CNI Program Description & Application* document, contact Novell Education through the CNI program administrator at the following address and phone number:

CNI Administration
Novell, Inc.
122 East 1700 South, MS A-22-1
Provo, Utah 84606 USA
Phone: 1-801-429-5445
Fax: 1-801-429-3900

1. Contact Novell by phone or mail to receive an application form.

2. Ensure that you meet the minimum qualifications as outlined earlier.

3. Submit to Novell a completed and signed SNI application form along with a signed CNI agreement, a copy of your resume (which must include three references), an order form for an instructor's kit for your target certification course, and payment of $500 for your first IPE (Instructor Performance Evaluation).

4. Once your application is approved, take and pass those Novell prerequisites required for your certification. Chapter 2, "Preparing to Become NetWare Certified," discusses those prerequisites in detail.

5. Attend the course that you have chosen as your target course for your IPE. You can attend a course from a local NAEC, NEAP or Novell training site.

6. Make a copy of your certificate for the course you attended and send the copy to Novell at the address previously shown.

7. If you have not already done so, take and pass the CNI-level test for your target course.

8. Complete any necessary training to ensure that your presentation skills are adequate to pass the IPE.

Note Although Novell provides a list of the presentation skills that you need to pass the presentation skills portion of the IPE, Novell does not provide detailed information to help you develop or improve your presentation skills. However, Chapter 5, "Becoming a Certified NetWare Instructor," provides you with detailed information on developing your presentation skills as needed to successfully pass that portion of the IPE.

9. Register to attend the appropriate IPE. You must register at least two weeks before you plan on taking the IPE. However, because IPE's are offered on a limited basis, register for the IPE as soon as possible.

10. Attend and pass the IPE. You do not find out whether or not you have passed the IPE on the same day that you take it. You are notified in writing at a later date.

Certifying for Additional Courses

You can certify to teach additional courses in the same product group, as well as in another product group.

To become certified to teach any other course within a product group for which you have taken and passed an IPE, you need only to take the course, submit proof of attendance to Novell (usually a copy of the course certificate) and pass the CNI test for each additional course that you want to teach. Keep in mind that CNIs must score a higher passing grade than CNE or ECNE candidates.

To become certified to teach a course in another product group, you must complete all of the same steps you took for your original certification, including the submission of an application and approval by Novell to enroll in a subsequent IPE for your target course.

Using What You Learn

To answer this question, go back to the beginning. If you are not already doing any of those things listed in the first paragraph of this chapter, you certainly can consider doing them now. If you want, you can do the following:

◆ Work for a company that has Novell NetWare installed

◆ Continue your college Computer Science studies with a specialization in networking

◆ Start or buy your own small-business and run it more efficiently and effectively with Novell NetWare connecting your various computer resources

◆ Apply what you have learned in your present position to get the most out of your Novell network

◆ Update your resume to reflect your new networking skills and knowledge that prospective employers need and look for

Obtaining Novell certification opens many doors to you. For example, you may choose to become a network administrator in a corporate organization. You may also choose to become a consultant, helping companies to set up, install, and train in-house personel. Or you may choose to teach NetWare courses, either as a CNE working for one large comapany, as an independent and on-call CNI, or as a CNI affiliated with a particular NAEC or NEAP. Regardless of what you decide, the opportunities are there.

Some of these opportunities may come to you because you became part of a limited group of individuals recognized as skilled and knowledgeable in their chosen field. Your contacts with others in your field may also provide opportunities for personal growth and professional advancement that were not available to you before.

However, few people would suggest that you simply sit back and wait for those opportunities. Most of the time, if you want to have opportunities presented to you, you must do two things.

The first thing to do is to prepare for those opportunities so that you can act on them when they are presented to you. Once you take the initiative and become Novell certified, you have also taken the first step toward opportunity.

The next step is to seek opportunity wherever it may be. If you want to change positions or increase your responsibilities at your present job, then look for ways to use your new networking skills. Actively seek out assignments and volunteer, if necessary, to take responsibility for the company's network or other related services.

If you want to change jobs or companies, look for networking opportunities everywhere you can think of.

Where To Look for Employment Opportunities

One of the best places to look for employment opportunities is in trade journals and magazines. Several of them provide classified advertisement listings of job opportunities in networking, and in particular, in networking with Novell's operating systems.

There are many trade journals and magazines that carry classified advertisements. Some of those are included in table 1.1.

 Table 1.1 is NOT an exhaustive listing. It is provided to give you some idea of what is out there and where to start looking.

For a more exhaustive listing, go to your local public or university library (particularly if that university or college teaches Computer Science and/or networking) and seek out the Reference Librarian. He or she can help you research other trade publishers and publications.

Table 1.1
Brief List of Trade Publications

Title	Description	Publisher
Communications Week	"The Newspaper for Enterprise Networking"	CMP Publications, Inc. 600 Community Dr. Manhasset, NY 11030
LAN Times	"McGraw-Hill's Information Source for Network Computing"	McGraw-Hill, Inc. 1221 Ave of Americas New York, NY 10020

Title	Description	Publisher
Computerworld	"The Newspaper of Information Systems Management"	CW Publishing, Inc. P.O. Box 9171 Framingham, MA 01701
Network Computing	"The Magazine for Client/Server Computing"	CMP Publications, Inc 600 Community Drive Manhasset, NY 11030
LAN	"The Network Solutions Magazine"	LAN Magazine P.O. Box 58123 Boulder, CO 80322

Not all trade publications and magazines are a wealth of classified advertisements for Novell NetWare specialists. Even if you cannot find current openings in the trade publications, you can still find valuable information about companies and the networking products they use, including NetWare. If you find information about a company that looks particularly interesting to you, consider sending a blind resume to the Personnel Director, or someone at the company who is responsible for their network. Some of the best jobs at a company never show up in the classified advertisements.

Trade publications are not the only places to look. You can also seek out classified advertisements in the appropriate section of your local newspapers. (Often you find these positions listed under Computers or a similar heading.)

Novell itself can help you indirectly with your job search. Novell provides a listing of NAECs (Novell Authorized Education Center) and NEAPs (Novell Education Academic Partner) in your area, just by electronically asking them for it. To get a listing call Novell's FaxBack line at 1-801-429-7051. Follow the prompts to request a listing of NAECs and NEAPs in your area.

While most NAECs and NEAPs do not directly hire Novell certification candidates (with the exception of Certified NetWare Instructors), these places have many industry contacts and may be able to steer you toward companies who are currently hiring, particularly if you have taken courses from them. If nothing else, these places may be able to give you other ideas of where to look for positions.

As NEAPs are colleges and universities that teach Novell-certified courses as part of their curriculum, the employment offices at these colleges and universities may also be able to guide you toward a position in this field.

You might consider joining one or more organizations that specialize in networking technology, and perhaps in Novell's networking technology in particular. The CNEPA (Certified NetWare Engineer Professional Association) is one such organization. They can be reached by mail at:

> CNEPA
> 122 East 1700 South
> MS E-31-1
> Provo, Utah 84606-6194.

Or you can reach them by calling 1-800-9CNEPRO or 1-801-429-7536. If you have a fax machine handy, you can send them a fax at 1-801-429-5565.

The CNEPA is a good organization to join if you want to do some personal networking with other professionals in the field. Getting to know some of these individuals might well bring your name to the attention of a company who is looking for someone who has your specific set of skills. At the very least, you might be able to find out what the phone number is for the company's job line, if they have one. Then you can keep a weekly ear tuned to job openings at specific firms.

You might also consider contacting consultants who regularly advertise in your local phone directory and newspapers. Look for those who specialize in networking technologies, and in Novell in particular. Even though you may not be looking to become a consultant yourself, many consultants work for companies who are looking for full-time professionals, in addition to the consultants that they use. If you can develop a business relationship with a local consultant, you may be able to learn about current or potential openings within a company.

Do not overlook the professional companies who make a living by placing people with businesses. Some of these companies charge the potential employee for their services, and some charge the employer. The type of firm you choose is up to you. However, consider working with firms that have a good reputation and know the networking industry. The placement agency's contacts in the industry can make all the difference between just finding you a job or helping you with advancing your career.

If you have the certification but no experience and find that this hinders you in your job search, consider obtaining experience that matches the certification.

Where To Get Networking Experience

If you are already working in a company that has a NetWare network, seek out your boss and find out if there is any possibility of you taking on some responsibility for that network. In other words, volunteer to take on added responsibility. Just make sure that it is networking-related so that your experiences can be added to your resume.

If you do not currently have an employer that uses Novell NetWare, see if any of your local community colleges or universities have Computer Science labs that run NetWare. You can go see the Lab Manager and offer to work as a Lab Assistant.

If the Lab Assistant positions are paid positions and they are not hiring right now, volunteer to be a Teacher's Assistant in a networking class. If that is not an option, talk to the school about being a tutor for network courses. Many of these positions are paid positions, though the amount they pay is generally quite minimal.

Also, you might consider working as a part-time volunteer for a non-profit organization that uses NetWare. Maybe you will even be fortunate enough to find one that has not yet installed NetWare, but who will be doing so soon. This opportunity may let you in on the ground floor and give you good experience, though your pockets may be empty.

Do you know anyone who works for a company that uses NetWare? Perhaps your friend or acquaintance can give you some insight into any programs that the company has for hiring knowledgeable but inexperienced NetWare personnel.

If you are currently enrolled in a Computer Science or other degree program at a college or university, ask them about corporate-sponsored work programs. Many companies have work-study programs that hire part-time temporary students as part of their training program.

You might think about using a temporary employment agency. Even though the only positions you can get through such an agency would provide you with limited network access and use, having some network experience to show on your resume is definitely better than no experience at all.

Do you know any consultants who work with clients who use NetWare? Perhaps you can volunteer some of your time to assist these clients. If you like to teach, you can offer to provide a basic course to the clients' users. (This is also one way to get some of the teaching experience that is a prerequisite for getting your CNI.)

Consider contacting your local school district's adult education division. If any of the local schools have adult education programs and a Novell Netware network, you can offer to teach a course in networking. This is yet another way to meet the teaching prerequisite for Novell's CNI certification.

If all else fails, and you have access to at least two computers, buy two copies of Novell's Personal NetWare product. Install the copies on your PCs, setup the network, use the network, and then you will have some experience with Novell's networking products.

This is a valid option for gaining NetWare experience. Although Personal NetWare uses a different operating system than Novell's other networking products, the client software (the programs that let a PC access a Novell NetWare network) are the same in Personal NetWare as they are in Novell's other DOS-based NetWare operating systems.

In addition, the networking hardware is the same. So you will have real networking experience that you can add to your resume; it will just be experience on a smaller scale.

Summary

Now that you have finished reading this chapter, you should have a good idea of which Novell certification program you are most interested in pursuing, and how to go about pursuing it. Of course, you may have decided that you want to pursue more than one certification.

The CNA program lets you choose to become certified just in the NetWare OS that you work with or administer, or you can choose to obtain more than one CNA, and learn about Novell's other NetWare Operating Systems.

The certification program you decide to pursue should be chosen based on your own needs and interests. The ability to choose elective credits in the CNE and ECNE programs allows you to pursue Novell networking information beyond just knowledge of the networking Operating System.

The CNI program lets you pick and choose which courses you teach, requiring only a minimum of prerequisites for certification as an instructor of Novell products.

No matter which certification you choose to pursue, you should find your certification experience and networking knowledge to be useful in your professional career, as well as interesting to learn.

Chapter 2 covers the details of the prerequisites that you must meet in order to obtain one or more of Novell's certifications. If you have decided which certification to pursue, read the sections that discuss that certification. However, if you are still undecided as to which certification to pursue, reading the chapter may help you to decide.

Preparing To Become NetWare Certified

Prerequisites for Each Certification Program

If you enroll in a certification or degree program at your community college or local university, the programs—as well as many of the courses you take—have prerequisites. Some basic knowledge or skill is necessary before going on to learn advanced information about a specific topic or a given field of interest.

The skilled and technical trades are the same. For example, if you want to be a carpenter, electrician, or plumber, you must first learn the basics of construction, wiring, or plumbing. You are then often required to spend time in an apprenticeship before you can become licensed or certified in your trade.

The field of networking technologies is no exception. You need to have some basic knowledge of microcomputers—including microcomputer hardware and software—and DOS before you begin learning about networking.

The Novell certification programs also have prerequisites, some of which are as simple as having to first enroll in the program.

After reading this chapter, you will know the following:

◆ The prerequisites for each of Novell's four certification programs

◆ The process you must go through to become certified in each of the four Novell certification programs

Prerequisites for the CNA Program

The CNA program is designed for those of you who administer a Novell NetWare LAN at your employer's office, your small business, or your home. Obtaining this certification shows that you have sufficient knowledge to successfully administer, monitor, and maintain a Novell network.

Before you can obtain the CNA certification, you need to have some basic knowledge of microcomputers and DOS (or UNIX) fundamentals. While this knowledge is not a specific requirement for registering into the CNA program, and no specific DOS or microcomputer questions are asked on the CNA test that you take, the knowledge is a prerequisite to understanding the information you learn about networking with NetWare or UnixWare.

There are several ways that you can obtain the information needed to meet this requirement of the CNA program, including:

◆ Formal education

◆ Experience

◆ On-the-job training

◆ Self-study

If you are already working with microcomputers and DOS, you may have sufficient knowledge of DOS and microcomputer concepts. You may still feel that you need some type of training or study in these topics, however.

Several training options are available to you. If you do well studying on your own, you have several self-study options, including the following:

◆ Third-party books published on the topics of DOS and microcomputers (such as *NetWare Training Guide: Networking Technologies, Inside MS-DOS 6.2,* and *Keeping Your PC Alive,* all published by New Riders Publishing)

◆ Reference manuals written by microcomputer manufacturers such as Intel, Compaq, and others

◆ Video and audio tapes available from Novell and some third-party companies

◆ Textbooks such as the student manuals included in each Novell course student kit

◆ Computer-based training (CBT) available from Novell

◆ Trade publications and related newspapers or magazines, such as those listed in Chapter 1, "Introducing the Novell Certification Programs"

If you prefer a hands-on approach, CBT programs are often useful, as well as video and audio tapes. Some CBT programs enable you to practice what you learn while actually using the program.

Some video tapes and audio tapes are also designed to be used while you sit at your computer and follow the instructions.

If it is easier for you to learn from a more structured classroom environment, you may be better off enrolling in one of the courses in microcomputers and DOS that many colleges and universities offer. If a college classroom is a little too structured for you, try one of the many adult education programs that also offer courses in these two topics. Although college-level credit is not granted for such courses taken through adult education, most adult education courses usually do not last as long as college courses or require that you take tests.

All of these options have their own pros and cons. For example, a structured classroom may provide you with the deadlines you need to successfully complete your work. On the other hand, formal classes may only be offered during working hours, and thus be unavailable to you. You need to choose the study option that best fits your needs and lifestyle.

Knowledge of DOS and microcomputer concepts is considered a prerequisite here because the CNA tests assume you have knowledge of both of these topics, although no direct DOS or microcomputer questions are asked. The tests are written with the expectation that you have already gathered this knowledge through experience or prior training.

Enrollment in the CNA program is another prerequisite for obtaining a CNA certification. Fortunately, enrollment is quite simple. You become enrolled in the program automatically when you sign up to take the NetWare or UnixWare CNA test.

When you call the DATC (*Drake Authorized Testing Center*) for the first time, they record information about you and enroll you in the certification program that you choose, including the CNA program. In order to become enrolled in a program, you need to provide the DATC with information about yourself. This information includes the following:

◆ Social Security number. If you do not have an SSN or prefer not to reveal your SSN, Drake personnel will assign a Drake ID number to your records. This number is used instead of your Social Security number to track information about your testing attempts and results.

◆ Last name, first name, and middle initial (if any).

◆ Name of the company you work for or, if self-employed, the name of your business.

◆ Telephone numbers, both work and home.

◆ Mailing addresses, both work and home. You can specify where you want materials sent.

◆ A fax number, if you have one.

◆ Number or name of the test you want to take.

◆ Method of payment for this test. Your options include using a credit card (VISA/MasterCard/American Express), check (Drake Training and Technologies bills you and you return the billing stub with your payment), or voucher. (NAEC's have vouchers available for purchase. If you purchase a voucher, Drake requests that you give them the voucher number over the phone.)

◆ The date and time you want to take the test. If paying by credit card, you can take the test the same day. Otherwise, you cannot schedule the test until Drake receives payment. Then you can schedule to take the test that same day, or within six weeks from the date of your phone call.

◆ The Novell certification program in which you want to be enrolled.

As mentioned previously, enrollment is also considered a prerequisite, but is handled automatically the first time you call the DATC and provide the information listed in the preceding paragraphs.

Prerequisites for the CNE Program

The CNE program was the only entry-level certification program until Novell introduced the CNA program.

Unlike the CNA program, the CNE program does require that you take a specific test in DOS and microcomputer concepts. This does not have to be the first test that you take, however. You may take the required certification tests in any order. You might find it quite useful to take the test on DOS and microcomputer concepts first, however; a basic knowledge of these two topics is a prerequisite to understanding networking technology and NetWare.

As with the CNA program, another prerequisite to the CNE program is enrolling in this certification program. Enrollment for the CNE is handled in the same way as enrollment for the CNA. To enroll in the CNE program, complete the following steps:

1. Gather and read information about the CNE program.

 This book provides you with most of the information you need. However, Novell changes its program requirements and procedures periodically to meet the changing demands of the marketplace. In addition to reading this book, you might also want to contact Novell to obtain the latest version of their documentation that discusses the CNE program and related requirements.

2. Decide which NetWare OS (or UnixWare OS) you want to choose as your CNE certification track. Your options include the following:

    ◆ NetWare 2.2

    ◆ NetWare 3.1x/3.11

    ◆ NetWare 4.x

    ◆ UnixWare

3. Select the first test for which you want to study and pass.

 DOS/Microcomputer Concepts, test number 50-15, or UNIX OS Fundamentals for NetWare Users, test number 50-107, are recommended as the first tests to take (depending on which OS you are going to study). The information that you gain by studying for and passing one of these tests helps you become better prepared for learning about NetWare.

4. Study for the test, taking the related Novell authorized course, if necessary.

5. Call the Drake Authorized Testing Center (1-800-RED-EXAM) and register for the CNE program and your first test.

6. Take the test at the date, time, and place that you registered to take it.

7. Sign and return the CNE/ECNE Agreement card.

The signature card is attached to the CNE agreement, which you receive after taking your first test. You can also obtain the agreement from Novell's FaxBack line by calling 1-800-NETWARE and choosing option 1, then choosing option 1 again, or by choosing option 3, following the prompts, and then asking administration for a copy of the CNE/ECNE brochure.

8. Sign up for, study for, and take the remaining CNE tests for certification.

The remaining tests that you must take depend on which NetWare or UnixWare track you chose to follow. As a minimum, you must pass the System Manager and Advanced System Manager tests or the Administration and Advanced Administration tests for your chosen track. Then you must also pass the Installation and Configuration test for your track, plus the NetWare Service and Support and the Networking Technologies tests. These last two tests are taken regardless of the track you chose. In addition, you must take a minimum of two more tests chosen from the electives list to total four elective credits.

Once you enroll in the CNE program, Novell keeps track of your progress. All test results are sent to Novell, as well as to you. When you have successfully completed all required tests, Novell sends you a CNE *Welcome Aboard* kit, which includes a letter stating your certification, CNE logo sheets, and additional items Novell considers important.

Prerequisites for the ECNE Program

The most important prerequisite for the ECNE program is to obtain your CNE certification. You must still be a CNE in good standing when you enroll in the ECNE program.

From the time you enroll in the ECNE program until you obtain your ECNE certification, you must continue to be a CNE in good standing. That is, you must complete any CNE continuing education requirements within the time specified and not give Novell cause to decertify you, such as by violating any aspect of the CNE Agreement, or you risk becoming decertified as a CNE. Decertified CNEs cannot obtain an ECNE. In order to obtain an ECNE, you must recertify as a CNE before continuing on for your ECNE.

Obtaining your CNE certification before enrolling in the ECNE program requires that you complete the steps outlined in the previous section. However, you may have noticed that in the CNE program, you can choose the NetWare 2.2 track. That track is not available in the ECNE program because NetWare 2.2 is not an OS designed for enterprise-wide networking. NetWare 3 and NetWare 4 are enterprise-wide networking solutions. Therefore, you must choose one of these two tracks for obtaining your ECNE.

If you think that you may want to obtain an ECNE after obtaining your CNE, you may want to consider taking the NetWare 3 or NetWare 4 track during your CNE studies. If you do, your transition into the ECNE program will be easier, simply because NetWare 2 is not an OS track option in the ECNE program. By taking the NetWare 3 or 4 CNE track, you will have already met most of the OS track options for the ECNE program.

As with the CNA and CNE programs, the prerequisites and other requirements may be changed from time to time. Therefore, you may want to call Novell at 1-800-NETWARE and ask for a copy of the latest CNE and ECNE program brochures.

Prerequisites for the CNI Program

You may have noticed that as you go through each level of certification, the prerequisites for certification increase proportionally. This is still true when you reach the level of CNI certification.

The CNI certification program helps to ensure that individuals who are taking Novell product courses through an authorized education center (NAEC or NEAP) are being taught by individuals who are specialists in their field and who have gone through a demanding certification process. This ensures that they are truly knowledgeable about the subjects they are teaching.

Novell CNI certification candidates must have a good working knowledge of the computer field before they apply to become CNIs. Novell expects each CNI candidate to have a great deal of experience and industry exposure in computer science and networking.

To ensure that a candidate is ready to go through the CNI certification process, each candidate must meet several prerequisites:

◆ First, a CNI candidate must have a working knowledge of microcomputers and their operating systems. If your primary interest is in DOS-based machines, you must have a good understanding of how DOS-based microcomputers work and of the DOS operating system. If your primary interest is in UNIX-based computers, you must have a good understanding of how UNIX computers work and of the UNIX operating system.

◆ The second prerequisite is that of technical experience and knowledge in the field of network computing. You must have at least one year of hands-on experience in the area in which you want to specialize as an instructor before you apply for certification as a Novell instructor (CNI).

◆ Third, you must have fully developed presentation skills. That does not necessarily mean that you must have a great deal of experience at giving presentations or teaching. You are only required to have a minimum of one year of experience teaching adults.

You must also have taken some type of presentation skills course. Novell does not offer such a course, or even recommend a specific course to take. Therefore, you have to find one on your own. You need to research that for yourself and find one that seems to fit your needs, then take and successfully complete the course you selected.

Many universities and colleges offer presentation skills courses. You can also find organizations that offer courses of this nature in a time frame that is substantially shorter than attending a full semester or quarter at your college or university. If you need a recommendation for such a course, you can ask your regional Novell contact for information about any courses in your area. To find your regional Novell contact, call CNI Administration at 1-800-429-5445, or refer to Appendix B in this book.

Author's Note Once you are enrolled in the CNI program, to become certified you must take and pass one of Novell's Instructor Performance Evaluation (IPE) classes. Each IPE is designed to test your technical knowledge of the subject course you want to teach, as well as your skills as a presenter/instructor. You are graded against a list of presentation skills, which are discussed in detail in Chapter 5, "Becoming a Certified NetWare Instructor." I would recommend that you know which presentation skills you will be graded on before you enroll in a presentation skills course. Then, choose your presentation skills course according to whether or not each of those presentation skills are taught in that course.

◆ The fourth prerequisite is an ability to clearly communicate technical information. This requires that you have a thorough knowledge of the information that you are planning to teach.

Before you enroll for your IPE, you must decide which course you want to teach. You are expected to fully learn the material related to your chosen course before you attend the IPE course. For many of the courses, just reading the course book is not enough. You may have to become thoroughly acquainted with the materials in the Novell manual set as well.

◆ The fifth prerequisite is the ability to manage a classroom of students effectively. You can best meet this prerequisite through your experience as a presenter or instructor. Factors related to this prerequisite that are important include the following:

> Ability to answer questions

> Skill at handling difficult students

> Adaptability to the varying requirements of an adult classroom

> Experience at presenting information so it is understandable and interesting

◆ The last prerequisite is one that cannot really be learned; you must simply possess it. You should display a positive and enthusiastic attitude reflecting your knowledge and feelings about both teaching and Novell's products. If you have decided to become a CNI, you probably already have a positive and enthusiastic attitude. If not, you might want to reconsider your decision before you invest too much time and money.

The Certification Process

Now that you know the prerequisites for each of the certification programs, it may help you to know the process you go through to become certified.

This section discusses the certification process for each of the four Novell certification programs.

For CNAs

To obtain your CNA, you must first meet all prerequisites, as discussed previously. One of the prerequisites includes choosing the Novell operating system for which you want to obtain a certification. Table 2.1 shows you what tests you must take for certification in each of the CNA tracks.

Table 2.1
Tests for the CNA Program

Test Number	Description
NetWare 2 Certification	
50-115	Certified NetWare 2.2 Administrator
NetWare 3 Certification	
50-116	Certified NetWare 3.11 Administrator
or	
50-130	Certified NetWare 3.1x Administrator
NetWare 4 Certification	
50-122	Certified NetWare 4.0 Administrator
UnixWare Certification	
50-134	Certified UnixWare System Administrator

One of the prerequisites requires enrolling in the program, which is done at the time you sign up for your CNA test.

When the date of your test arrives, go to the DATC and take your test (remember to bring a photo identification card with you).

After taking your CNA test, both you and Novell are notified of your score. If you have a passing score, the certification process continues.

Note If you did not pass the test, you must study again, sign up and pay the $85 fee to take the test again, and then pass the test. If you take the test without passing it three successive times, you must take the related Novell course. You are not allowed to take the test a fourth time until you have taken the related course and submitted a copy of your certificate to Novell.

Once Novell receives notification of your passing score, Novell sends the CNA paperwork to you. Included in this paperwork is a request for a passport-sized photo. Once you return the photo to Novell, Novell issues a CNA badge to you.

That is all there is to the CNA certification process. You are now a Certified NetWare Administrator and may use that designation on your business cards, letterhead, resume, and other paperwork.

The following checklist will guide you step by step through the certification process.

Steps To Follow for CNA Certification

☐ 1. Learn about microcomputer concepts and DOS or UNIX fundamentals for NetWare users.

☐ 2. Choose the operating system track for your CNA.

☐ 3. Study for (or take courses for) your chosen operating system track.

☐ 4. Call the Drake Authorized Training Center to enroll in the CNA program and sign up for the CNA test.

_____   _____   _____
Date scheduled   *Time*   *Location*

☐ 5. Gather identification (with picture) and go to the DATC to take the test.

☐ 6. Pass the test

_____
Date notified

continues

63

☐ 7. Receive your *Welcome Aboard* kit. (You should receive it within 3 or 4 weeks of being notified of passing the test.)

For CNEs

The certification program for CNEs is more complicated than that of the CNA program.

The first step in the CNE certification process is to decide which Novell CNE track you want to follow and then choose your required electives. In essence, you should plot out your course before steering straight ahead. Table 2.2 shows you the tests you must take, depending on the track you choose to follow.

Table 2.2
Tests for the CNE Program

Test Number	Description (Credits)
Prerequisite Requirement (2 Credits)	
50-15	DOS/Microcomputer Concepts (2)
or	
50-107	UNIX OS Fundamentals for NetWare Users (2)
Operating System Requirements (5 Credits)	
50-20	NetWare 2.2 System Manager (3)
and	
50-44	NetWare 2.2 Advanced System Manager (2)
or	
50-130	NetWare 3.1x Administration (3)
and	
50-131	NetWare 3.1x Advanced Administration (2)
or	
50-91	NetWare 3.11 System Manager (3)
and	
50-82	NetWare 3.11 Advanced System Manager (2)
or	

Test Number	Description (Credits)
50-130 and	NetWare 3.1x Administration (3)
50-82	NetWare 3.11 Advanced System Manager (2)
or	
50-91 and	NetWare 3.11 System Manager (3)
50-131	NetWare 3.1x Advanced Administration (2)
or	
50-122 and	NetWare 4.0 Administration (3)
50-123	NetWare 4.0 Advanced Administration (2)
or	
50-134 and	UnixWare System Administration (3)
50-135	UnixWare Advanced System Administration (2)

Core Requirements (8 Credits)

50-132	NetWare 2.2 and 3.1x Installation and Configuration (2)
or	
50-146	NetWare 4.0 Installation and Configuration (2)
and	
50-46 and	NetWare Service and Support (5)
50-80	Networking Technologies (3)

Electives (4 Credits)

Choose tests to equal 4 elective credits. Appendix A contains a list of tests that meet this electives requirement.

You may apply any operating system track NOT used to meet the requirements specified under the *Operating System Tract* section as elective credits. Also, you may choose from a list of electives to meet this requirement.

The second step in CNE certification is to enroll in the program. As with the other programs, enrollment is handled automatically when you call the DATC to sign up for your first test. Of course, because signing up for a test is the first step, you may want to be certain you have studied for the test before you enroll. Therefore, you may either want to do some studying on your own, take a course, or do both.

After passing your first test, study for and take all the additional required tests.

Each time you take a certification test, both you and Novell are notified of your results. Once Novell has verification that you have passed all of your required tests, Novell sends you the CNE *Welcome Aboard* kit.

When you receive your CNE *Welcome Aboard* kit, complete all the required paperwork, including obtaining and submitting to Novell a passport-sized photo so Novell can send you a CNE identification badge.

Once you receive your kit, you can use the Novell logos and the CNE designation on your business cards, letterhead, and any-where else that Novell considers the use of its logo appropriate.

The following checklist will assist you in charting your progress during the CNE certification process.

Steps To Follow for CNE Certification

☐ 1. Learn about DOS and microcomputer concepts or UNIX fundamentals for NetWare users.

☐ 2. Call DATC and sign up for the DOS/Microcomputer Concepts test (50-15) or the UNIX fundamentals for NetWare Users test (50-107), which also enrolls you in the CNE program.

☐ 3. Sign and return your CNE/ECNE agreement card.

_____

Date returned

☐ 4. Gather identification (with picture ID) and take it with you to the testing center.

_____   _____   _____

Date scheduled   *Time*   *Location*

☐ 5. Choose the operating system track in which to obtain your certification:

   ☐ NetWare 2.2
   ☐ NetWare 3.1x/3.11
   ☐ NetWare 4.0
   ☐ UNIX

☐ 6. Sign up for, study for, and pass each required test for the operating system track that you chose:

NetWare 2.2
   ☐ 50-20 NetWare 2.2 System Manager
   ☐ 50-41 NetWare 2.2 Advanced System Manager

NetWare 3.1x
   ☐ 50-130 NetWare 3.1x Administration
   ☐ 50-131 NetWare 3.1x Advanced Administration

NetWare 3.11
   ☐ 50-91 NetWare 3.11 System Manager
   ☐ 50-82 NetWare 3.11 Advanced System Manager

UnixWare
   ☐ 50-134 UnixWare System Administration
   ☐ 50-135 UnixWare Advanced System Administration

☐ 7. Sign up for, study for, take, and pass the Installation and Configuration course for your chosen operating system track.

   ☐ NetWare 2.x/3.1x Installation and Configuration workshop
   ☐ NetWare 4.0 Installation and Configuration workshop

continues

67

☐ 8. Sign up for, study for, take, and pass Networking Technologies test 50-80.

☐ 9. Sign up for, study for, take, and pass NetWare Service and Support test 50-46.

☐ 10. Sign up for, study for, take, and pass four credits worth of electives.

☐			
Test #	Description	Date passed	Credits

☐			
Test #	Description	Date passed	Credits

☐			
Test #	Description	Date passed	Credits

☐			
Test #	Description	Date passed	Credits

☐ 11. Submit the required Novell paperwork, including a passport-sized photo.

☐ 12. Let others know that you are a Certified NetWare Engineer.

For ECNEs

The ECNE certification process encompasses the complete certification process for CNEs; current possession of a valid CNE is a prerequisite to obtaining your ECNE.

Once you are a Certified NetWare Engineer in good standing, you can begin the ECNE program.

To begin the ECNE program, decide which of the tracks you want to follow and then design your program accordingly.

You must choose either NetWare 4 or NetWare 3 as your track through the ECNE program. If you gained certification in one of these during the CNE program, you may have already met one of the requirements for certification in the ECNE program. If you gained certification in NetWare 2, your NetWare 2 courses can be applied as electives to your ECNE program.

When you have chosen the track you want to follow, you must pass each of the required courses.

You can take any of the Novell certification tests without ever taking a single Novell course. Some people learn better by taking courses, however. If this is your preference, sign up for the related course.

Two tests that are difficult to pass without some hands-on experience include the Installation and Configuration course and the related NetWare Service and Support course. These two courses require a great deal of work with installing, configuring, troubleshooting, and maintaining a Novell network.

If you do not have access to a network and cannot perform the tasks assigned in these courses, consider taking these courses so you can have access to a Novell network.

You can also prepare for these course tests by studying specific third-party books, such as the *NetWare Training Guide* series published by New Riders Publishing. Otherwise, you will have to study not only the course book for each of these tests, but all of the related Novell red manuals as well.

To obtain your ECNE, choose your NetWare Operating System preference (either the NetWare 4.0 OS track, or the NetWare 3.1x/3.11 OS track), and then study for, take, and pass the required tests. You must then choose sufficient elective credits to complete your ECNE requirements, for a total of 19 credits (available electives are listed in Appendix A).

Table 2.3 shows you the required tests for both the NetWare 4.0 and the NetWare 3.1x/3.11 OS tracks.

Table 2.3
Tests Required for ECNE Certification

Test Number	Description (Credits)
Operating System Requirements *NetWare 4.0 OS Track (7 or 10)*	
Required:	
50-122 and	NetWare 4.0 Administration (3)
50-123	NetWare 4.0 Advanced Administration (2)
	and one of the following options:
Option 1:	
50-45*	NetWare 3.11 OS Features Review
	and 12 additional elective credits
Option 2:	
50-130 or	NetWare 3.1x Administration (3)
50-91*	NetWare 3.11 System Manager (3)
and	
50-131 or	NetWare 3.1x Advanced Administration (2)
50-82*	NetWare 3.11 Advanced System Manager (2)
	and 9 additional elective credits

Test Number	Description (Credits)
NetWare 3.1x/3.11 Track (7 or 10 Credits)	
50-130	NetWare 3.1x Administration (3)
or	
50-91*	NetWare 3.11 System Manager (3)
and	
50-131	NetWare 3.1x Advanced Administration (2)
or	
50-82*	NetWare 3.11 Advanced System Manager (2)
	and one of the following options:
Option 1:	
50-124	NetWare 3.11 to 4.0 Update (2)
	and 12 additional elective credits
Option 2:	
50-122	NetWare 4.0 Administration (3)
and	
50-123	NetWare 4.0 Advanced Administration (2)
	and 9 additional elective credits

Note The test numbers in table 2.3 that have an asterisk (*) next to them are only available until May 12, 1994. After that date, you must take the other tests shown in that part of the table.

As you take each test, both you and Novell are notified of your test results. Once you have passed all required tests, Novell will send you a copy of the Novell ECNE *Welcome Aboard* kit.

This kit contains some paperwork that you must complete and return. In particular, you need to provide Novell with a passport-sized photograph of yourself. Once you have done so, Novell will send you an ECNE identification badge.

You do not have to wait for the arrival of your identification badge to begin promoting your new certification. The Welcome Aboard kit contains Novell ECNE logos that you can start using on your business cards, letterhead, advertisements, and so on.

Once you receive your identification badge, the certification process is complete. You may be required to fulfill continuing education requirements, however.

If any continuing education requirements are established, Novell notifies you of what they are and how long you have to meet them. If you do not meet the continuing education requirements within the specified time limit, you are decertified.

If you are decertified and you want to reestablish your ECNE certification, you must start the ECNE certification process over again. As long as you are still a CNE in good standing, you do not have to repeat that part of the process. However, if you have lost your current CNE status, you must first go through the CNE program again to reestablish your CNE certification, and then go through the ECNE program again to reestablish your ECNE certification

The following checklist will assist you in charting your progress during the ECNE certification process.

Steps To Follow for ECNE Certification

☐ 1. Obtain your certification as a CNE.

    _____   _____

    Date certified   *CNE number*

☐ 2. Determine your operating system track:

    ☐ NetWare 3.1x/3.11
    ☐ NetWare 4.0

☐ 3. Call DATC and sign up for the ECNE program and the required test. (Call DATC for each test after you finish studying.) Complete the following tests:

NetWare 4.0
    ☐ 50-122 Administration
    ☐ 50-123 Advanced Administration

and

    ☐ 50-45 NetWare 3.11 OS Features Review
or
    ☐ 50-130   or   ☐ 50-91
    ☐ 50-131   or   ☐ 50-82

NetWare 3.1x/3.11
    ☐ 50-130   or   ☐ 50-91
    ☐ 50-131   or   ☐ 50-82

and

    ☐ 50-124
or
    ☐ 50-122   and   ☐ 50-123

☐ 4. Sign up for, study for, take, and pass enough elective credits to reach a total of 19 credits.

☐
| _Test #_ | _Description_ | _Date passed_ | _Credits_ |

☐
| _Test #_ | _Description_ | _Date passed_ | _Credits_ |

☐
| _Test #_ | _Description_ | _Date passed_ | _Credits_ |

☐
| _Test #_ | _Description_ | _Date passed_ | _Credits_ |

☐
| _Test #_ | _Description_ | _Date passed_ | _Credits_ |

☐
| _Test #_ | _Description_ | _Date passed_ | _Credits_ |

continues

___	_____	_____	_____
Test #	*Description*	*Date passed*	*Credits*
___	_____	_____	_____
Test #	*Description*	*Date passed*	*Credits*

☐   5. Submit the required Novell paperwork, including a passport-sized photo.

☐   6. Let others know that you are an Enterprise CNE.

For CNIs

You do not have to be a CNA, CNE, or an ECNE to become a CNI.

To become a CNI you must first meet the prerequisites, and then enroll and be accepted into the CNI program. After studying for and passing the tests required for your certification, you must pay the $500 fee, and then take and pass the *Instructor Performance Evaluation* (IPE) class for one of the Core/OS Products.

While there are three areas in which you can obtain a CNI, you must first pass an IPE in the Core/OS Product option before you can take an IPE in either of the other two certification options.

Unlike the CNA, CNE, and ECNE certification programs, you *must* take each course you plan to teach, in addition to passing the related test and the IPE for the category (certification area) into which the course fits.

Table 2.4 shows you the requirements for obtaining your first CNI, which must be in the Core/OS Product Courses category.

Table 2.4
Tests Required for CNI Certification

Test Number	Test Description
Certification for Teaching Your Chosen Core/OS Product Courses:	
50-15	CNI DOS/Microcomputer Concepts
	and one of the following IPE-eligible courses:

Test Number	Test Description
50-81	Networking Technologies
50-230	NetWare 3.1x Administration
50-231	NetWare 3.1x Advanced Administration
50-222	NetWare 4.0 Administration
50-223	NetWare 4.0 Advanced Administration
50-225	NetWare 4.0 Design and Implementation
50-237	Printing with NetWare
50-218	NetWare Service and Support

When you have met all the CNI requirements and passed the necessary tests and the IPE, you receive a letter of certification that lists the courses you are eligible to teach. Once you receive this letter, you may begin teaching any course for which you are certified.

 Note Passing grades are set higher for CNI certification than they are for CNE and ECNE certification.

In addition to the certification letter, you also receive the CNI *Welcome Aboard* kit. Included in this kit is a Novell Order Entry form. Use this form to purchase instructor kits for each additional course you want to certify to teach.

Unlike the CNA, CNE, and ECNE certifications, the CNI certification requires annual renewal. The renewal involves meeting any continuing certification requirements defined by Novell, if any, and submitting an annual recertification fee.

Presently, the annual recertification fee is $700. However, you should check with Novell each year to see if the fee has changed, as well as to determine if there are any continuing certification requirements to be met. This fee is due every year at the same time, generally during the month of September. If you paid $500 for IPE certification in July, you will need to pay the $700 annual recertification fee in September of the same year. This fee covers the costs of keeping you informed. It includes course kits for which you are certified, free update training, NSE Pro CD, education bulletins, and Appnotes (Novell's application notes that usually come out on a monthly basis).

The following checklist can assist you in charting your progress during the CNI certification process.

Steps To Follow for CNI Certification

☐   1.   Submit your application and resume for admission into the program.

☐   2.   Select the IPE course.

☐   3.   Complete the prerequisites for your chosen IPE target course.

☐   4.   Attend the course you selected for your IPE and submit a copy of your completion certificate to Novell.

☐   5.   Pass the CNI test.

☐   6.   Study and practice your presentation skills.

☐   7.   Study and become very familiar with your chosen course materials.

☐   8.   Sign up for, study for, take, and pass the IPE.

☐   9.   Receive your letter of certification from Novell and let everyone know that you are now a CNI.

☐   10.   Certify in other courses by attending them and passing their tests.

☐   11.   Take additional IPEs if you want to certify in other non-Core/OS courses.

Summary

Now that you have read this chapter, you should have a better idea of which certification(s) you want to obtain. You should also know what prerequisites, if any, you need to complete before enrolling in one or more of the programs. Finally, you should know what is required for each of the certification programs.

Once you choose a certification program to pursue, the checklists provided in this chapter can be used to help ensure that you meet the prerequisites and successfully accomplish each certification step.

Chapter 3, "Training to Become NetWare Certified," guides you through the types of training available to you so you can prepare to take your chosen certification tests.

Training to Become NetWare Certified

CHAPTER 3

This book is designed to help you select the certification that is best for you, as well as choose the path to certification that is the quickest and easiest for you and your particular needs. This book would not be complete without a discussion of your options for learning the information that you must learn to become Novell certified.

This chapter discusses the types of training available to you as a Novell certification candidate. It explains ways to learn the necessary information to complete a certificate through self-study, on-the-job training, using Computer-Based Training (CBT) or tutorials, or taking courses from Novell Authorized Education Centers (NAECs) or Novell Education Academic Partners (NEAPs).

This chapter explains how to obtain additional information about any of the Novell certifications, and how and where to get the training that you need. In addition, this chapter discusses Novell's FaxBack program. FaxBack is a quick way of getting the most current certification program information via facsimile.

This chapter also provides hints and tips for studying the information that you need to know in order to successfully pass the required tests, as well as correctly and efficiently perform the duties that are expected of you as a Novell Certified Administrator, Engineer, or Instructor.

After reading this chapter you will be able to do the following:

◆ Make the most of hands-on and self study

◆ Use CBTs and tutorials for maximum effectiveness

◆ Select and take the right courses to meet your certification needs

◆ Get more information on Novell courses

Making the Most of Hands-On and Self-Study Options

Hands-on study requires that you become involved in working with the information that you are studying. For example, if you were taking a botany course, the hands-on portion of that course might include plant dissection, diagramming, seed germination, and other approaches to working with the topic of botany. In studying computers and networking, hands-on techniques might include opening up a computer and installing a LAN card, troubleshooting a communication failure on an existing network, or just sitting at a computer and entering different DOS commands to watch the results. There are several ways to obtain useful hands-on experience while learning network-related topics. Several hands-on learning options are discussed in this section.

Self study involves learning material by reading it, asking and answering questions, and applying other techniques that cause you to understand and learn the information through your own efforts. Self-study is most often accomplished with the aid of written study materials such as books and periodicals.

This section also shows you how to use several effective self-study techniques so that you can learn necessary information about DOS, microcomputers, UNIX, NetWare, or UnixWare without having to first attend courses. You might also find that you can apply the hands-on and self-study techniques learned from this section can be applied to your course materials, if you decide to take one or more related courses from an NAEC or NEAP.

Ways To Make the Most of Hands-On Learning

Much of the information needed to pass the Novell certification tests can be learned by studying the appropriate written materials. For some, that is more difficult than for others. But if you are someone who enjoys studying and knows how to translate what you learn from your books into practical experience, you can do very well.

The problem is that, in addition to our studies, most of us need some kind of hands-on learning to effectively grasp a topic. If that is true for you as well, you may benefit from the following suggestions that are aimed at helping you find and use hands-on exercises to supplement your studies.

If you take Novell courses, you have no problem getting hands-on experience in a Novell networking environment. Each Novell course includes a great deal of hands-on time. All the Novell courses have assignments for you to complete and computer labs in which you can complete those assignments.

If you elect to study for the tests without taking Novell-authorized courses, you will need to find alternative approaches to obtaining practical hands-on experience. There are several options open to you, although you may not be able to take advantage of all of them.

Finding and taking advantage of practical hands-on experience in any field requires accessing the tools of the trade. For example, if you want to learn to scuba dive, you can study the books, practice proper breathing techniques, and even practice swimming. However, none of those options gives you real-life experience with scuba diving. To get that experience, you must acquire a wet suit, scuba tanks, a regulator, swim fins, a face mask, and a place to go scuba diving, such as the ocean. To obtain hands-on experience in a Novell networking environment, you must find or build such an environment. In other words, you must have access to the tools of the trade.

Novell networks are found in many places. An inexpensive way to obtain practical experience on a Novell network is to take courses at a college or university as part of Novell's NEAP (Novell Education Academic Partner) program. Contact your local college or university to find out if it is an NEAP, or call Novell for a list of NEAPs.

If an NEAP is located near you, you have a couple of other study options. You can enroll in a networking course that provides lab access. This can be time-consuming for someone who wants the experience very quickly, because a single college or university course runs a full semester or quarter, usually around 15 weeks.

If taking a course is not an option for you, perhaps you could obtain access to the lab on your own. If you know someone who works at the college lab, you might be able to work out an arrangement, such as working in the lab during slow lab periods. Of course, you should make sure that this will not cause you or your acquaintance any problems.

If you cannot arrange to study in the lab on your own time, you might be able to become a lab assistant or a private tutor. Either of these options might also make it possible for you to have some hands-on time in the school's networking lab.

The use of personal resources may also be an option for you. Perhaps you know someone who works for a company that runs a Novell network. Perhaps your friend would agree to tutor you or give you access to the network after hours. You cannot get full networking hands-on experience with this method unless your friend is the network supervisor or administrator. You can, however, obtain some practical experience that might benefit your studies.

NAECs (Novell Authorized Education Centers) also offer lab-only courses for people who already understand NetWare. That does not mean that you have to already know everything there is to know about NetWare. If you have studied and learned all you can without having any hands-on experience, you might want to contact your local NAEC and arrange to take one of their lab courses. These courses are taught by a CNI and usually last one week. This type of course often has predefined lab experiments or lessons set up for you. The instructor explains the lesson to you and helps you if you need help. For the most part, however, you do the lab work on your own, just as you do in the lab portions of regular NetWare courses.

The main advantage to this approach is that you do all of your lab work in an intensive one-week effort. It is a quick way to get the hands-on learning that you need. It is also less expensive than attending each Novell instructor-led course.

If you already work at a company that has a Novell network installed, you can get all or at least some of your experience where you work. Even if you do not normally work with the network, you may be given clearance to work with it by asking permission from the right people. If you have already completed your self-study of the Novell materials, it is likely that you have learned enough about networking to start working in the actual environment and performing some of the recommended lab experiments.

Techniques and Tips for Making the Most of Self Study

Self-study involves any method that you employ to learn a given topic. In this case, *self-study* refers mainly to using Novell student manuals and third-party books, such as those published by New Riders Publishing, to learn about Novell's networking and related products.

There are different sources for self-study materials. There are even self-study programs offered by Novell through the NAECs. By contacting an NAEC, you can obtain self-study course materials and can later sign up for a related lab course, if one is available.

If, however, you prefer to learn exclusively from the student manuals or third-party books, you may find some of the self-study suggestions in this section to be of use to you. Even if you decide to take one or more of the Novell courses from a NAEC or NEAP, the information in this section can still help you improve your chances of passing the certification tests by providing you with techniques that improve your retention of learned material.

Before you begin to study for any of the certification tests, it is in your best interest to know exactly what Novell expects you to have learned. You find this out by obtaining a copy of the course/ test objectives for each test that you intend to take.

You can obtain the course/test objectives several ways. This book provides lists of objectives for several tests. Also, if you have a copy of the Novell student manual for the course, objectives are listed at the beginning of each section. In addition, you can call the FaxBack line and have lists of course/test objectives sent to you. Once you obtain a copy of the objectives and the student manual, third-party book, or other reference material that you are using for your studies, you are ready to begin.

If you have taken any college courses at all, you have probably learned such recommended study techniques such as the following:

◆ Studying in bright light to reduce fatigue and depression

◆ Establishing a regular study schedule and following it

◆ Turning off the television and other distractions, or going into a quiet room

◆ Studying in the same place each time so that you have all your materials at hand and readily available

There are additional common study recommendations, most of which you have probably heard. Many of these recommended study techniques, including those in the preceding list, are effective.

There are also some other self-study techniques that are less commonly taught, but are, none the less, very useful. These techniques are discussed in this section.

Author's Note

Before I discuss some less commonly known study techniques, I want to point out an additional issue related to the last technique mentioned in the preceding list.

Although it is convenient to have all of your study materials in one place, and to subsequently always study in the same place, this habit does not necessarily facilitate test-taking.

Your certification tests are given in a testing environment that is likely to be substantially different from your study area. If possible, you should either vary the location where you study and/or study in surroundings similar to those of the testing center. This approach helps to reduce some of the stress and distractions associated with taking tests in strange places. In addition, some recall of material may be made possible because of a conscious or unconscious association with your surroundings during a previous study time. Therefore, if you can study in an environment similar to the test center, or at least know what it looks like and keep it in mind while studying, you may do just a little better at test time.

If possible, I recommend that you find out where your closest testing center is (call DATC and ask them), then visit the testing center to see how it is set up before you schedule to take your first test. Ask for a tour of the testing center. By becoming familiar with the testing center and keeping it in mind when you study in your own study area, you may make your actual test-taking more relaxed.

Studies have shown that a topic must be studied seven different times before the information becomes part of our long-term memory. Therefore, when you plan your studies, plan to review your material at least seven different times, and, preferably, on seven different occasions.

If this seems like a great deal of studying, well, it could be. It depends, among other factors, on how truly new the material is to you. Because your mind is adept at sorting new information into categories, and filing that information into long-term memory storage next to information that it already knows, it may not take more than one or two study sessions to commit material to your long-term memory. It is likely that only a small percentage of the information you learn will require several repetitions in order for you to readily remember and retrieve the information. However, you should consider designing your study sessions in such a way as to maximize the benefits of your mind's learning abilities.

Another useful fact about memory that research has determined is that people best remember things presented first and last to them. In other words, if you are studying a long list of items, your mind finds it easier to remember those items that were presented first and last on the list.

You can take advantage of this discovery by designing your study sessions so that when you are studying a list of facts, you can modify the order in which they are reviewed. Each time you study, shuffle the items around so that on at least one occasion, each item in the list falls into either the first or last position on the list.

In the earlier NLIST example, NLIST had several parameters that could be used to specify the type of information for which NLIST would search. Though only three parameters were discussed using NLIST—/A, /S, and /D—the list of parameters that you need to learn for any given command is often substantially longer. To use the study technique of reordering your review materials, you can list and describe each parameter on a separate slip of paper. Then each time you study these parameters, you can change the order in which you study them by shuffling the slips of paper.

Although this example may seem fairly simple, the technique is very effective when you have a long list of similar information to learn. Human memory research has shown that when you study or read, you should be very active in your participation. Active study is easy if you do a little preplanning for each review session.

When you begin your session, quickly skim the material you are going to study. Write down any questions that come to mind as you are skimming. Then actively search for the answer to those questions as you are reading and reviewing the material.

Another active study technique involves guessing the contents of the material, before you actually start reading and studying it. Start by skimming the material to be read or studied. As you skim, notice any headings, subheadings, figures, tables, graphics and so on that are in the material. Try to guess the types of information you expect to find while reading these sections or when reviewing the figures, tables, and graphics. Then, when you actually read the material, see if your guesses were correct.

Novell also provides you with an excellent way to become actively involved in your studies. When you study, actively look for the answers to the course/test objectives in your study materials. When you find the answers, you might want to use the next recommended study technique—taking effective notes.

Though you often speak in complete sentences, your mind thinks very cryptically. It abbreviates the information that you are gathering so that it can effectively categorize and properly store it. Because you think in key ideas, you can also take effective notes by writing down only those key ideas.

As you will see when you begin taking Novell's certification tests, test questions do not always cover just key ideas, but often also cover many details. The previous NLIST example can be used to advantage here as well.

The key idea in this instance is that you can use NLIST to search for objects in the NDS tree. The type of test question you must answer in this case, however, is more likely to be detailed and very specific—in other words, along the lines of the sample question shown earlier. Therefore, take cryptic notes of key thoughts when studying conceptual or other relevant information, but be careful not to miss important details such as command syntax.

One final study suggestion relates directly back to repetition of study. The suggestion is that if you have or can obtain a tape recorder, record in a concise form the information you need to memorize. Then play back the recording as often as you can. Some people do much of their studying while they drive back and forth to work. They read the material they need to study, take concise and cryptic notes, record the information onto a tape, and repeatedly listen when they are too busy doing other things to sit down and reread their notes. You may find this an effective technique for studying as well

Hands-On Learning and Test Taking

Working with the network can quickly and substantially increase your NetWare or UnixWare knowledge. Because many people learn more by doing than they do by merely reading and studying, a little hands-on experience can go a long way.

The methods you employ in hands-on training affect how well you do when you take the certification tests. The certification tests are written to determine whether or not you have sufficient knowledge of the Novell networking information that Novell considers important. To make sure that you know what Novell considers important networking information, each Novell course and its accompanying certification test has a list of objectives associated with it. Test questions are written based on these course/test objectives. Obtaining hands-on experience that parallels the course/test objectives, therefore, gives you a much better chance of successfully passing the test.

For example, Novell's NetWare 4.0 Administration course (number 520) and its accompanying CNE certification test (number 50-122) has the following item as an objective:

> Access NDS information from the command prompt using NLIST and CX.

To obtain hands-on experience that is sufficient to meet this course/test objective, you need to connect to a Novell NetWare 4 Directory Services tree and run the NLIST and CX utilities.

To accomplish this, once you have connected to an NDS (NetWare Directory Services) tree, you might type **NLIST** at the DOS prompt. When you type **NLIST**, you see the help screen (see figure 3.1) that shows you the correct syntax for using the NLIST utility in the NDS environment.

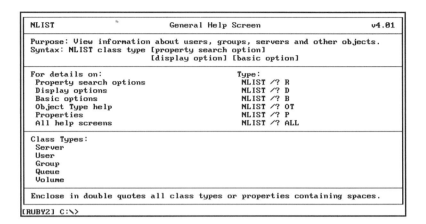

```
NLIST                    General Help Screen                      v4.01
Purpose: View information about users, groups, servers and other objects.
Syntax: NLIST class type [property search option]
                         [display option] [basic option]

For details on:                           Type:
  Property search options                 NLIST /? R
  Display options                         NLIST /? D
  Basic options                           NLIST /? B
  Object Type help                        NLIST /? OT
  Properties                              NLIST /? P
  All help screens                        NLIST /? ALL

Class Types:
  Server
  User
  Group
  Queue
  Volume

Enclose in double quotes all class types or properties containing spaces.
[RUBY2] C:\>
```

Figure 3.1

NLIST General Help screen.

The fact that you see the NLIST General Help screen after you type NLIST at the DOS prompt in this environment tells you that you have not used the correct NDS syntax for this utility. However, it also tells you a great deal more, however, such as what the proper syntax is, the types of classes about which you can obtain information, and ways to bring up additional NLIST help screens.

If, for example, you follow the syntax instructions for additional help, type **NLIST /? ALL**, and then press Enter, you can page through all of the help screens for this utility.

These help screens contain examples of ways to use this utility to accomplish certain NLIST search tasks on the network. For example, the second help screen, the Basic Options help screen, tells you that to see all logged-in users that are active on the network you must type **NLIST User /A**. Once you page through all of the help screens, type **NLIST User /A,** and press Enter, you see something similar to the following:

```
Object Class: user
Current context: OU=ACCT.O=BUZYB
Conn      =    The server connection number
*         =    The asterisk means this is your connection
User Name =    The login name of the user
Address   =    The network address
Node      =    The network node
Login Time=    The time when the user logged in
```

```
User Name                          Address      Node
- - - - - - - - - - - - - - - - - - - - - - - - - - - - - - - - - - - - - - - - - - -

    Guest                        [ 1010108][    1BAD2DEF]
    Ssmith                       [ 1010108][    1BAD2103]
    Dtomlin                      [ 1010108][    1BADCA11]
A total of 3 user objects was found in this context.
A total of 3 user objects was found.
```

Implementing the steps as discussed is an example of hands-on learning. But how does this relate to passing the certification tests?

Well, in the case of the NetWare 4.0 Administration test, accessing NDS information from the command prompt using NLIST is part of a course/test objective. By typing NLIST at the DOS prompt, reviewing the associated help screens, and trying out one or more of the commands on your networked computer, you fulfill a portion of this objective using hands-on learning.

Now, you must relate the information you learned to the ability to answer test questions about what you learned.

To continue the previous example, if you have a copy of the Novell NetWare 4.0 Administration revision 1.0 student manual, you notice that page 5-20 of that manual shows a table: *Table 5-6: Common Tasks Accomplished with NLIST*. One of the entries in that table tells you what you must do to "View active users (currently logged in to the network." Beneath the table you see an example of what performing a conditional search listed in that table looks like on your computer monitor if you run one of these searches. The following page in that manual (page 5-21) contains an exercise that gives you hands-on experience in "Accessing NDS Information from the Command Line." Your first task is to "Display all users in the current context." To do that you type **NLIST User /A**, and press Enter.

As you may have figured out, Novell considers the ability to use NLIST to be an important responsibility of a certified NetWare 4.0 Administrator, Engineer, Enterprise Engineer, and Instructor. This ability is a specific course/test objective. In addition, two pages in the student manual are dedicated to showing you ways to use this utility, and giving you hands-on experience in the form of a lab exercise. All of this attention to NLIST on Novell's part, means that there is a good chance that you might have to answer one or more questions about using NLIST on your certification test.

One of the best ways to study for answering test questions related to this particular course/test objective, is to try to figure out ways one or more test questions might be written.

> **Author's Note** Although Chapter 4, "Testing," also provides information on taking certification tests, such as how to write your own self-study test questions, understanding the concept of test questions and the relationship of test questions to course/test objectives may help you get more out of your studies. These issues, therefore, are discussed briefly in this chapter as well.

Table 5-6 in the student manual and the NLIST help screens show you different options to use with NLIST in order to find out different types of network information. Some of the options that you can use with NLIST include the following:

- ◆   /A   Active users, those currently logged in to the network

- ◆   /S   Sub-container search for the object type you defined

- ◆   /D   Details for a given object such as user or group

Given the course/test objective noted previously, the information on which the student manual concentrates, and the lab exercises, you might, therefore, expect to see questions on your certification test that are similar to the following:

> Which of the following commands would you use at the prompt in order to see all active users currently logged in to the network?
>
>   A. NLIST Users /All
>   B. NLIST User=All /S
>   C. NLIST User
>   D. NLIST User /A

When you answer test questions, you are instructed to choose the best answer (or sometimes to select the best two or three choices). In the above question, the best answer is D. Answer A is incorrect because the student manual tells you to use /A. You use /All to view all of the help screens for NLIST, not to see all of the users. Answer B is incorrect because no equal (=) sign is used in the NLIST syntax unless it is followed by a specific object type such as User. In this answer, no object follows the equal sign. Therefore, the answer is incorrect. Answer C is incorrect because, without the /A, you do not get a list of active users, and **Active** is a key word in the test question.

If you familiarize yourself with the course/test objectives, study the relevant material, and then pre-test yourself by creating your own potential test questions, you have a much better chance of passing the test questions on each certification test. You also receive an added bonus for understanding and using this study technique, because you learn and remember much more of what you study by this method.

Using CBTs and Tutorials for Maximum Effectiveness

Computer Based Training (CBT) is a study tool that helps you learn information about a given topic. A tutorial is also a study tool for learning. CBTs and tutorials are discussed in more detail in this section.

An Overview of the Novell CBTs

Many CBTs use graphics to show you information in a visual form, which you can use to supplement standard text. Many CBTs are also capable of some interaction. This interaction usually takes the form of things such as moving freely between units of the CBT, or taking tests for which you are provided some feedback as to correct and incorrect answers.

Novell recognizes the need of individuals to study information on their own, and the importance of variety. Therefore, Novell has several CBTs that you can obtain, at no charge, if you are a certification candidate.

The CBTs that Novell provides are all based on the Microsoft Windows interface. If you are familiar with Microsoft Windows, you will probably find that the CBTs are relatively easy to use and a fun way of learning networking.

Of course, in order for you to run any of Novell's CBTs, you must have access to the proper equipment. The minimum requirements for running the NetWare 4 CBT are greater than for running the other CBTs. Therefore, to ensure that you can run any of the CBTs, try to meet the following minimum requirements.

- IBM 386 or fully-compatible PC
- Microsoft Windows version 3.0 or above
- A mouse that is compatible with Microsoft Windows
- Novell DOS or Microsoft DOS version 3.1 or above
- A minimum of 4 MB of RAM
- VGA graphics adapter and monitor
- 5.5 MB of available hard disk space

The requirements in the preceding list are for the NetWare 4 CBT. If you are running other CBTs, you may be able to run them with at least 4 MB of RAM, a minimum of 15 to 20 MB of hard disk space, and Microsoft Windows 3.0 or a later version.

CBTs are nice to use because they are more graphical than workbooks or study guides. Novell's CBTs are designed so that you can easily leave an electronic bookmark. This allows you to come back to a particular location in the CBT, or skip forward to an entirely different section. Novell's CBTs can be loaded on individual PCs, or on a network, if you purchase the version of the CBT that comes with a server license. Another benefit of using the CBTs is that they enable you to study when time permits, and do not commit you to having to take a three- to five-day course.

The cost of each CBT is very similar to the cost of taking a course. The biggest plus, however, is that you do not have to pay for accommodations, meals, entertainment, and transportation on top of the cost of the course when you choose to study by using a Novell CBT.

Each CBT contains at least some practice questions and hands-on practice. If you find that the CBT does not have enough practice test questions, you also can get a copy of the CNE assessment disk. CBTs also contain many features, including the following:

◆ Menus and maps to help you navigate through the CBT

◆ Glossaries so that you can look up terms you are not familiar with

◆ Help designed to give you information about the CBT itself

◆ Navigation buttons to let you move freely through the different lessons

◆ Indexes for the lessons so you can find specific information

◆ Go To and Course Topic Search options so that you can search for, find, and then jump to a particular topic you are interested in studying

Although the full CBTs must be purchased from Novell or from a NAEC, you can obtain a free copy of the CBT sampler. The sampler shows you all of the features that Novell's CBTs provide, and gives you some networking information.

You can obtain a free copy of the CBT sampler by calling Novell's After Market Products division at 1-801-429-5508, or your local NAEC. To install the NetWare 4.x CBT sampler, complete the following steps:

1. Insert the first disk in the packet into drive A of the workstation onto which you want to load the CBT

2. Start Windows

3. Select Run from the Program Manager File pull-down menu

4. Type **A:SETUP** in the Command Line box, then select OK.

5. Select Yes when prompted with *Do you wish to continue?*

 The NetWare 4 CBT sampler also requires a minimum of 5.5 MB of disk space. This first window lets you exit out of the CBT sampler if you do not have enough disk space to install it.

6. When prompted, select either Standalone Workstation or Network Server.

 If you select to install the CBT sampler on a standalone workstation, the group and item are created automatically by the install program. If you choose to install the CBT sampler or a network server, you must create the group and item for each network workstation.

7. When prompted, enter the drive letter for where you want the CBT sampler to be installed. If you are installing the CBT sampler on your local hard disk, for example, type **C:**.

8. When the Setup Options Menu appears, select Install Novell CBT Sampler.

 If you follow steps 1 through 8 to bring you to this Setup Options Menu, you also can uninstall the CBT sampler at this point, if you previously installed it.

9. Continue to follow the prompts, inserting disks as requested, until the CBT sampler is installed.

Once installed, you can run the CBT sampler by choosing the Novell CBT Sampler icon from the NOVCBT group.

An Overview of Novell Tutorials

A tutorial is a software program that takes responsibility for guiding you through the things you need to learn about a given topic. Novell's NetWare 4 tutorial, for instance, takes you through various NetWare 4 networking procedures. The NetWare 4 tutorial can be described as a thin version of the NetWare 4.0 Administrator CBT.

What Is Available

NetWare 4.0 ships with the NetWare 4 tutorial. If you have access to a NetWare 4 server then you also should have access to the tutorial, assuming you have the rights to the tutorial.

CBTs are separate Novell products that can be purchased directly from Novell or through an NAEC. Novell presently has seven CBTs available for purchase. An eighth CBT is scheduled for release in the first or second quarter of 1994.

The following list contains the CBTs that are currently available, along with their current single-user purchase price:

- ◆ NetWare User Basics, $395

- ◆ Introduction to Networking, $295

- ◆ NetWare 3.11 System Manager, $895

- ◆ NetWare 3.11 Advanced System Manager, $995

- ◆ NetWare 4.0 Administration, $895

- ◆ Networking Technologies, $895

- ◆ NetWare Expert for NMS, $595

 Note Prices are subject to change. Contact After Market Products by calling 1-801-429-5508 or 1-800-346-7177, 7 A.M. to 5 P.M. MST, for the latest pricing.

The NetWare 4.0 Advanced Administration is the eighth CBT, and the one which is expected to be released during the first or second quarter of 1994. Its planned price is $995 for a single-user version.

Each CBT is available in either a single-user version, or a server license version. If you purchase a single-user version, you can only load and run the CBT on one PC without violating copyright laws.

Server license versions of the CBTs, also referred to as network versions, are available as well. The network version costs either $4,475 or $4,975 depending on the CBT you choose. The Advanced System Manager and Advanced Administration CBTs are the more expensive of the server license CBTs.

Whether you order a single-user version or a server-license version of the CBTs, Novell pays the shipping charges, but you must include sales tax at your state's sales tax rate when paying for the CBT.

Where To Find the CBTs and Tutorial

The NetWare 4 tutorial comes with NetWare 4 when you purchase it. Both the CBTs and the CNE Assessment Disk, mentioned previously, are available through NAECs. However, you also can purchase the CBTs directly from Novell's After Market Products division, a practice that Novell encourages.

To find out which NAEC is closest to you, contact Novell's FaxBack system and follow the phone prompts. You also may be able to obtain access to a CBT through your local college or university, if they are an NEAP. The FaxBack system can tell you which colleges and universities are NEAPs, or you can call your local college or university and ask if they are an NEAP.

CBTs must be prepaid if you order them from Novell's After Market Products division. To prepay, you can use a credit card. Novell currently accepts American Express, VISA, and Master Card. You also can set up an account with Novell if you are representing an organization that regularly does business with

Novell's After Market Products division. You also can send a check or money order directly to Novell's After Market Products division at the following address:

Novell, Inc., After Market Products
Mail stop A-23-2
122 East 1700 South
Provo, Utah 84606

How the CBTs and Tutorial Work

Because the CBTs and tutorial are Microsoft Windows-based, you start the CBT or tutorial by running Windows and choosing the appropriate icon. Figure 3.2 shows the main screen for the NetWare 3.11 Advanced System Manager CBT.

Figure 3.2

NetWare 3.11 Advanced System Manager CBT main screen.

From the main screen of this CBT, you can choose to start by taking a tour of the course itself. Taking a tour explains each individual CBT feature, such as maps, menus, and navigation buttons. Once you are familiar with using Novell's CBTs, you may find that a course tour is not necessary.

If you choose not to take the course tour, you can select any of the main options from this first screen. The NetWare 3.11 Advanced System Manager main screen lets you select from the following:

◆ Advanced System Management

◆ Network Performance Optimization

◆ Advanced System Management Features

◆ Network Protocol Support

If you are using a CBT to study for a certification test, Novell recommends that you go through the CBT from start to finish, rather than jumping around through the lessons. This method helps to ensure that you have sufficient knowledge in one area before moving on to the next. There are other techniques and study tips that are useful when using the CBTs or a tutorial to study for certification tests.

Novell Certification Assessment Disk

As mentioned previously, there also is a Novell Certification Assessment disk available to further test your networking knowledge before you take actual certification tests. You can obtain a copy of this diskette by contacting Novell's After Market Products division, or CNE Administration, or by asking for it from your local NAEC or NEAP. There is no charge for this disk. Refer to Appendix B or contact FaxBack for phone numbers.

The disk contains brief tests for several of the Novell certification tests at different levels. You start the program running by inserting the disk into a drive, changing to that drive, typing **CERT,** then pressing Enter. After you answer questions about your name, you can then choose to take CNE/ECNE/CNI-level tests or CNA-level tests.

If you choose to take a CNA-level test, you can then select from three specific tests including:

- ◆ Certified NetWare 2.2 Administrator

- ◆ Certified NetWare 3.11 Administrator (This one may be updated to NetWare 3.1x by the time you read this book)

- ◆ NetWare 4.0 Administration

If you choose to take a CNE/ECNE/CNI-level test, you can then choose from several tests listed on each of three different menus. The first menu is presented to you automatically. You can choose from 10 tests on this menu, including the following:

- ◆ DOS/Microcomputer Concepts for NetWare Users

- ◆ NetWare 2.2: System Manager

- ◆ NetWare 2.2: Advanced System Manager

- ◆ NetWare 3.11: OS Feature Review

- ◆ NetWare 3.11: System Manager

- ◆ NetWare 3.11: Advanced System Manager

- ◆ NetWare 3.11 to 4.0 Update

- ◆ NetWare 4.0: Administration

- ◆ Networking Technologies

- ◆ NetWare Service and Support

You also can select Menu 2 and choose from any of the following 10 tests:

- ◆ NetWare TCP/IP Transport

- ◆ NetWare NFS

- ◆ NetWare for Macintosh Connectivity

- ◆ LANtern Services Manager

- ◆ NetWare Asynchronous Connectivity

- ◆ NetWare for SAA

- ◆ NetWare Internetworking Products

- ◆ NetWare Global MHS

- ◆ UnixWare Personal Edition: Installation and Configuration

- ◆ UnixWare Application Server: Installation and Configuration

From this second menu, you can choose Menu 3 and take the following test:

- ◆ UNIX Systems Skills Prerequisite Exam

It is likely that in versions later than 2.0 of the Novell Certification Assessment disk, additional sample tests will be added.

Once you select a test, you can then choose to cover a specific section (a single section) or to cover all sections. If you choose to take a test on a single section, you must then choose the section for the test. Figure 3.3 shows a test question chosen from the NetWare 4.0 Administration CNA test for the Connecting to the Network and Using 4.0 Resources section.

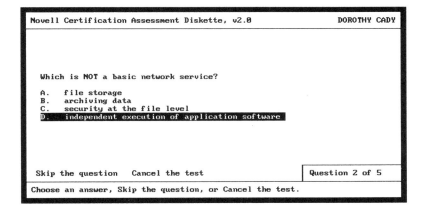

```
Novell Certification Assessment Diskette, v2.0          DOROTHY CADY




    Which is NOT a basic network service?

    A.    file storage
    B.    archiving data
    C.    security at the file level
    D.    independent execution of application software




    Skip the question   Cancel the test            Question 2 of 5
    Choose an answer, Skip the question, or Cancel the test.
```

Figure 3.3

A CNA NetWare 4.0 Administration sample assessment test question.

Once you complete a test, you can evaluate how you did on it. You are told how many questions you answered correctly. Figure 3.4 shows the test results for the NetWare 4.0 Administration test, Connecting to the Network and Using 4.0 Resources section.

Figure 3.4

The Assessment Test
Score screen.

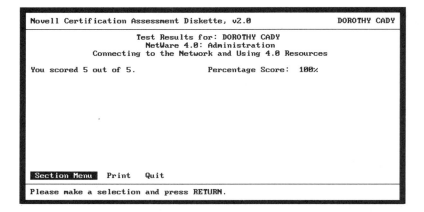

<author's note panel>

Author's Note

If you did not answer all test questions correctly, there is only one way to find out exactly which ones you missed. You must retest on the section using a trial-and-error method.

Go through the test again and make a note of the content, not the associated letter of the answers you gave to each test question. Each time you take this test, the questions are presented in a random order. Do not, therefore, try to write down number-and-letter answers. Instead, write a note that tells you the answer chosen to the specific test. For example, figure 3.3 shows you one test question. As a note, I would write down the word *Independent.* That way I would know which answer I chose for this question.

Then, reanswer all test questions with the same answers as before, except for one of them. On one test question, choose what you feel is the next most likely answer. When you finish the test, compare the score and see if you did better or worse. Then you will know whether or not the one question you changed was right or wrong the first time.

You may have to repeat this process several times until all test questions are answered correctly, but at least by then you will know which answers are correct for the test questions.

This technique does not give you the right answers to the actual certification test, as the certification tests ask different questions. But knowing your weak areas and what made your answers incorrect may help you do better on the actual certification tests.

When you have finished taking all of the tests you want to take, you have three types of reports that you can see:

◆ Report on a single section

◆ Report on all-section test

◆ Summary report

If you implement the strategy explained in the previous Author's note and choose to see a report on the section, the report shows you how many questions you answered correctly for each attempt. It also tells you the percent of correctly answered questions for this test.

Use these Novell Certification Assessment disk tests to help improve your chances of passing the actual certification tests on your first try.

Techniques and Tips for Getting the Most Out of CBTs and Tutorials

You can apply almost any study tip and technique previously recommended for learning networking to studying with CBTs.

One way to make certain that you get the most out of using a CBT or tutorial to help you pass the related certification test is to use active study techniques. In particular, use the CBT or tutorial to ensure that you are studying material directly related to the Novell course/test objectives, as defined for the particular test you are planning on taking. Remember that the test questions are created based on those objectives. You may, therefore, want to make certain that you clearly understand the information that you are required to learn in relation to each course/test objective.

Another way to get the most out of the CBTs and tutorials is to take their related tests. Use these tests not only to see how well you understand the information presented, but also as a study method. Although you cannot expect to see the exact questions used in the CBTs and tutorials on the actual certification tests, you can expect that similar questions on these topics may be presented to you on the actual test.

You also should obtain the Novell Certification Assessment disk and take those tests as well. The more comfortable you become with taking Novell's sample tests, the more comfortable you will be when you take the real certification test.

In addition, the course materials and third-party books that you study have questions to answer. Study these materials and answer their questions as well. New Riders' published networking books are a good example of third-party books that present you with test questions for study purposes as well. The *NetWare Training Guide* series, for example, provides a host of questions at the end of each chapter.

The test questions provided on the CBTs, those provided with the Novell Certification Assessment disk, and those provided by other means such as course manuals or third-party books, should provide you with enough experience answering test questions that you are much more comfortable with test-taking when it is time to take the real certification tests.

Choosing and Taking the Right Courses To Meet Your Certification Needs

The courses you take—even the decision to take courses, versus the exclusive use of CBTs, tutorials, self-study materials, and so on—depend heavily on the certification program you are pursuing, as well as your own personal needs and interests.

This chapter has already discussed ways to get the most out of self-study efforts, including the use of CBTs and tutorials. But if total self-study is not sufficient for your needs, you may decide to take one or more Novell-certified courses. This section guides you through the process of selecting and getting the most out of any Novell-certified courses you choose to take.

Taking Courses from NAECs versus NEAPs

Because there are companies out there who teach NetWare and networking technologies courses, but who are not certified by Novell, this section discusses taking courses from these independent and uncertified businesses.

Uncertified Courses

There are many companies that teach NetWare and networking-related courses even though they have not been certified by Novell. These independent and uncertified companies cannot use official Novell course materials, course outlines, or Novell logos, but must design their own courses and course materials. To ensure that they do not violate copyright laws, these courses and materials must be designed differently from Novell's course curriculum and materials.

You may choose to take courses from unauthorized companies. Sometimes these courses are less expensive than Novell-certified courses. Much of what you learn in noncertified courses is very useful. There can, however, be significant differences between taking a course from a NAEC or NEAP and from a noncertified company.

Noncertified companies cannot claim to be teaching a certified course. To teach certified courses using certified materials and course curricula, these companies must be certified NAECs. Unless they are certified NAECs, or NEAPs in the case of colleges or universities, their instructors may not be Certified NetWare Instructors. In addition, their curricula and materials will not be Novell-certified, and may eventually prove to be insufficient to give you all of the skills and knowledge necessary to properly administer a Novell network and pass the certification tests. Therefore, if you plan on becoming certified, consider taking only certified courses.

If you are planning on becoming a CNI, you must take certified courses, as course certificates signed by a CNI are part of the requirements for certification.

NAEC Courses

An NAEC is fully certified by Novell to teach Novell courses. NAECs also are independent businesses, but they have met stringent guidelines in order to be able to teach Novell's certified courses.

NAECs use Novell's certified course materials. These are the same materials from which Novell's certification tests are created. If you take a course from a NAEC, Novell guarantees that the related certification test reflects the contents of the student materials for at least six weeks from the time you took the course.

Novell requires that NAECs use Certified NetWare Instructors to teach their courses. This requirement assures you of well-trained and technically competent instructors.

Certain minimum equipment requirements for classrooms and networking labs must also be met in order for an NAEC to obtain and keep its certification. When you take a course from an NAEC, therefore, you know that you will have the required lab equipment with which you can perform the exercises contained in Novell's certified course materials.

When you take a course from an NAEC, you can usually plan on it lasting three to five days. Different courses have different time requirements.

The NetWare 3.1x Administration course, for example, is three days long. The accompanying NetWare 3.1x Advanced Administration course is two days long. Most NAECs schedule these two courses back-to-back so that you can take one and then the other without having to make two separate trips to the area in order to complete both courses.

NAECs usually advertise in the local telephone directory. In addition, many NAECs run advertisements in trade publications and local newspapers. If you cannot find a NAEC near you, you can contact Novell for a list of NAECs. The FaxBack program discussed later in this chapter under the section titled "Getting More Information on Novell Courses" explains ways to obtain information about NAECs.

NEAP Courses

NEAPs are colleges or universities that have incorporated certified NetWare courses into their regular curriculum. They, too, have to meet stringent requirements for course content and lab equipment, and must hire a Certified NetWare Instructor to teach their courses.

The biggest advantage of taking your networking courses from an NEAP is the fact that you receive full college credit for the courses that you take. The biggest disadvantage of taking courses through an NEAP is the length of time it takes to complete a course. Because the courses offered through NEAPs are full college courses, it takes a full semester or quarter to complete your course.

Some people believe that taking this much time to complete the course is an advantage rather than a disadvantage. In the three to five days it takes to complete a course through an NAEC, there is little time for extra study. With courses taken through an NEAP, you usually attend three hours of class a week. You can spend as much time as you can spare studying what you have learned between those classes.

Another drawback of taking courses through an NEAP is that not all certification courses are necessarily available. Because NEAPs are colleges and universities, they have boards that must approve the courses that they offer. If a course does not fit within their degree or certification programs, the NEAP may simply not offer it, even though you may need it in order to obtain the Novell certification that you are seeking.

What Courses Are Available?

The courses that are available for you to take depend on where and how you choose to take them. If you plan on doing all or most of your studies taking CBT-based courses, your choices are shown in table 3.1.

Table 3.1
CBT-Based Courses

Course Number	Course Name
1102	NetWare User Basics
105C	Introduction to Networking
505C	NetWare 3.11 System Manager
515C	NetWare 3.11 Advanced System Manager
520C	NetWare 4.x Administration
525C	NetWare 4.x Advanced Administration
200C	Networking Technologies
730C	NetWare Expert for NMS

If you choose to take your courses in the form of self-study workbooks, which you can purchase from Novell's After Market Product division or through an NAEC, you have the course options shown in table 3.2:

Table 3.2
Workbook-Based Courses

Course Number	Course Name
1101	Microcomputer Concepts for NetWare Users
1603	Using LAN WorkPlace for DOS 4.1
1760	Administering SNADS for NetWare Global MHS
1770	Administering SMTP for NetWare Global MHS
1125	LANalyzer for Windows
1150	NetWare Management MAP for OS/2
1120	NetWare Lite

Not all of the workbooks have associated certification tests.

If you choose to take your course using a Novell video, course number 505V for NetWare 3.11 System Manager is available.

If you choose to take an instructor-led course from an NAEC or NEAP, the courses shown in table 3.3 are available, although not every course may be available at every NAEC or NEAP.

Table 3.3
Instructor-Led Courses

Course Number	Course Name
904	Btrieve: An Overview
205	Fundamentals of Internetwork and Management Design

continues

Table 3.3, Continued
Instructor-Led Courses

Course Number	Course Name
105	Introduction to Networking
601	LAN WorkPlace for DOS 4.1 Administration
708	LANtern Services Manager
501	NetWare 2.2 Advanced System Manager
502	NetWare 2.2 System Manager
802	NetWare 2.2/3.1x Installation and Configuration
526	NetWare 3.11 to 4.0 Update
508	NetWare 3.1x Administration
518	NetWare 3.1x Advanced Administration
520	NetWare 4.0 Administration
525	NetWare 4.0 Advanced Administration
804	NetWare 4.0 Installation and Configuration
100	NetWare Buyer's Guide
911	NetWare Database Administrator
715	NetWare Dial-in/Dial-out Connectivity
611	NetWare FLeX/IP
615	NetWare for Macintosh Connectivity
720	NetWare for SAA: Installation and Troubleshooting
750	NetWare Global MHS
740	NetWare Internetworking Products
730	NetWare Management Systems for Windows
610	NetWare NFS

Course Number	Course Name
625	NetWare NFS Gateway
940	NetWare Programming: Basic Services
941	NetWare Programming: Protocol Support
701	NetWare Service and Support
605	NetWare TCP/IP Transport
200	Networking Technologies
304	Product Information Course for Authorized Resellers
905	Programming with Btrieve
912	Programming with NetWare SQL
220	UNIX OS Fundamentals for NetWare Users
676	UnixWare Application Server Installation and Configuration
675	UnixWare Personal Edition Installation and Configuration
907	Xtrieve PLUS

What It Costs To Take a Course

The cost of a given course varies—depending on the type of course, the length of the course, and where you take the course. Courses that you take at NEAPs, because they are constructed just like regular college or university courses, are priced accordingly. Courses that you take from an NAEC vary in price depending on the length of the course. As a general guideline, you can expect to pay anywhere from approximately $900 to $1,400 for a course at a NAEC. Contact your local NAEC for actual course fees.

CBT courses range in price from $195 for the least-expensive single-user version to over $4,900 for the most expensive server-licensed course.

Workbooks vary in price as well. Contact a NAEC or Novell's After Market Products division to get more information about purchasing workbooks.

Third-party books, such as New Riders' *NetWare Training Guide* series, also vary in price. Contact a local bookstore that carries these types of books for information on the price range.

How Taking a Course Can Help You

CBTs, workbooks, third-party books and other courses can help you learn the information that you need to know in order to pass the Novell certification tests. Some benefits of using these types of courses have already been covered in this chapter. There are, however, some good reasons for taking classroom instruction in addition to or instead of taking these other types of courses.

Some of the ways that classroom instruction can benefit you include the following:

◆ Hands-on and practical experience in using Novell's products.

◆ Novell's Customer Satisfaction Guarantee, which ensures your complete satisfaction when you take a course that meets the specified guidelines, and which gives you the opportunity to receive your money back or to retake the course at no charge.

◆ Quick answers to your questions from a technically competent instructor.

◆ Interaction with other individuals who are studying the same information as you.

◆ Real-world hints, tips, and practical solutions to networking problems that you can learn about from other students as well as the instructor.

- Access to original Novell course materials that are guaranteed to match the related certification test for at least six weeks from the day you complete the course.

- A completion certificate which you can display, and copy to send to Novell as proof of attendance, one of the requirements for obtaining your CNI.

No matter which certification program or courses you choose, taking Novell courses benefits you, because of the industry recognition it provides you, and all of the benefits that come with that recognition.

Hints and Tips for Getting the Most Out of a Course

The hints and tips for studying and preparing to take the certification tests you can readily apply to getting the most out of a course, no matter which course approach you choose. In addition, if you take a course from a NAEC or NEAP, there are some specific suggestions that may benefit you.

Arrive at class early enough to choose a seat that is close to the front—in the front row if possible. Being close to the front provides several benefits, including the following:

- You can readily see any overheads, flip charts, or board work that the instructor uses.

- It is easier for the instructor to see you, so any questions that you have are likely to be answered more quickly.

- With only the instructor in front of you, you are less likely to be distracted by others in the classroom.

- You can hear the instructor better, as well as any questions that are asked by other students.

Try to complete all lab assignments, as the hands-on experience is very useful for memory recall, particularly when you are studying for or taking any of the certification tests. If time permits, many instructor-led courses have additional lab work for those who finish their assignments sooner than the time allowed. If possible, attempt to do some of those extra assignments, even if it means a shorter lunch or break period.

Take the time to get to know some of the other students in the classroom. Having a network of others to contact and ask questions of or share problems with after the class ends can stretch your learning far beyond the actual number of class days.

Share your own experiences with the class whenever it is appropriate. This encourages others to share their experiences as well, and all of you can learn from the experiences of others.

If you take notes during class, consider writing them right in your student manual so that the information you need is located exactly where you can find it. Sometimes it is easy to lose little slips of notepaper. And if you do take notes, follow the recommendations given earlier about note-taking.

If you follow some of these suggestions, you can get more out of the course than you may have thought possible.

Getting More Information on Novell Courses

There are several ways for you to learn more about available Novell courses. Reading a book such as this one is one way. You can call a NAEC or NEAP and ask about Novell courses. You also can call Novell directly, or use Novell's FaxBack system to have information sent directly to you.

Calling Novell for Information

Novell provides several routes for obtaining information. Often the number you call depends on the information that you want. If you need information directly from Novell, you can contact them at any of the following numbers:

NAECs and NEAPs

To obtain a list of NAECs or NEAPs in your area, and to find out which courses each NAEC or NEAP is certified to teach, call 1-800-233-EDUC, if you are calling from within the United States or Canada. Outside the United States or Canada, call 1-801-429-5508. These numbers put you in touch with Novell's Education division at the corporate offices in Provo, Utah.

Self-Study Products

To obtain Novell self-study products, such as CBTs, contact Novell's After Market Products division at 1-800-346-7177, if you are calling from within the United States or Canada.

CBT Samplers

To obtain samples of the CBTs available, call 1-800-233-EDUC or 1-801-429-5508.

Certification Testing

To learn more information about taking the certification tests, or to register for testing, call the Drake Authorized Testing Centers (DATC) at 1-800-RED-EXAM. If calling from outside the United States or Canada, call 1-612-921-4190.

Certification Programs

For more information about Novell's CNA, CNE, ECNE, and CNI certification programs, call 1-801-429-5508, or contact the nearest Novell office (check your phone book).

Regional Information

For information more directly related to your area of the world, you also can contact any of Novell's other offices for help and information. Novell currently has offices in many states as well as the following countries:

Australia	Italy
Belgium	Japan
Brazil	Mexico
Canada	Spain
France	Sweden
Germany	Switzerland
Hong Kong	United Kingdom

Using FaxBack

If you want to receive copies of various Novell documents and you have a facsimile machine, you can call Novell's FaxBack line and order various documents. When you call the FaxBack line, you can only request two documents at a time. If you need more than two documents, wait at least two hours, or until your first FaxBack order arrives, then call the FaxBack number again and order additional materials.

To reach the FaxBack system, call either 1-800-233-EDUC or 1-801-429-5363. When the FaxBack hot line answers, you can obtain a list of NAECs in or out of your area, order a master catalog that lists all available FaxBack documents, or order a specific document.

To place an order, follow the prompts. Once you choose an order, you are asked to enter information that FaxBack needs in order to send your FaxBack order to you. This information includes:

Area code and phone number of your fax machine

Cover sheet information (name or phone number)

You can choose to have cover sheet information included on your document when it arrives at your fax machine. If you want your phone number placed on the cover sheet, enter your phone number and press the pound (#) key when finished.

Entering your name is a little more difficult. Enter your name by pressing the phone button containing each letter of your name, one after the other. The trick is, if the letter you want to type is not the first letter listed for that button, then you have to quickly press the button more than once. In other words, if the letter you want to enter is B, then press the 2 button twice (22). After you press a button to select a letter, wait until FaxBack answers with the letter you have chosen. Then choose the next letter.

For example, to have the name TOM entered on your FaxBack cover sheet, press the following phone keys:

8	Wait for FaxBack to respond with T
666	Wait for FaxBack to respond with O
6	Wait for FaxBack to respond with M
#	Wait for FaxBack to respond with T O M

Now you can continue answering the prompts as they are presented to you. When you have made all of your selections, FaxBack tells you how soon the requested documents will be sent to you. If no other requests are waiting to be sent before your own request, FaxBack tells you that your order will be sent immediately. If there are two other orders in front of yours, FaxBack tells you that your order is third in line to be sent.

When you have finished placing your FaxBack order, hang up the phone. Remember to wait at least two hours, or until your ordered documents arrive, before calling again. If you do not wait, your second order may never arrive. Although the FaxBack system retries to send your order if it encounters a busy signal from your fax machine, it limits the number of those retries and then it cancels your order.

When using the FaxBack system, the first order you need to place is for the FaxBack catalog. This catalog contains all the document numbers for each FaxBack document you can order through the FaxBack system. Some of the types of information that are listed in the FaxBack catalog include the following:

◆ **General education information,** such as a Course Schedule Legend (1001), an Overview of Novell Education Programs and Products (1101), Answers to Common CBT Support Issues (1102), and others.

◆ **Novell Authorized Education Center (NAEC) courses,** such as NAECs for each of the US. Western (5501), Southern (5502), Northern (5503), South Eastern (5504), North Eastern (5505), and Canadian (5506) Regions, and others.

◆ **Novell Education Academic Partner (NEAP) courses,** such as NEAP List (1235), NAEC and NEAP 4.0 Training List (1240), and others.

◆ **Certified NetWare Administrator (CNA) program information**, such as the CNA Program Overview (1305), and the Test Objectives for NetWare 2.2 (6005), NetWare 3.11 (6006), NetWare 3.1x (6508), and NetWare 4.0 (6520).

◆ **Certified NetWare Engineer (CNE) program information**, such as the CNE/ECNE Agreement (1445), CNE and ECNE Progress Charts (1447/1446), and others.

◆ **Certified NetWare Instructor (CNI) program information,** such as CNI Program Overview (1450), CNI Presentation Skills Requirements for IPEs (1453), CNI Course Groups for IPEs (1452), and others.

◆ **Testing objectives,** such as Adaptive Testing Overview (1550), Test Objectives (the catalog lists different numbers for each different test, including all the numbers in the 6000 series), and others.

◆ **Course information,** such as Product Information Study Guide (1600), Course Revision Numbers (1610), and others.

◆ **Instructor-led course descriptions,** such as for Introduction to Networking #105 (2105), Networking Technologies #200 (2200), NetWare 2.2 Advanced System Manager #502 (2502), and others. You can order each course description by putting a 2 in front of the course number to create a four-digit FaxBack order number, as shown in the previous sentence.

◆ **Self-study product descriptions,** such as Computer-Based Training (CBT) and Video Product List (1460), DOS for NetWare Users workbook #1100 (3100), and other workbook product descriptions. You can order these descriptions by replacing the first digit of the four-digit course number with a 3 (i.e., course number 1603 becomes FaxBack product description order number 3603, and the Computer Based Training and Video Product List number 1460 becomes 3460). You can order individual CBT course descriptions by putting the number 4 in front of the CBT order number and dropping the letter C (for example, CBT course number 515C becomes FaxBack product description order number 4515).

The descriptions and related order numbers in the preceding paragraphs are subject to change at any time. Though you can attempt to order the correct FaxBack document number from the information presented here, it really is in your own best interest to order your own copy of the FaxBack catalog from the FaxBack line. You can then use the listed numbers to order the exact FaxBack documents that you need.

This list of FaxBack document subjects is not complete. There are other categories of information that were not included, because they do not apply to you as a certification candidate.

Summary

Now that you have finished reading this chapter, you should be well versed in the types of training available to you as a certification candidate, ways to go about choosing the best training for your needs, and where to get the training you have chosen. In addition, you should know ways to obtain additional information about any of the Novell certification programs, as well as information on just about any related topic.

If, after reading this chapter, you still have questions about the certification programs and training options, you can use Novell's FaxBack system to get quick answers to your questions, as well as the most current certification program information.

Now that you know how, where, and what information you need, you are ready to learn about the testing program itself. Chapter 4, "Testing," helps you prepare for taking your certification tests.

Testing

The most stressful part of any certification or degree program is proving that you have learned the required information. Test-taking is the primary method used to prove your competence. It is no different with the Novell certification programs. To become a CNA, CNE, ECNE, or CNI, you must prove your competence by taking one or more required tests.

Most people find that taking a test—regardless of whether it is a written test, an oral test, or a competency test—is very stressful. Studies show that the more stress you feel, the less capable you are of doing your best. When you are taking one or more tests that could determine your future, an added level of stress exists.

The goal of test-taking is to do your best. To ensure that you do your best on any test, you must overcome the stress and relax as much as possible. You can use techniques such as meditation and yoga to help you relax. These techniques only go so far, however.

Studies show that people who are well-prepared and self-confident are naturally relaxed and often perform better in stressful situations. Therefore, one of the best ways to overcome test-taking anxiety, and to do your best when taking the Novell certification tests, is to not only know the material thoroughly, but also to be confident about your ability to master test-taking techniques.

You can learn how to confidently take and pass the Novell certification tests by first learning about and understanding the testing process, how the Novell certification test questions are designed, the cost of taking the tests, where and how the program is administered, and the different types of tests.

In this chapter you will learn the following:

◆ To understand the testing process

◆ How to answer typical test questions

◆ How to pretest yourself

◆ Where to obtain information on taking the tests

Understanding the Testing Process

Each of the Novell tests, with the exception of the CNE assessment test and the IPE, is taken at a Drake Authorized Testing Center (DATC). Therefore, the process of enrolling and preparing for taking the tests is the same as well. The differences involve the type of test you take. These differences are explained later in the section on the different types of tests.

How the Testing Process Works

The first step in the testing process—once you have studied for the test you are going to take—is to decide where you want to take the test. In many instances this is already determined for you. You generally take the test at the nearest DATC. However, you do have the right to take the test at any DATC.

 To find out where your nearest DATC is located, call 1-800-RED-EXAM.

After you have chosen the DATC at which to take your test, you should complete the following steps:

1. Gather the information that you need to register for the test. This information includes:

◆ Your Social Security or Drake ID testing number

◆ The number of the test you want to take

◆ The date and time you want to take the test

◆ How you plan on paying for the test

2. Call Drake Training and Technologies to register and pay for (or arrange for payment of) the test.

3. Continue to study until the day before the test, then get a good nights sleep.

4. Arrive at the testing center fifteen minutes early. Be sure to bring a photo ID and one other form of identification with you.

5. Take the test.

Once you finish taking the test, your test is electronically scored immediately. Novell has predefined cut-off scores for each test. If your score exceeds the cut-off score, the computer tells you that you passed the test. If your score does not exceed the predefined cut-off score, you must make arrangements to retake the test at a later time.

If you do not pass and have to retake the test, you must go through the same steps as you went through originally to schedule and take the test.

Once you pass the test, the DATC forwards your score to Novell. Even though Novell tracks your score electronically, you should keep a copy of each test verification report for your records should any discrepancies arise.

If for some reason you cannot take a scheduled test, you can cancel the test without having to pay for it, as long as you call Drake Training and Technologies at least 48 hours before you are scheduled to take the test. If you do not cancel at least 48 hours before the test, you forfeit your test payment.

What Do the Tests Cost?

Presently, the cost of taking a Novell certification test through Drake Training and Technologies is $85.

Note This price is the current fee for taking a test. It applies to all tests except for the CNE assessment test, and the IPE. Because testing fees are subject to change without notice, you should verify the testing fee before you sign up to take a test.

There are some exceptions to the $85 testing fee. If you take seven tests through Drake Training and Technologies, and you took the first six of those tests after August 1992, you can take the seventh test at no charge.

The CNE assessment test is not taken at a DATC. You take this test on your own computer. Therefore, there is no fee for taking this test, and no grade.

One other test that you must take if you are pursuing a CNI certification is the IPE (Instructor Performance Evaluation) test. This is a two-day class that ends in a presentation given by each student, on which each student is scored. You must pass the IPE test/class to become a CNI.

The current cost of the IPE test is $500. However, this fee is also subject to change, so ask about the current fee when you call to inquire about or register for your IPE.

Where Are the Tests Administered?

You take the Novell certification tests from either your local DATC, or from your area education manager (AEM) if there is no DATC near you. AEMs are Novell employees who are assigned to handle Novell education-related matters for different areas of the United States and Canada. You can call FastBack or CNE Administration for a list of AEMs.

Note DATCs are available throughout the United States and Canada. If you do not live in the United States or Canada, then contact your AEM to register to take your Novell certification tests.

To register for most of the certification tests, call the Drake Training and Technologies registration line at 1-800-RED-EXAM. This line is open Monday through Friday from 7:00 a.m. to 6:00 p.m. central daylight time. You can also find out where the nearest DATC is located when you call the registration line.

The IPE and the CNE assessment tests are not taken through a DATC, as are all of the other tests.

The IPE is a combination course and test that runs for two days. You are required to teach a section of the course in which you have chosen to become certified. IPEs are taken through a Novell Technology Institute (NTI) or an authorized international site.

To find out where the nearest NTI is located, as well as to get more information about and register for the IPE, call 1-800-233-3382, or 1-801-429-5508. If you need to register for or take the IPE outside of the United States, contact your local AEM or Novell education center.

CNE assessment tests are provided by Novell at no charge. You can take them on any available computer. CNE assessment tests are intended to help you decide whether or not you are ready to take the certification test. They are only practice tests.

Taking the Different Types of Tests

There are two types of Novell certification tests: adaptive tests and form tests.

In addition, to help you prepare for your certification tests, you can answer sample test questions provided on the CNE assessment test disk. This disk contains several tests that are designed to help you determine whether or not you are ready to take an actual certification test.

This section discusses the CNE assessment test, as well as the two types of certification tests: adaptive tests and form tests. In addition, this section also provides hints and tips for taking these tests, regardless of the type of test you are taking.

CNE Assessment Test

The CNE assessment test disk contains a series of computer-based practice tests intended to help you decide whether or not you are ready to take one of the certification tests.

You can get a copy of the CNE certification assessment disk from Novell or from your local NAEC (Novell Authorized Education Center). Some NEAPs (Novell Education Academic Partners) have copies of the CNE assessment test as well.

The CNE certification assessment disk actually contains several tests and is applicable to more than just the CNE test. Many of the practice test questions on the CNE assessment test disk can help you prepare to take the CNA, ECNE, and CNI tests as well.

To start one of the CNE assessment tests, insert the disk into a disk drive, change to that disk drive, then type **CERT** and press Enter.

After you page through the introductory screens and type in your first and last name, the CNE assessment program lets you choose to take either the CNA-level test, or the CNE/ECNE/CNI-level tests. After you choose the level of test you want to take, you are presented with a list of the available tests for that level. Figure 4.1 shows the Test List for the CNA-level test.

If you choose the CNE/ECNE/CNI-level tests, you see the Test Lists shown in figure 4.2.

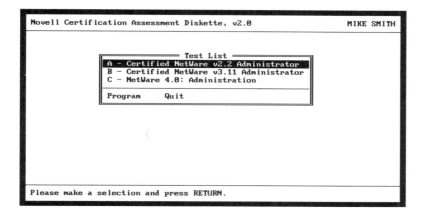

Figure 4.1

The CNA test list from the CNE assessment disk.

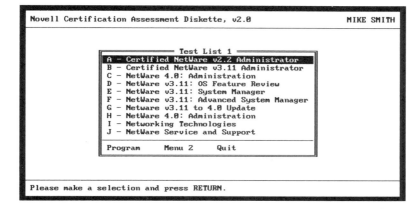

Figure 4.2

CNE/ECNE/CNI test list 1.

Although passing the CNA assessment test does not guarantee that you are prepared to pass the actual CNA certification exam, it does help you determine where your weak areas are, so that you can continue your studies in those areas. In addition, it familiarizes you with the types of test questions you can expect to see when you take the actual certification test.

Unlike the CNA test list, the CNE/ECNE/CNI test list has three separate menus from which to choose the tests you want to take. Figure 4.2 shows the first menu for this test list. The other two menus let you choose from the following additional tests:

127

- ◆ NetWare TCP/IP Transport
- ◆ NetWare NFS
- ◆ NetWare for Macintosh Connectivity
- ◆ LANtern Services Manager
- ◆ NetWare Asynchronous Connectivity
- ◆ NetWare for SAA
- ◆ NetWare Internetworking Products
- ◆ NetWare Global MHS
- ◆ UnixWare Personal Edition: Installation and Configuration
- ◆ UnixWare Application Server: Installation and Configuration
- ◆ UNIX System Skills Prerequisite Exam

After you choose the test you want to take from either the CNA or CNE/ECNE/CNI test lists, you can choose to answer test questions for a single section (topic) or for all sections. If you choose to take a test for only a single section, then you are asked to choose which section. See figure 4.3 for the list of sections from which you can choose if you take a single-section test from the DOS/Microcomputer Concepts for NetWare Users CNE/ECNE/CNI level test.

Figure 4.3

Single-section test choices.

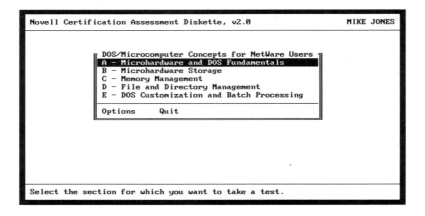

```
Novell Certification Assessment Diskette, v2.0                    MIKE JONES


                    ┌ DOS/Microcomputer Concepts for NetWare Users ┐
                    │ A - Microhardware and DOS Fundamentals        │
                    │ B - Microhardware Storage                     │
                    │ C - Memory Management                         │
                    │ D - File and Directory Management             │
                    │ E - DOS Customization and Batch Processing    │
                    │                                               │
                    │ Options      Quit                             │
                    └───────────────────────────────────────────────┘




  Select the section for which you want to take a test.
```

After you choose the test you want to take, you are presented with test questions. Each question appears one at a time on its own screen. The lower right corner of the screen indicates which question number you are answering, as well as the total number of questions the test. Figure 4.4 shows you how a typical test question is presented.

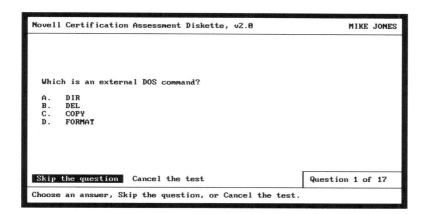

Figure 4.4

A typical CNE assessment test question.

You answer the test question by typing the letter (usually A through D or E) that you believe is the best answer for the question, and then pressing Enter. If you are unsure of the best answer and prefer to come back to answer the question later, you can choose to **S**kip the question. You can also choose to **C**ancel the test.

Once you have finished at least one test, you can see a report on a single section, all sections, or a summary report of all of the tests you have taken. The report shows you the section of information on which you were tested, how many questions you were asked, and how many questions you successfully answered.

Because the CNE assessment test disk requests your name when you use it, it tracks all tests you have taken using this disk. The reports let you know how well you did on all of the tests that were taken under your name.

Adaptive Testing

Adaptive testing functions much as its name implies. An *adaptive test* chooses test questions that adapt to your level of knowledge, which is determined by whether or not you successfully answer test questions which are rated for their level of difficulty.

For example, when you take an adaptive test, the questions you are presented with may start out to be quite easy for you. As you successfully answer the easy questions, the computer chooses harder test questions for you. If you are not able to answer the more difficult test questions, the computer adapts to your level of knowledge by choosing an easier question as the next question it presents to you.

With adaptive testing, you may only have to answer as few as ten questions. The questions you answer are scored based on their level of difficulty. Therefore, the computer determines whether or not your level of knowledge is sufficient, based on comparing the points granted to you by the questions you answered correctly, and then determining if your score exceeds the predetermined cut-off score. If your score is higher than the cut-off score, you pass the test. If your score is not higher than the cut-off score, you must retake the test at a later date.

Because each test contains a large database of potential test questions—each rated for its level of difficulty—you can take the same test several times without ever seeing the same test questions.

A disadvantage of adaptive testing is that, unlike the CNA assessment tests and form tests, you cannot review previously answered test questions.

Adaptive tests also have some advantages. They usually require less time to take than the form tests. Adaptive tests are completed within 30 minutes, whereas form tests average an hour to an hour and a half to complete.

Adaptive tests are also generally considered to be more accurate than form tests because they determine your level of knowledge based on the difficulty of the test questions you answer. Test questions selected at random—such as those used in the form test—may provide a disproportionate number of easy or difficult questions. If the form test questions you are given have too many easy questions, you can pass the test with less knowledge than that required of someone who is given a higher percentage of more difficult test questions.

Most adaptive tests range from 10 to 25 questions. The computer is able to determine within those boundaries whether or not you have sufficient knowledge of the testing topic to pass the test.

If you do not pass the test the first time, you can retake the test. You must retake the test on a different day; you are not allowed to retake the test on the same day.

The primary requirement—after you start the CNE program by taking your first test—is that you take and pass all of the required tests within one year of the date that you took the first of the required tests.

Though adaptive testing is designed to present you with challenging test questions, the format of the questions themselves is the same as the format of the questions for the other types of tests. Multiple choice and fill-in questions are used, regardless of the type of test you take.

Form (or Standard) Testing

Not all certification tests are adaptive in nature. A single test question on an adaptive test must be answered by hundreds of people before sufficient statistics can be gathered to properly identify the level of the question and the number of points that should be assigned to it.

Novell has only been using adaptive testing since November 1991. Since then, courses and test questions have been revised and added as well. Because of the time involved in establishing the difficulty level and points for the test questions, many of the certification tests that you take use form (or standard) tests.

Form tests consist of a predetermined number of test questions. Each form test presents you with 60 to 75 questions. They are the same type of questions as the adaptive test (multiple choice and/ or fill-in-the-blanks). However, the questions on the form tests are not chosen based on their level of difficulty, or on your ability to answer them correctly. Form tests do not have the immediate feedback from the computer as do the adaptive tests.

When you take a form test, you have 60 to 90 minutes, depending on the test, to answer all of the test questions. The form test presents questions to you one at a time, as do the adaptive test and the CNE assessment test.

Author's Note Although the CNE assessment tests do not count toward your certification, I have spoken with several certification candidates who found it helpful to take these tests so that they knew what to expect from the actual tests.

As Novell is still collecting statistics on various test questions, many of the certification tests are still form tests, instead of adaptive tests. Working through the related CNE assessment test questions gives you a feel for the type of tests you are likely to be taking, when you take your actual certification tests.

Form tests are graded based on the percentage of questions that you answered correctly. The test results of the form tests are reported in two measurements.

First, your certification examination score report tells you what you score is, whether your passed or failed the test, and what the required passing score was.

Second, you see an analysis of each section of the test, and the percentage of questions that you answered correctly.

For example, if you took the NetWare 3.11 to 4.0 Update test, the section analysis would list such topics as NetWare 4.0 Overview, and Client and Utility changes. Next to each section, your score is shown as a percentage of 100. The sections where you did not score well are the sections you might want to pay special attention to when studying (if you did not pass the test and have to retake it).

Hints and Tips for Doing Your Best on the Tests

Test taking is rarely easy, although some people find it less stressful than others. One way to reduce your level of stress associated with taking the Novell certification tests is to take advantage of some of the hints and tips that follow.

Novell certification tests are computerized, and most of the questions are multiple-choice in format. Except for the adaptive tests, you are given the opportunity to go back and review or change your answers to any test question. When taking the standard tests, a few suggestions that apply to any test you take may be useful to you when taking certification tests.

Because Novell certification tests are timed, you should go through the test quickly, answering those questions to which you feel certain you know the answer. You should use the computerized marking option to mark those questions you answer, but which you feel should be reviewed. You can also leave blank any questions for which you do not readily know the answer. If time permits, you can go back and answer those questions that you initially skipped, or which you marked for review.

When you choose your answer(s) to a test question, always select the best possible answer, given the whole question and the potential options. Sometimes a question may not seem to have a totally correct answer. Remember that the test questions are written from the material in the related course. Sometimes, the material in the course may be a little different than actual experiences you may have had. Therefore, the optional answers may not always seem to be correct. You should choose the best answer from the available information.

When you answer fill-in-the-blank questions, look for key words to help you determine the best word or words to fill in. Also, when answering test questions based on a scenario, be certain to take into account all information given in the scenario.

Finally, while preparing for a Novell certification test, be certain that you thoroughly understand the objectives associated with the course related to the test. Course objectives and test objectives are the same. Therefore, if you have not already done so, be certain to get a copy of the course objectives for the test you are planning to take. Being able to successfully meet each test objective determines whether or not you can succeed at passing the certification tests.

The following section helps you to better understand the test questions you can expect to see on your certification tests, so that you can do your best during the test.

Answering Typical Test Questions

The approach that you take in answering Novell certification test questions can be affected by several factors, many of which are related directly to the test questions themselves. Some of these factors include the following:

◆ Who writes the test questions

◆ How is the validity of the test questions determined

◆ What relationship exists between the course/test objectives and the test questions

◆ What are test questions typically like

Who Prepares Test Questions?

Most Novell certification test questions are written by the individuals who wrote the course manuals. This may mean that one or more people are responsible for writing test questions. However, often only one person writes the test questions for any given course.

A single author for a course may not be the only individual with input into the test questions. Most test questions are reviewed and answered by Novell's staff of Certified NetWare Instructors. Other individuals (volunteers from various Novell sites) may take pre-released versions of the tests on paper long before they are put through a more formal process of validating the test questions. This helps establish a more valid set of questions by weeding out those questions that statistically prove to be too easy or difficult, or just vague and unusable.

What you want to keep in mind is that the individual who wrote the course is often the one most responsible for writing the questions for the related certification test. If you keep this in mind when studying the course materials, then you may begin to see questions that come readily to mind as you are reading through the course materials.

How Are Test Questions Checked for Validity?

Certification test questions are checked for validity before being introduced to the public for certification purposes. Several hundred people may review the test questions or take the test before you ever see it.

Novell performs in-house beta-testing of its test questions before the final list of available certification questions is released. That means that many different people answer the test questions before you answer them. If beta-testing statistics indicate weak test questions, or questions that seem ambiguous or inappropriate, the questions are removed from the final certification tests. You only see test questions that have successfully passed some type of review before they are released.

When answering certification test questions, if the question seems to be poorly written, out of context, or incorrect for your knowledge and skills, chances are pretty good that your viewpoint of the question is not the same as what was taught in the course material. Try to think back to the course material itself, and answer the test question accordingly.

How Do Course Objectives and Test Questions Relate?

As test questions are tested before you ever have the opportunity to answer them, the questions that you are expected to answer should be considered to be valid questions. That is, by the time you take the certification test, those questions that are too easy, too difficult, inappropriate, poorly worded, and so on, will have already been eliminated from the test.

You may occasionally come across test questions that do not seem to fit what you have learned. The key is to consider the questions in relationship to the objectives of the related course, even if the most logical of all the available answers still does not seem to be correct.

In order to establish a consistent base of technical knowledge, as well as to let the student know what they can expect from taking a given NetWare-related course, each course contains a specific list of course objectives.

 Course objectives for each course are found at the beginning of each section in the Novell student manual.

In addition, you can obtain a copy of the course objectives for each of Novell's courses by requesting it from Novell's FaxBack system, or by calling CNE Administration.

To request a list of objectives for a particular course, call the FaxBack line at 1-800-NETWARE. When prompted, choose Option 1, followed by choosing the second Option 1 offered.

You have to know the document number for the course whose objectives you want to obtain. If you do not know the exact document number, you can first request a copy of the FaxBack catalog. Once you receive the catalog on your fax machine, then you can call the FaxBack line again and request the specific document that you need.

Each test question is based on one of the objectives for the related course. Occasionally, something may change or an error accidentally may be admitted into the course material text. This error or change may or may not appear in a related test question. If an error does appear in a test question, you should answer the question based on what you know about the material contained within the official related Novell course material.

If you always keep in mind the fact that certification tests are written from the course objectives and the information contained within the course materials, your job of correctly answering test questions will be simplified.

What Are Typical Test Questions Like?

As previously mentioned, Novell certification tests are computerized. Test questions are presented to you one question at a time and most are multiple-choice in format. The tests enable you to select the best possible answer(s) for the question presented.

When more than one answer is required for a specific test question, you are specifically told to choose more than one answer. Usually, the question is stated to tell you to choose the *two* or *three*

continues

137

best answers. If you are not specifically told to choose more than one answer, choose only the best possible answer.

Many of the newer tests that require multiple answers change the shape of the answer that you mark. For example, if only one answer is required, the answer choices may be preceded with a square box. If you are required to choose more than one answer, the answer choices may be preceded with a round checkbox.

Regardless of the type of question presented, all tests, except for the adaptive tests, give you the opportunity to go back and review or change your answers to test questions. If you cannot immediately answer a test question, you may leave it blank and return to it later. If you think you know the answer but are unsure, you should choose the answer you believe is best, then choose the "mark" button to mark the question and come back to it later.

After you finish answering all of the other test questions, you are shown which questions you have marked and which questions were left unanswered. If there is any time remaining on the test (all tests are timed), you may go back and change answers or answer the questions that you originally left blank.

As with paper and pencil tests, it is still a recommended strategy to go through a test quickly and answer all of the questions about which you feel confident. Then, if time permits, you should go back and answer the questions about which you were unsure. The computerized test version makes this approach even easier as it displays for you a list of which questions were not answered, or which questions you marked to be checked again later.

With Novell's computerized testing system, this approach is particularly useful. Computerized test questions are chosen randomly (except in the case of adaptive testing). Though you may be required to answer anywhere from approximately 30 to 85 questions, well over 300 questions are commonly written for any given course. Therefore, it is possible that you may see two or more different questions written about the same course objective. One of those questions may stimulate your memory for the other question, giving you the extra information you need to choose the best possible answer for the first question. If you have left the answer to that first question blank, or if you have marked it to go back and review later, you can go back and answer or change your answer as you see fit.

Author's Note It is probably best not to assume that you will remember to check back on a particular question. My experience has shown me that you are not likely to remember which question covered a given topic, if you did not mark the question for review or in some way single it out.

When taking a nonadaptive test, you are only given one opportunity to answer the question. Whether you answer the question correctly or incorrectly determines the level of the next question. Therefore, you cannot apply the technique previously described to adaptive tests.

No matter what type of test you are going to take, however, you can prepare by pretesting yourself with test questions that you create.

Pretesting Yourself

The more comfortable you feel with answering test questions, the better you are likely to do on a test. One way to become comfortable with answering questions on Novell's certification tests is to take the tests more than once. However, because each test costs $85, taking certification tests for practice can very quickly become costly.

A reasonable alternative is to create your own test questions, then practice with these questions before you take the actual certification tests.

Of course, it is not going to be of much use to you to answer random test questions that do not resemble the type of questions you can expect to see on Novell's tests, or that do not directly relate to the material. You must be able to create practice tests with questions that are similar to Novell's test questions, in order to get the most use out of pretesting. This section shows you the following:

- What to keep in mind when writing your test questions
- How to create test questions that emulate Novell's test questions
- How to relate the test questions to the course objectives
- How to use your own questions to review and prepare for the actual certification tests

This section also tells you where to go to get more information on taking the actual tests, once you are prepared and ready to sign up for the certification tests.

Why and How To Create Your Own Test Questions

One of the best ways to determine whether or not you have gained sufficient knowledge to take the tests and become Novell certified is to write your own test questions, particularly if you write them so that they are similar in nature to the Novell test questions.

Creating your own test questions and testing yourself is an accepted method of study. This section explains the benefits of creating your own test questions, and how to create them.

Why Create Your Own Test Questions?

As you now know, Novell certification test questions are based on the information in the official Novell course materials, which includes the course objectives. This might lead you to believe that the best way to study for the certification tests is to get a copy of the student manual for the course and begin studying. While this might be sufficient for some people, there are reasons why this is not a sufficient study approach for most people to pass the certification tests.

First, some of Novell's student manuals do not always contain all of the details that you need to know in order to pass the certification tests. Novell's certification tests sometimes ask questions that are not spelled out in the student manual, but are only answered for you if you have performed the related laboratory exercises. Therefore, you often must also complete the laboratory exercises explained in the student manuals. Just the process of completing these exercises provides you with much more information than does just reading the student manual.

Second, the student manuals may refer you to some of Novell's red manuals (the documentation set that ships with the particular Novell product). When the student manual refers you to a topic in one or more of the red manuals, you are responsible for reading and learning that material. You may be tested on the information in the red manual, even though the only related student manual information is a reference to the red manual. Creating your own test questions from the material found in the red manual set helps you focus on what is important in this large volume of information.

Both of these problems can be countered in one of several ways. The first way is by taking the actual Novell course related to the test that you are taking. This gives you access to a laboratory to perform the required exercises, access to the related red manual, and access to the valuable insight and knowledge of a Certified NetWare Instructor.

If taking the course is not an option for you, then you can study by setting up your own laboratory according to the minimum requirements for the Novell product about which you are learning, or by doing some of your learning on the job. For example, if you work for a company that has Novell products installed, you can ask administration to help you. In addition, you should still make certain that you have access to the appropriate red manual set. While you can obtain most of the experience and information you need to know using these methods, they can be very time consuming.

A third alternative is to purchase and study from third-party books such as the New Riders' *NetWare Training Guide* series. Third-party books are often written by individuals who have real-world experience with NetWare, who have been through one or more of Novell's certification programs, and who have access to and use of laboratories, student/instructor manuals, and Novell's red manual set. If you cannot take the actual course, third-party books are a reasonable and effective alternative.

In addition to providing you with much of the information that you need to know, third-party books give you practice at answering test questions. Unfortunately, these books do not have the space to provide you with an unlimited number of test questions from which you can practice. This is where writing your own valid practice test questions can really make a difference for you when you take the real certification test. It is important, however, that your test questions resemble the type of test questions on the actual Novell tests.

Statistics show that many college students do better on the second test that they take from a given professor than they do on the first test from that same professor. The reason is due to the fact that most students do not know what types of questions to expect when they take the first test. By the time they have taken the second test from the same professor, however, they generally have a better feel for the types of questions that the professor may ask, and what the professor feels is important. This allows them to focus their studies on the more important materials. Creating your own study test questions in preparation for taking the official Novell certification tests can do the same thing for you.

If you create your own test questions, regardless of how you choose to learn the material to begin with, you reap several benefits including:

◆ Increased concentration on the material while you are studying

◆ Readily-available review materials (test questions and answers)

◆ A feel for the types of questions that will be on the certification tests

◆ A better understanding of what knowledge Novell considers to be important

How to Create Your Own Test Questions

No matter how closely your test questions resemble the official certification test questions in format and style, if they are not testing you on the material that Novell considers important, you are not likely to pass the official certification tests. Therefore, the most important thing to consider when creating your own practice test questions is the material from which you write your questions.

The way that Novell has designed its courses, and the supplemental materials that Novell provides, make it easy for you to know exactly what information you should be studying in order to pass a certification test. The first step in creating test questions is, therefore, to obtain a list of objectives for the test that you are planning to take.

As previously mentioned, you can get a list of course objectives from the student manual (each section lists its own objectives) or from Novell's FaxBack line.

As you study the materials related to the course objectives, try to think of ways in which you might ask comprehension questions about the material. Pretend that you must teach or explain the material to someone else. What questions would you ask someone to determine whether or not they understand the information that you have just taught them. Because most of Novell's tests are multiple choice, you must also provide multiple-choice answers. Also, because the answers must be contained within the course manual, the related laboratory exercises, or the red manuals that the course may reference, your potential answers must come from these sources as well.

Writing test questions becomes easier with a little practice, though it may seem totally foreign to you at first attempt. The following shows you how to write test questions and possible answers, based on course objectives.

As NetWare and networking may seem foreign to you at this point in time, the first objective and related set of sample questions starts with more generic information. The first set of questions relates to nutrition. The second objective and set of related questions then covers a networking topic.

The intention here is to show you objectives and potential questions, then to give you some hints or recommendations for creating test questions and answers that will make Novell's certification test questions more familiar to you.

You are shown how to create test questions by first being given an objective, followed by the related information. Next you are given some recommendations to keep in mind when creating your own test questions, or when answering the questions on Novell's certification tests. Then you are told the right answer to the question, and why it is the best answer.

This first example involves determining the minimum protein needs for an individual. It assumes that you are studying nutrition. The objective—that is, the information that you must learn—is stated as follows:

Objective: Discuss one method used to determine the minimum protein requirements for an individual.

Information: The minimum quantity of protein required by any individual is determined by measuring the quantity of nitrogen (*a nonmetallic element, occurring as a colorless, odorless, and almost inert gas that is found in various minerals and in all proteins*) that the individual expels over a period of time, when placed on a protein-free diet. Such an approach shows how much protein the body requires to function. This provides the minimum protein requirement for any given individual.

Notes on creating test questions: How many test questions do you think can be created from the above sentence—one, ten, an unlimited number? If you look at the Objective and then write test questions that fulfill that objective, you find that more than one question can be written. However, you also find that in order to meet the specific objective, the number of potential questions is limited.

Possible test questions:

1. Which of the following is not a method of determining minimum protein requirements for a young child?

   a. Collecting excretions and measuring them for residual nitrogen

   b. Asking the child to keep a log of his/her daily intake of protein

   c. Placing the child on a protein-free diet and measuring nitrogen excretions

   d. Both A and C are acceptable procedures for determining minimum protein requirements in a young child

2. If you are on a protein-free diet, which nonmetallic element should be tracked in order to determine your minimum daily protein requirements?

   a. Oxygen

   b. H2O

   c. Nitrogen

   d. Carbon Dioxide

3. Which of the following are not necessary when determining the minimum daily requirement of protein for a 5'5", 180 pound male patient? (Choose two answers.)

   a. A protein-free diet

   b. Measuring the amount of nitrogen expelled during the test period

145

    c. Tracking the amount of protein eaten by the patient on a daily basis

    d. Requiring the patient to report any minerals supplements that they are taking

As you can see, three separate and distinct questions were created from one paragraph of information. With a little effort, you can probably create other questions. Creating as many test questions as you can that relate to the objective for the material substantially increases your chances of seeing a similar question on the actual certification test.

What are the correct or best answers for the preceding three questions?

In the first question, you should consider the key words "method of determining minimum protein requirements." Because these key words are used in the objective, they are important in this test question. The answer to this question is C. It is not A because no mention is made of a protein-free diet. However, a protein-free diet is key in obtaining accurate test results. It is not B because no mention in the written material is made regarding logging protein intake. In addition, the material states that you must be on a protein-free diet. Therefore, what protein intake is there to log? D is not the answer because A has already been ruled out as an acceptable answer.

Things to keep in mind when writing or answering test questions as learned from the first sample question include the following:

◆ Know the objective of the material that you are learning

◆ Relate key words in test questions to key words in the material

◆ Understand that half-true statements are not usually the best answer

◆ Note that information that is unrelated to the objective should not be considered in relationship to the test question

In the second question, although the fact that nitrogen is a non-metallic element is not specifically listed in the objective, the information is presented in the text. Therefore, it is valid to use small details of this nature when creating test questions. The answer to this question is C, because nitrogen is the only element on the list that is discussed in this section. However, it is likely that had you seen the entire chapter or text related to this topic, each of the other answers might have seemed valid because they may have been mentioned.

Things to keep in mind when writing or answering test questions as learned from the second sample question include the following:

◆ You need to pay attention to detail information in relationship to the course objective and ultimate test question

◆ That just because options listed as potential answers may have been mentioned somewhere in the text does not make them the best answer

In the third question, you are asked to give more than one answer. Some Novell test questions are written that way. Therefore, you should write some of your practice test questions that way as well. The answers to this question are A and B. If you answered only A or only B, you would be incorrect. Two correct answers are required for this question. C is not the answer because the individual is not suppose to be eating any protein at all. D is not the answer because nothing in the text indicates that minerals can or cannot be taken, or that their consumption should be tracked. The correct answers are A and B because the nitrogen expelled shows how much protein is required. However, more protein may be expelled (via nitrogen) than is required, simply because it was consumed. Therefore, the diet must also be free of protein.

Things to keep in mind when writing or answering test questions as learned from the third sample question include the following:

◆ More than one correct answer may be chosen, if the question tells you to choose more than one answer

◆ The best answer is the answer that relates directly to the material being taught

◆ Just because information is given, such as that relating to minerals and nitrogen, does not mean that the information is correct when it comes to the specific wording of the question

The next sample objective and test questions relate to a networking topic. You should begin to have a feel for how to relate objectives to test questions, regardless of the topic (nutrition or networking).

Objective: Identify client-related changes in the NetWare 4.0 environment.

Information: The NetWare DOS Requester replaces the older NetWare Shell. Using the DOS Requester requires that changes be made to several configuration files including the CONFIG.SYS, AUTOEXEC.BAT, and NET.CFG files. In addition, changes to accommodate NetWare 4.0 are required in the user's login script environment. Login scripts are now properties of NDS objects, of which there are three types: SYSTEM, PROFILE, and USER.

Notes on creating test questions: Test questions are easier to create if you consider two important points. First, consider the key words used in the objective itself. Second, consider the key words used in the text which accompanies the objective. Key words in the objective and text above include, but are not limited to: client-related changes, CONFIG.SYS, AUTOEXEC.BAT, NET.CFG, login-script environment, NDS objects, SYSTEM, PROFILE, and so on.

Possible test questions: The following test questions are just two of several questions that you could write from the preceding paragraph of information.

1. The three types of login-script related NDS objects include SYSTEM, USER, and _____.

2. Which of the following configuration files does not require modification under NetWare 4.0?

   a. CONFIG.SYS

   b. PROFILE.SYS

    c. AUTOEXEC.BAT

    d. NET.CFG

The first question requires that you fill in the answer from memory. There are no multiple choice options to guide you. You simply have to remember the pertinent information, in this case, the word PROFILE. This may require rote memorization techniques. Questions of this nature are valid, and you can expect to see them on the certification tests.

Things to keep in mind when writing or answering test questions as learned from the first sample question include the following:

◆ Memorize information that can be learned as a list. Write test questions and be prepared to answer test questions that do not provide a list of choices from which you must select the best possible answer(s).

◆ Look for key words in the questions and answers that clue you as to the relevancy of the question to the answer. In the first question, the fact that the question is looking for a list of NDS objects (specific to NetWare 4.0) is important to the answer you choose. If you just answer based on a list of login script types, you may have given a NetWare 3.x answer such as DEFAULT.

The answer to the second question is B, "PROFILE.SYS." First of all, there is no such file as PROFILE.SYS though the term PROFILE and the extension of SYS are common. This technique of giving seemingly valid answers is one method of determining if you really know the answer.

Things to keep in mind when writing or answering test questions as learned from the second sample question include the following:

◆ Some questions may have answers that, at first glance, appear to be valid, such as the PROFILE.SYS choice, but which are in fact not valid answers.

◆ Test questions may expect you to choose the one answer that does NOT fit, not just the best answer that DOES fit. Read and carefully word these types of questions.

149

After you have created test questions, you can sit down and answer them, then memorize them as part of studying for the actual certification test. However, this is only one way to use test questions to further your knowledge and prepare to take the Novell certification tests.

Using Your Own Test Questions To Review and Prepare

In addition to collecting all of your questions and answering them as if you were taking the real test, you can use the questions in other ways.

First of all, you can use the act of creating the questions themselves to focus your attention when you study the course materials or related third-party books and study guides. As you read each particular course objective, you should create a list of potential questions.

For example, in reading the objective, "Identify client-related changes in the NetWare 4.0 environment," the following questions may come to mind and should be written down:

What is a client?

What makes up a NetWare 4.0 environment?

How important are client-related changes?

The number of questions that come to mind is unimportant. Writing the questions down starts you thinking about asking questions, and gives you something to look for as you read the related information.

Next, as you read the related material, refer back to your questions and see if you can find answers to the questions you wrote. Continuing with the previous example, as you read about client-related changes, you learn that the NetWare 4.0 client environment includes several files: CONFIG.SYS, AUTOEXEC.BAT, and NET.CFG. This information answers, at least in part, your question about the importance of client-related changes.

Finally, now that you are studying and asking questions, it will help you later on to try to write the test questions as you are studying the material, rather than waiting until you have finished studying. Writing test questions while you study accomplishes two things.

First, it creates questions which, when you answer them later, will seem fresher to you. You will not have memorized the answers to them as readily as if you study all of the materials, create all of the questions, and then go back and answer all of the questions. Writing questions while you study will provide a better assessment of what information you have and have not learned and remembered from your studies.

Second, you are less likely to skip creating test questions at all, if you write them a few at a time. When confronted with cramming at the last minute, or just running out of time to study, it is unlikely that you will go back through all of the material to create test questions. You are more likely to just skim through your notes or the material you have read. Having a set of questions already prepared so that you can do a self-test to find the areas where more study is required can focus what study time you do have available to the areas most in need of review.

Where To Obtain Information on Taking the Tests

After you have completed your studies, or are close enough to begin thinking about taking the actual tests, you may need more information on taking the tests.

Call the DATC (Drake Authorized Testing Center) to get more information about taking the certification tests, even if you are not ready to sign up for a specific test. The DATC number is 1-800-RED-EXAM.

You can also call, FAX, or write to any NAEC or NEAP. These people are often willing to answer any certification questions that you may have.

The NetWare Users International (NUI) organization can also answer questions for you, though their answers may be somewhat limited. To contact the NUI call 1-800-228-4NUI.

Novell's FaxBack system (1-800-NETWARE) provides additional information on the Novell certification programs, as well as on certification testing.

Summary

Taking tests to prove your knowledge on a given topic can be either a stressful or rewarding experience. The more rewarding experiences are usually realized by being fully prepared to take the test, and then of course, by passing the test.

This chapter has attempted to help you become better prepared to take the Novell certification tests by teaching you to:

◆ Understand the Novell certification testing process

◆ Understand the different methods to use when answering typical test questions

◆ Prepare for testing and pretest yourself to determine and eliminate areas where your networking knowledge is limited

For more information on passing the IPE and becoming a Certified NetWare Instructor, see Chapter 5, "Becoming a Certified NetWare Instructor."

Becoming a Certified NetWare Instructor

If you want to become a Certified NetWare Instructor (CNI), you must meet the prerequisites discussed in the the section titled "Increasing Your Chances of Getting Accepted into the CNI Program" later in this chapter, fulfill the requirements, and pass the Instructor Performance Evaluation (IPE) course. You must also attend the course you plan to use for your IPE, and submit a photocopy of the certificate that you receive for that course to Novell's CNI administration.

You do not have to first obtain any of Novell's other certifications in order to become a CNI, as you do for other Novell certifications. For example, if you want to become an Enterprise Certified NetWare Engineer (ECNE), you must first become a Certified NetWare Engineer (CNE). That is not true for the CNI program. You do not need to earn a Novell CNE, ECNE, or Certified NetWare Administrator (CNA) certificate before applying to become a CNI.

That does not mean, however, that the CNI program does not have prerequisites of its own. This chapter not only discusses the CNI prerequisites, but explains the IPE, and provides information about the mastery of teaching techniques that Novell considers to be important. After reading this chapter you will be able to:

◆ Prepare to become a CNI

◆ Increase your chance of getting accepted into the CNI program

◆ Understand the IPE

◆ Develop IPE-relevant teaching skills

◆ Decide where to go from here

To become a CNI you must fulfill several requirements, which include:

◆ Sufficient experience as an instructor, and/or successful completion of a presentation skills course

◆ A minimum of one year's experience working in the field of network computing, with hands-on experience in your intended area of specialization

◆ A properly completed and submitted application

◆ An approval from Novell to enroll in the CNI program

◆ Attendance as a student at the certified course you choose for your IPE

◆ A valid copy of the completion certificate for your IPE-related course

◆ A passing score on both the prerequisite test and on the test associated with your chosen IPE

These requirements are discussed in detail in the following section.

Preparing To Become a CNI

In order to become a CNI, you must first be accepted into the CNI program. Acceptance into this program depends on several factors, each of which are described in the section titled "Increasing Your Chance of Getting Accepted into the CNI Program." The most significant factor, and the one that may be the most difficult to obtain, is experience as an instructor. Novell will consider your having taken a presentation course as a possible substitute for teaching experience. However, teaching experience is important, and if you do not yet have any teaching experience, you need to get some. It may even be in your own best interest to take a presentation skills course first and then get some teaching experience. Other preparations you must make include:

♦ Completeing and submitting your application and related documents

♦ Contacting Novell for the required documents and any assistance that you need

Attending a Presentation Skills Course

Many colleges, universities, and private companies offer presentation skills courses. If you have no teaching or presentation experience, you should consider taking a good presentation skills course.

Consider several factors when choosing a course. The most important factor is that the course teaches you the skills that you need to pass Novell's IPE.

When you take the Novell IPE, you are evaluated on two areas of presentation skills, as well as on technical proficiency. The two presentation skill areas include:

♦ Presentation characteristics

♦ Presentation mechanics

Each area includes a list of separate characteristics on which you are evaluated. You should, therefore, evaluate the presentation course you are considering in relationship to its ability to teach you successful mastery of these presentation skills.

Those presentation skills which you are expected to master are covered later in this chapter under the section titled "Developing IPE-Relevant Teaching Skills."

Getting Experience

The prerequisite of instructor experience may be the most difficult requirement for you to meet. This prerequisite exists to help assure that students attending certified Novell courses are being taught by individuals who have mastered the basic skills of teaching adults.

If you have already been teaching courses or training seminars for adults, and if you have the equivalent of one full year of experience, then you should be able to meet this requirement, although the experience you list is subject to review and consideration by Novell.

If, however, you do not already have experience as an instructor, obtaining that experience is possible. There are several approaches that you can take. The main goals to keep in mind are that your experience must relate to educating adults rather than children, and that the experience must equal a minimum of one year of full-time teaching.

Where you begin your search for teaching experience depends on your current situation. For example, if you are a full-time employee doing a job other than teaching, you may prefer not to quit your job for a full-time teaching position, particularly if it pays less, or if you are not yet sure that you want to become a full-time instructor.

On the other hand, if pay is not a problem, you are sure that you want to teach full time, and you can find someone who is willing to hire you, then becoming a full-time instructor might be the best choice for you. If you, however, want to continue in your present job and get as much teaching experience as quickly as possible, here are a few suggestions to get you started.

Adult Education Courses

Most communities have some sort of adult education program available to their residents. The administrators of many of these programs are flexible in their approach to who they hire and what courses they teach. They look for individuals who have skill or expertise, and are not necessarily concerned about whether or not their instructors have a teaching certificate or a great deal of teaching experience. Therefore, as an inexperienced instructor, your local adult-education program may be a good place to get started.

If you do not have a great deal of experience in computers or networking, you can begin your teaching experience by teaching other types of courses. Though teaching in a technical field such as computer science might be preferable, Novell does not require that your teaching experience be restricted to that particular field. You can, therefore, choose to teach any course for which you are reasonably qualified as an instructor. So, how do you decide what courses to teach?

You can begin by looking at your present list of skills and knowledge, and deciding which area is your strongest. Consider your work experience, as well as your hobbies and other interests. For example, if you presently work in retail sales, you may find that you enjoy selling. If this is the case then you can consider teaching a course in sales.

If you cannot think of a particular subject that you want to teach, try looking at the catalog of courses offered by your local adult-education division. You can start by reviewing that list to determine the following:

- ◆ If they list any courses that you believe that you can teach
- ◆ Whether or not they have any obvious holes in their curriculum, one of which you might be able to fill

After reviewing the list of courses, if you find any courses listed which you think you might be qualified to instruct, there are three options.

First, you might consider working with the current instructor as a volunteer teaching assistant. This usually entails little teaching. You will probably be helping more with paperwork and organization than with the actual teaching; however, this factor does not mean that you should rule out this option. Instructors who have

157

large classes can often use help, and welcome not having to pay you.

Teaching assistant work does not necessarily have to be done gratis. You may be able to arrange some type of compensation for your services.

Once you establish a rapport with the instructor, you can then ask to teach a few of the classes, or at least a small part of them. This is actual teaching experience, and you can include this experience on your CNI application.

If you want to gain further experience, ask the instructor to let you plan and develop course material for the class.

You may encounter resistance from some instructors. It is, therefore, important that you do your research first, and be open and honest with the instructor as to why you are doing this and what you hope to get out of it. Never give the instructor the impression that you hope to someday replace them in their current position. Consider how you might react if the situation was reversed.

The second approach you can take is to contact the adult-education office and offer your services as a substitute instructor. If you take this approach, you should have a great deal of knowledge in the subject area of the course(s) for which you are volunteering. The more courses you are technically qualified to teach, the better your chances are of actually being asked to teach a class as a temporary substitute.

If being paid for obtaining your teaching experience is important to you, this second option and the next one are possible choices. A substitute instructor is usually paid by the regular instructor.

Author's Note

The adult education division usually does not take responsibility for paying a substitute instructor. You must make arrangements with the regular instructor to receive payment for teaching.

Many adult education programs do not pay the instructors until the course has ended. Consequently, the regular instructors may be hesitant to pay you until they have been paid. By that time, everyone may have forgotten about the money you are owed, so be prepared to have to wait for it, and maybe even to have to ask for it.

If this happens to you and the income is as important to you as the experience, then you must remind the instructor that you have not yet been paid. The problem with reminding the instructor is that, if he or she becomes in any way offended despite your best intentions, you may not be called upon again to substitute for any instructors at that adult education program. While most instructors are very conscientious and would never deliberately cheat you, you may want to consider all of your options under such a circumstance.

Your third alternative is to come up with an idea for a new course, and then propose that course to the adult-education division personnel. You will need to be creative in your ideas, and develop a course that adults in the area may be interested in attending. If you decide to teach a course in sales or salesmanship, for example, the first thing you will need is an interesting course title. A title such as *Becoming a Salesperson* might be acceptable, but a title such as *Making Great Money in Sales* may be a better attention-getter. You must be able to sell the adult-education manager on your course, and his or her decision may depend on if your course sounds interesting enough to attract people.

Once you have an effective course title, develop a rough outline of the course. Because many adult-education courses run approximately one night a week for eight weeks, you should have seven worthwhile main topics in your outline. List two or three subtopics for each main topic, and type up your outline neatly. Find out who runs the local adult-education program, and make an appointment to meet with that person or persons if possible. Take your outline, explain that you would like to add this course to their curriculum, and tell them you will be willing to teach the course for a percent of the receipts. That way, if only a few people enroll in the course, it costs the adult-education division only the time and use of the room for you to try out your new course. Even if you only have five or six students, the teaching experience you gain is still the same. You will earn a few dollars, the adult-education program earns a few dollars, and everyone gets what they need out of the program.

Tutoring Adults

If starting off as a teaching assistant or teaching your own class seems more than you feel comfortable handling the first time out, you might consider tutoring as a first choice. There are several tutoring options open to you.

First, you can contact your local community college. Consider your area of expertise, such as math or history, and contact the chairperson for that department. Explain that you would like to become a tutor. Most colleges and universities have some type of tutoring assistance program established. They should be able to point you in the right direction. College tutoring programs often pay a small sum as well.

If you do not presently have a special subject that you feel confident about tutoring, you can contact your local library. Many libraries often have reading assistance programs, and use volunteers to help teach adults how to read. Their programs are usually carefully designed. They often need tutors, and generally have a training program for their tutors so that you do not have to start cold without any idea of what to do.

You can also consider private tutoring if either of the previous options do not suit you. You can let local high schools, colleges, and universities know that you do private tutoring. These institutions may provide you with referrals. You can also run advertisements in your local newspaper, or post notices on public bulletin boards, such as those found at your public library and outside your local grocery store.

Tutoring alone does not give you enough experience to qualify for enrolling in the Novell CNI program, but it can give you a start. It does not really matter which approach you take, so long as you do whatever you feel most comfortable doing. You must get started somewhere.

Part-Time College Instructor

If you have a college degree and work in the same field as your degree, you may be able to join the adjunct faculty of your local community college.

Because of tight budgets and increasing enrollments, many community colleges use part-time contract staff to teach a variety of their college classes.

Author's Note

Before I enrolled in Novell's CNI program, I began my teaching experience working in adult education. I later joined the adjunct faculty staff of my local community college. The experience I gained doing both types of teaching was invaluable in becoming a CNI.

One interesting fact I learned while a member of my local college's adjunct faculty was that 60 percent of their teaching staff was adjunct faculty. Budget and enrollment constraints puts ever-increasing pressure on the college to hire more and more adjunct faculty. Because persons hired as adjunct faculty are paid a set fee under a contract, the college does not have to provide medical insurance, sick leave, or any of the other benefits that full-time staff receive. It makes it much easier for the college to hire you, and therefore much easier for you to be hired, and to get the experience that you need.

There are advantages to teaching as adjunct faculty. Most students treat you with respect. You earn a little extra income while you are gaining the experience that you need. You get to mingle with other teachers and learn from them.

In addition, the college generally provides everything you need in order to teach the class. That means that you do not have to develop the curriculum yourself, come up with test questions, or choose the books for your students to read.

With some classes, you even have a student teacher assigned which means that you have some help with all of the paperwork.

Private Training

If none of these previous options appeal to you, you can consider doing some private training. Many companies hire individuals to teach specialized courses for them. This sort of teaching may require that you have extensive knowledge in a particular area. Your local gun club, for example, may need someone to teach a course in handgun safety. The YWCA may need someone who can give a class on first aid. Or your local boy scout troop may need someone to teach knot-tying skills.

If you are trained in any specialty, and you keep your eyes open, you may find something suitable. If, however, you do not want to wait until something comes along, you should search the newspapers, and get the word out to your friends and relatives of your desire to teach private classes. In addition, check the phone book for companies and organizations that might need your special skills, and call or write them. Offer your services as an instructor. If you have something to offer them at a price they can afford, you are likely to find some companies or organizations that will let you teach for them.

Completing and Submitting Your Application and Related Documents

Once you have sufficient teaching experience to meet the experience prerequisite, and you have met the other Novell prerequisites for enrollment in the CNI program, you can fill out and submit your application and other related documents. Start by requesting those documents from Novell.

To obtain a copy of the Certified NetWare Instructor Application and related documents, contact Novell's CNI Administration at:

CNI Administration
Novell, Inc., MS # A-22-1
122 East 1700 South
Provo, Utah 84606 USA

You can also request these documents by calling the CNI Administration directly at 1-801-428-5445, or by calling 800/NETWARE and choosing the appropriate option numbers.

You can also contact Novell CNI Administration by FAX. Send your FAX request for a copy of the *CNI Program Description and Application* brochure to 1-801-428-3900. This document includes the following information:

◆ An overview of the CNI program

◆ A list of the CNI program prerequisites

◆ A review of CNI certification requirements

◆ Information about professional development and support provided to CNI candidates and certified CNIs

◆ Details about Novell's commitment to quality and how they implement it

◆ A list of contacts that include the CNI Program Administration, course and test registration, Novell Technology Institutes (NTIs), international Novell training sites, and regional CNI program contacts

◆ A CNI application checklist

◆ The CNI application

◆ A copy of the Novell Certified NetWare Instructor agreement form

◆ An order form for requesting your IPE Instructor Kit

When you receive your copy of the *CNI Program Description and Application* brochure, pull out the application along with the IPE Instructor Kit order form, and the Novell Certified NetWare Instructor (CNI) Agreement. You must complete and submit all of these documents at the same time.

The Application

It is important for you to type or clearly print the required information on the Certified NetWare Instructor Application form. Your acceptance into the CNI program is determined primarily by the information that you include on this form and the accompanying required documents.

Information that you are required to complete as a CNI candidate includes:

◆ The IPE product type you want to certify to teach. You can choose to take the Core/OS Products IPE, the Advanced Products IPE, or the Development Products IPE. If this is your first IPE, however, you must take and successfully pass the Core/OS Products IPE before you can take either of the other two available IPEs.

◆ The course number and name of the course for your IPE. This course must be one of the allowed IPE courses. The list of courses from which you can choose and IPE target course (the course you choose to teach during your IPE) is included on the IPE Instructor Kit order form.

◆ Your social security number. If you do not have a social security number, then you can alternately use the Test ID number assigned to you by Drake Training and Technologies when you register to take your first Novell test.

◆ Your full name and address, including your country, phone number, and, if available, your fax number.

◆ Information about how you are paying for the IPE. Your choices include an enclosed check or money order, a credit card (be sure to include the credit card type, number, and date of expiration), or a Purchase Order (PO). You must include the purchase order number and indicate if the PO is included, or another method of payment which has been prearranged with an Area Education Manager (AEM).

 Note You can only use a PO for payment if you are working with a Novell Authorize Education Center (NAEC) or Novell Education Academic Partner (NEAP) that is in good standing, and the NAEC or NEAP is issuing the PO. Whenever payment is being made by a PO, a copy of the PO must be included with this application.

You can choose the Other option only if you are taking the IPE outside of the U.S., or are making your application for the IPE from outside the U.S.

◆ An indication as to whether you will be teaching Novell courses solely for an NEAP or if you will be entering the CNI program as a contract CNI. A contract CNI has no specific NEAP affiliation, but may teach for any NEAP, NAEC, or private company.

◆ Your signature, placed on the line designated as *Candidate signature*.

◆ The date on which you completed and signed this application.

Whether you are going to teach solely for an NEAP, or you are going to be an independent CNI contractor, you must also fill in the NAEC/NEAP Information section. If you are teaching solely for an NEAP, you can have the NAEC/NEAP contact fill it out for you if you prefer. This section must include the following information:

◆ The name of the sponsoring NAEC/NEAP. If you are applying to the CNI program as a contract CNI candidate, include the name of your employer or support company.

◆ The address, country, telephone and Fax numbers, E-mail address, and name of a contact person at the sponsoring organization.

When you have completed the application, include it with all of the other forms listed here, as well as a copy of your resume and three references. Submit the entire package, INCLUDING PAYMENT FOR THE IPE, to Novell's CNI Administration at the address previously listed. (See Appendix B.)

 If you need assistance from Novell or any affiliated organization, use the following list of contacts to find the right person, department, or affiliate.

To register for an IPE or obtain general information:

Call 1-800-233-3382 or 1-801-429-5508, from within the U.S. or Canada

Contact your local Area Education Manager (AEM) if you are outside the U.S. or Canada

If you do not know who your AEM is, you can obtain a list of AEMs by calling Novell's FaxBack line and following the prompts to request a faxed list of AEMs.

You can also call Novell CNI Administration to find out who your AEM is, if you do not have an available Fax machine.

To obtain any document from Novell's FaxBack line:

Call 1-800-233-3382 or 1-801-429-5363

To obtain information regarding certification testing and registration:

Contact Drake Training & Technologies at 8800 Queen Avenue South, Bloomington, Minnesota 55431 USA, or call 1-800-RED-EXAM or 1-612-921-4173

If you are outside the U.S. or Canada, contact your nearest Drake Training & Technologies office

To find and contact your nearest U.S. Novell Technology Institute (NTI), call or write to one of the following Novell, Inc. offices:

2850 West Golf Road, Suite 100
Rolling Meadow, Illinois 60008 USA
Phone: 1-708-228-7676
Fax: 1-708-228-7411
8 a.m. to 5 p.m. M-F(CST)

5080 Spectrum Drive, Suite 120 West
Dallas, Texas 75248 USA
Phone: 1-214-448-3650
Fax: 1-214-448-3660
8 a.m. to 5 p.m. M-F(CST)

122 East 1700 South
Provo, Utah USA
Phone: 1-801-429-5508
Fax: 1-801-429-3900
7 a.m. to 5 p.m. M-F(MST)

890 Ross Drive
Sunnyvale, California 94089 USA
Phone: 1-408-747-4000
Fax: 1-408-747-4242
8 a.m. to 5 p.m. M-F(PST)

continues

2323 Horsepen Road, Suite 600
Herndon, Virginia 22071 USA
Phone: 1-703-713-3500
Fax: 1-703-713-3641
8 a.m. to 5 p.m. M-F(EST)

To contact Novell's international training sites:

Write: European Training Centre
     Novell House
     London Road
     Bracknell
     Berkshire RG12 2UY
     United Kingdom

To find out what region you are in and who your regional NTI manager is:

Call 1-800-332-3382 or 1-801-429-5508

You can also find this information in the *CNI Program Description & Application* document.

The IPE Instructor Kit Order Form

When you apply for acceptance into Novell's CNI program, you must fill out the IPE Instructor Kit order form. When you are accepted into the CNI program, indicate on the form the Instructor Kit you want, your mailing address and method of shipment.

Include the following information on the IPE Instructor Kit order form:

◆ Your "Ship To" address. This address must be one to which UPS or Federal Express can deliver.

◆ Your telephone number and, if you have one, your fax number.

◆ Your shipping preference. Novell pays for UPS 10-day ground shipment. If you want overnight or second-day shipment, you can select either of these options. If, however, you choose either of these options, you must also include your Federal Express account number for billing purposes. Novell does not pay for Priority1 or Priority2 delivery.

◆ Your order date, which is effectively the date on which you complete this form.

◆ The Must Arrive By date, if you must receive your IPE Instructor Kit no later than a specific date.

◆ The IPE Instructor kit that you need for your target (chosen) IPE course.

The CNI Agreement

You must also read, sign, and submit the five-page Novell CNI Agreement included in the *CNI Program Description & Application* document.

This agreement specifies 13 items of information that you need to know and are required to read and acknowledge with your signature. The 13 items covered in this document include:

1. The purpose of the Novell CNI program.

2. A list of related definitions.

3. Information about your certification and Novell's reserved rights.

4. Specifics about your authorization (license) to teach Novell courses for affiliated NAECs.

5. The term of this agreement and information about rights and reasons for termination.

6. Your agreements as to how you conduct your business, which may reflect on Novell or its products.

7. Details about title and ownership of Novell products by Novell.

8. Information about Novell's belief in the quality of its licensed services.

9. Novell's reservation of rights and goodwill.

10. Your agreement not to make any trademark, collective mark, and/or service mark registration application(s).

11. Your responsibility and agreement to protecting Novell's rights.

12. An agreement by you to indemnification of Novell.

13. General provisions which cover topics including governing law, non-waiver of trade usage, course of dealing, assignment, independent contractor status, compliance with laws, and modifications to this agreement.

You must sign your name, print your name, print your title, and date the CNI Agreement in the specified spaces located on the last page of this document under the heading of Certified NetWare Instructor.

If you are accepted into the program, Novell, Inc.'s authorized representative also signs his or her name, and provides a printed copy that includes name, title, and date that this agreement was signed.

Increasing Your Chances of Getting Accepted into the CNI Program

Novell's CNI program exists to provide the training and resources that Novell's customers, resellers, and certification candidates need in order to participate and compete in an environment that is growing ever more complex and competitive.

Becoming a CNI means that you are joining a company that is on the cutting edge of networking technology. It also means that you have taken steps to improve your personal and career development.

To help you accomplish your goals—and Novell to accomplish its goals—Novell views the CNI as a partner in what it describes as an education alliance. The responsibility of this alliance is to ensure that Novell's customers get the technical support and knowledge that they need.

Novell considers this alliance and its CNI program to be an important part of a professional organization. One way to help increase your chances of becoming a CNI is to look upon yourself and your profession with a similar attitude.

As a CNI, you have a clearly defined role in Novell's education alliance. Your role includes a set of responsibilities. You will have the opportunity to demonstrate these responsibilities when you take your IPE. Others will be demonstarted in your everyday life and in your approach to your CNI training.

Your responsibilities as a CNI include:

- ◆ Representing Novell in a positive manner
- ◆ Conducting yourself and your business dealings in a professional and ethical manner
- ◆ Keeping your knowledge up-to-date with current technology
- ◆ Teaching authorized Novell courses at authorized facilities using original Novell course materials
- ◆ Completing continuing-education requirements when specified
- ◆ Teaching to and meeting the course objectives as defined by Novell course materials for each course that you teach

To increase your chances of becoming a CNI, you must make certain that you meet all of the CNI program prerequisites and that you meet all certification requirements. Once you have met the prerequisites, your application is processed to determine if you meet the first certification requirement, that of having your application approved.

Program Prerequisites

The first step toward meeting the prerequisites for certification as a CNI is to make yourself an expert in a given area of related technology. To do this you must fulfill several requirements including:

◆ A working-level knowledge of microcomputers and their operating systems

 Note You do not have to know everything about all hardware and operating systems. You do need to know enough about any one particular operating system, such as DOS or UNIX, and the microcomputer that it runs on, to be considered an expert in that area.

One way in which your expertise can be determined is by your experience or related college education. You may be considered sufficiently knowledgeable in this area even if you do not "feel" like an expert.

◆ A minimum of one year experience in the area of networking in which you want to specialize

◆ Strong presentation skills that can be demonstrated before you take your IPE through experience in adult education, or successful completion of a presentation skills course

 Note The presentation skills course should teach you the skills you will have to demonstrate when you take your IPE.

◆ The ability to communicate technical information so that it is clearly understood

◆ Skill at managing a group of students

◆ An outward attitude that reflects an inner feeling of enthusiasm and positive thinking

 When you submit your application for the CNI program, your admittance is decided based on whether or not your application successfully reflects these program prerequisites. Pay careful attention to the application, therefore, when you fill it out.

Make certain that you fill out the application completely. Neatness always counts, even though it is not listed as a prerequisite.

Fill out your application so that it reflects your experience and training. If you cannot sell Novell on your qualifications as a CNI candidate, how can you expect to sell your students on your abilities as an instructor?

Although Novell generally makes its determination to admit you into the CNI program based on the information contained within your application, they might also decide to conduct an interview with you.

If an interview is requested, your local Novell Technology Institute (NTI) manager or the Area Education Manager (AEM) will arrange the interview with you.

You can expect the interview to concentrate on your background, your experience, and other qualifications.

Certification Requirements

There are four requirements that you must fulfill in order to become a CNI. The first one has already been discussed. You must fill out and submit your application, and be approved for entry into the CNI program.

173

The second requirement is that you must attend, as a student, each Novell course that you want to become certified to teach.

 You only have to pass one IPE in order to become certified to teach any of Novell's core operating system courses. To teach other courses that do not fall into this category, you must pass one of two other possible IPEs. You cannot take the other IPEs, however, until you pass the operating system IPE.

To obtain your IPE you must, therefore, attend the course you plan on taking for the operating system IPE.

The third requirement is that you take and pass all required competency tests. This includes such tests as the DOS/Microcomputer Concepts test and the test for the operating system class you have chosen for your IPE.

The fourth requirement is successful attendance at and completion of the IPE. For most people, passing the IPE is the most difficult part of the requirements for the certification program. You cannot, however, take the IPE or continue with the other certification requirements until your application goes through the application process and becomes approved.

The Application Process

Unless Novell contacts you for additional information or to setup an interview, as mentioned previously, after you submit your application all you can do is wait.

The processing of your application will be easier and therefore quicker, however, if you make certain that you include with your application everything that Novell needs in order to determine whether or not you meet the minimum qualifications for the CNI program. It is, therefore, in your best interest to make certain that:

◆ You have neatly and completely filled out and signed your application

◆ You attach a copy of your resume that clearly shows your network computing and PC industry-related experience and education, as well as your professional teaching experience and three references

◆ You have signed and included a copy of the CNI Agreement

 A blank copy of the agreement is included in the *CNI Program Description & Application* document, available from Novell CNI Administration.

◆ You have completed and returned the IPE Instructor Kit order form

 This form is also available in the *CNI Program Description & Application* document. The instructor kit for your first IPE is included in the initial application fee.

◆ You enclose payment in full for the IPE

◆ You attach copies of any course certificates that you presently have for any Novell-authorized courses that you have already attended

◆ You specify the target course you want to use for your IPE

After Novell receives your application package and verifies that it is complete, you may be requested to attend an interview, as mentioned previously.

If your application is denied, your IPE fee is refunded. After your application is accepted, Novell forwards your instructor kit to you, along with a packet of instructions designed to help you prepare to take your chosen IPE.

You must sign up for your IPE at least two weeks before you want to take it. If you have not yet met ALL certification requirements other than attendance at the IPE, you are not allowed to register for it. Novell must have a copy of your certificate of attendance for the IPE course you plan to teach.

Once all prerequisites and requirements are met, you are enrolled in the IPE. The results of your IPE presentation are sent to you within 10 days of attendance.

After you pass the IPE, you receive an official letter of certification from Novell's CNI Administration. Once you receive this letter, you can teach any courses listed on the letter.

Approximately one week after receiving this letter, you also receive a CNI *Welcome Aboard* kit.

Understanding the IPE

The IPE is often cited as the most difficult part of certification, because of the narrow range of passing scores. To pass the IPE you must successfully demonstrate your mastery of each of the required presentation skills. You must also prove your technical knowledge in your chosen IPE target course.

Presentation skills are divided into two areas:

◆ Presentation characteristics

◆ Presentation mechanics

All of the presentation characteristics and mechanics are discussed in detail in the following section, "Developing IPE-Relevant Teaching Skills."

Your technical proficiency requirements are determined based on your target course. Your technical proficiency skill is based on your presentation of technical course materials, and is compared against:

◆ The objectives defined for your target course

◆ Technical information specified in the instructor's guide for your target course

◆ The use of instructional aids provided and/or recommended in the instructor's guide for your target course

◆ The technical reference materials included in the instructor kit for your target course

The IPE lasts for two days. During the first half of the first day, the IPE process is explained to you. The IPE evaluators tell you what you can and cannot do, and how much assistance and what type of assistance you can expect from the evaluator.

The evaluator then assigns you a portion of the target course that you will have to teach in order to pass the IPE. Your assignment may cover one full section in your target course, two sections in your target course, a mixture of two or more portions of your target course, or less than one section of your target course.

What you are assigned is governed by two factors:

◆ The amount of time that you are given for doing your presentation, because your presentation cannot exceed 45 minutes—although it can take less time if appropriate

◆ The luck of the draw as assignments are predefined and placed into envelopes

Once you have your assignment, you take the remainder of the first day to prepare for your presentation. The IPE evaluators can help you with presentation needs, such as getting your transparency sheets, making photocopies, and so on. They cannot, however, provide you with any technical assistance or presentation ideas, suggestions, recommendations, or anything related to how you do your presentation.

On the second day of the IPE, each of the six students (maximum) in your class deliver their respective IPE presentations.

At the time of your presentation, you will have access to a file server and a workstation, as well as various types of presentation equipment, such as an overhead projector, white boards, flip charts, and so on. How you make use of these items in your presentation is up to you.

177

Presentations are spaced so that each student has 15 minutes between the end of the previous presentation and the start of their own. Use this time to set up your presentation materials, and mentally prepare to deliver your presentation.

The IPE evaluator signals you to start when the 15-minute break is over, and the camcorder is set up and ready. All IPEs are recorded. The recording, however, is never viewed or used to determine whether or not you pass the IPE. It is ONLY used in the event that you do not pass the IPE, and you subsequently file a formal complaint. The video tape of your presentation is then viewed by independent evaluators to determine whether or not your original score was reasonable and unbiased.

How the IPE Is Scored

Your presentation, and subsequently your IPE score, is based on your demonstration of your abilities in two areas: technical proficiency and presentation skills. You must demonstrate your skills to the satisfaction of the IPE evaluators.

The score you receive is the result of a composite of all of your scores, which are given in each of the IPE evaluation criteria (technical proficiency, presentation characteristics, and presentation mechanics). Scores are based on a scale of one to five points.

If your composite score totals 3.5 or above, you pass the IPE.

If you composite score falls between 3.0 and 3.5, you pass the IPE, but with conditions (known as a Conditional pass). The Conditional pass lets you teach Novell certified courses; however Novell will monitor your performance as an instructor, and reserves the right to require that you perform one or more of the following:

◆ Take additional IPEs

◆ Take additional tests

◆ Participate in a team-teaching experience with another CNI

◆ Attend a presentation skills course

Note While Novell does not specify which presentation skills course you should take, you can contact Novell's CNI Administration department and ask for a list of presentation courses.

A score lower than 3.0 indicates that you did not successfully pass the IPE. You must retake the IPE.

Regardless of your score, Novell notifies you of the result of your IPE within 10 business days of the date that you took the examination.

Hints from Successful CNI Candidates

Different individuals who have successfully taken and passed the IPE have some suggestions to help you do your best when you take your IPE. These suggestions include the following:

◆ Take the IPE seriously. Spend all of your available time preparing for and practicing your presentation.

◆ Time yourself on several dry runs to make certain that you do not exceed the 45-minute maximum time allotted for your IPE presentation. Once you reach the 45-minute time limit, your presentation is cut off. If you have not done some things, such as your summary for example, you will lose points.

◆ As soon as you decide which target course you will be using for your IPE, begin earnestly studying and learning all related course information. You have no way of knowing which portion of the target course you will have to present until the first day of the IPE.

◆ If you have a technical question about any aspect of your presentation, ask one or more of the other prospective CNI candidates for their help. It is okay to ask other students for technical help, but you cannot ask nor will you receive it from the IPE evaluator.

No matter which target course you choose for your IPE, or when or where you take your IPE, try to relax and enjoy your IPE experience.

If you meet the prerequisites, fulfill all of the requirements, take seriously the goal of obtaining your CNI, and spend all of your available time preparing for and practicing your IPE presentation, you should be able to obtain a passing score on your IPE and become a Certified NetWare Instructor.

To make certain that you develop each of the required teaching skills, the next section of this chapter explains each required skill, and provides information to help you master them.

Developing IPE-Relevant Teaching Skills

As mentioned previously, your IPE score is determined by your presentation and your technical knowledge. Your presentation score is based upon your success in meeting the required presentation skills, which have been divided into two categories: presentation characteristics and presentation mechanics. All 25 presentation skills are explained in the following sections.

Presentation Characteristics

Your presentation at the IPE is scored based on eleven presentation characteristics, which include the following:

- ◆ Your confidence in presenting material
- ◆ Proper voice modulation
- ◆ Appropriate dress
- ◆ Your ability to maintain proper eye contact
- ◆ Speech that does not contain filler words and distracters

- Ability to maintain a pace that is appropriate for both the material and the audience

- An enthusiastic attitude toward the course and the subject materials

- Gestures and language which are not distracting

- Promotion of student autonomy

- Promotion of student security

- Encouragement of class belonging

Confidence

Showing confidence when you present materials is important. Students have the right to expect that they are being taught by someone who has a thorough knowledge of the subject. Whether or not your students believe that they are receiving quality education for the money they have spent depends on your confidence, or lack of it. Part of your IPE score, therefore, is determined by your display of confidence in yourself and the material that you are teaching.

The best way to build confidence is to thoroughly learn your material. When you take your IPE, you are assigned a section from your chosen course to use for your teaching session. Learn that section so thoroughly that you can teach it regardless of the circumstances.

When it is time for you to conduct your training session for the IPE evaluators, begin by setting up your teaching aids—then take a moment to catch your breath and tell yourself to relax before you begin. If you follow these steps, you are more likely to be poised and confident during your teaching session.

Voice Modulation

It is difficult for anyone to listen for any length of time to someone who speaks in a monotone voice. A voice that is particularly high or low in its tone also becomes difficult to listen to for an extended period of time. Not only must your students be attentive to your voice, but they must also be a captive audience. Most students are with you for a minimum of two full days. Therefore, properly modulating your voice is an important part of instructing students.

Proper modulation includes changing the tone of your voice when appropriate. Show occasional excitement when you are teaching a part you find particularly interesting. Show periodic enthusiasm in your voice as well. Raise and lower the tone of your voice to prevent monotonous droning; however, be cautious about letting your voice changes sound too phony. A little natural enthusiasm is often enough to provide the modulation that you need without going overboard.

Dress

Although you might think that how you dress has nothing to do with how good or bad your teaching skills are, it does affect the result of your teaching. You have heard the expression that first impressions are important because you can rarely change a person's first impression of you. The way in which you are dressed when you first meet someone leaves a lasting impression, and can influence whether you leave a positive or a negative impression.

Because students learn better if they approach the class with a positive attitude, the impression you give them by the way you dress can affect the way they perceive the course itself. If you give the impression that you are educated, knowledgeable, and business-like in your approach to teaching, the students begin the class expecting to learn. If you give the opposite approach, many students may make up their minds immediately that they are going to get little or nothing out of the class. When that happens, that is just what they get out of it.

Part of your IPE score is also determined by the impression you give your students. Therefore, to give the impression that you are a professional who knows how to do your job, you need to dress in a professional manner. Business suits for both men and women are appropriate; however, as long as you present a neat, well-groomed, professional appearance, your choice of clothing is up to you.

When considering how well-groomed you look, do not overlook the small details. Things such as scuffed shoes, chipped nail polish, uncombed hair, or an untrimmed beard are immediately noticed by most students, and by the IPE evaluators.

Eye Contact

Maintaining proper eye contact is another area on which your IPE presentation is scored. Some people feel distrustful of others who seem unwilling to look them straight in the eye. It does not matter if you have difficulty with direct eye contact due to shyness, or for any valid reason. Keeping proper eye contact with your students is important to keeping proper control of your classroom. Therefore, the ability to maintain proper eye contact is also an area of the IPE on which you are scored.

Filler Words and Distractions

Uh, you know how annoying it is to, uh, hear someone who, uh, always says, uh, you know, things that are, well you know, repetitive, and uh, distracting when you are just, you know, trying to learn, um, well, something? If that sentence was annoying and distracting to you, you can see how distracting and annoying it is to your students as well. Check your own speech to make certain that you are not randomly repeating and using filler words such as uh, um, you know, well, and so on. Record your presentation and play it back. If you find yourself using these types of words, make every effort to eliminate them from your speech.

Not only repetitive words annoy and distract your students, but nervous habits can bother them as well. For example, sometimes instructors pop the caps to white board pens on and off while they are speaking. Some instructors jingle loose change or keys in their pockets.

Many of us develop other nervous habits as well. You need to remove these annoying habits. Prevent yourself from snapping pen tops off and on by setting the pens down each time you stop writing. Empty the loose change out of your pocket before you come into the classroom. Keep your car keys out of your pockets. In other words, put anything that might inadvertently annoy your students away, where you cannot accidentally use it.

Some annoying habits are not as obvious as these. To determine if you have any less obvious but still distracting habits, ask a friend or relative to watch your presentation, looking specifically for annoying movements or sounds. Then make an effort to eliminate any that are pointed out. A habit that could become an annoyance to a student, may cost you additional points when you take your IPE.

Pace

It is difficult to establish a pace in writing. If not, I would write this paragraph so that you had to read it two or three times before you could understand it, to demonstrate the importance of using the correct pace for the topic.

Although your reading skills are the primary factor in establishing the pace for this book, it is also your teaching approach that establishes the pace for your students. Difficult material needs to be presented more slowly than does material which is considered simple or a class review. As the instructor, you set the pace. During the IPE, your ability to set the proper pace for the material you are assigned to teach is another area in which your presentation skills are evaluated.

Enthusiasm

If you give your students the impression that what you are teaching them is boring, they will be bored. If you show enthusiasm for what you are teaching, even if you have already taught the exact same topic 1,000 times before, the students will pick up that enthusiasm. Sometimes enthusiasm is contagious. It is definitely important, particularly when you take the IPE.

Those who do your IPE evaluation do not expect you to show enthusiasm and excitement all of the time. You must make sure, however, that you do not show boredom any of the time.

To make certain that your IPE presentation displays enthusiasm, find something about the topic you are assigned to teach that is interesting to you. Then try to develop some eagerness for it. One way to do that is to include a short example of how someone made good use of a particular piece of your assigned topic. Bring in a personal experience, either one of your own or one of your students, to help show your excitement.

Author's Note

When I took my IPE (it was called Train the Trainer at the time), my assigned topic was the section of my chosen IPE that covered SBACKUP. I had recently finished testing the SBACKUP software. During my testing, I had found a particularly useful way to implement backup after work hours. It gave me back the use of my file server for a few hours on Friday, which were originally dedicated to doing backups. I relayed this information to my students. Because I was enthusiastic about the benefit of that feature of SBACKUP, my enthusiasm just naturally showed through.

If you attempt to discover at least a little something that is exciting about your assigned topic, your enthusiasm will show as well.

Gestures and Language

Excessive use of filler words, or constantly jingling your keys, are not the only habits which students find annoying or distracting. Other personal habits can be distracting as well.

185

For example, if you frequently throw your hands up in the air when you talk, your students will get tired of seeing you throw your hands up. If the habit becomes too annoying, you may find some of your student talking among themselves about it, while you are trying to lecture.

One way to find out if you have any of these little habits is to have a friend or relative watch you lecture, and then give you some advice. You can also videotape your lecture and play it back. This is particularly useful if you think your friends or relatives may be inclined to be less critical than necessary.

Autonomy

Adult students need to feel as though they have control over their own learning environment. Autonomy is an important part of most adults' lives, and applies to their learning environment as well. For this reason, you should take advantage of every opportunity to provide your students with an autonomous environment. Your students will learn more, and the class as a whole will be more cooperative if it feels that it has some say in the course.

Some ways in which you can provide autonomy include such things as giving the students the option to choose between possible alternative laboratory assignments, or perhaps letting the students decide whether they prefer to take a short or a long break in cases where a long break would not disrupt the class schedule.

The point is, whenever you can let the students make their own decision without disrupting the class or interfering with other student's needs and rights, you should try to give them the opportunity to decide for themselves.

Security

Many adults that attend your courses may have been out of school for some time. Even those who attend courses of this type on a regular basis may find some discomfort in going to a new place. It is your job to make them feel safe and secure in your course. It is often the little things that you do which make the difference.

To help your students feel more comfortable, answer some of their unanswered questions up front. For example, tell them where the rest rooms are located. Let them know where there is a telephone they can use if they need to call their office or home. Tell them the times and lengths of scheduled breaks. Also inform them what time each day you plan on starting and ending the class.

You also need to determine if any of your students have any special needs and then do your best to accommodate those special needs. Give students the opportunity to move closer to the front if they are having any difficulty hearing you, for example.

The students also need to feel that it is okay to ask questions. If you prefer that students ask their question as soon as it comes to mind, then tell them so. If you prefer that the students hold their questions until you prompt them, tell them that as well. However, be sure that if you take this second approach, that you provide frequent question-asking opportunities.

When a student asks a question, be positive in your response to the student. Answer the question the best way possible. Never make the student feel as though the question was stupid or inappropriate. If it is a question you would rather answer at a later time, tell the students that it is a good or important question. Tell them also that you will be discussing that topic later and ask them to ask it again at that time. Let them know their question was worth asking.

Also, when you ask the students a question, encourage participation by responding favorably to each student's answer, even if it was not the answer you were looking for. Find something positive in their answer that you can respond to.

Let the students know that your goal as an instructor is to help all of them learn the information that you are there to teach them. They should understand that you want to do your best to help them feel comfortable with what they have learned.

It may help if you try to remember what it was like when you first attended a new class in unfamiliar surroundings. Then do your best to make each of your students feel comfortable, and to provide them with a positive and successful experience.

Class Belonging

Many adults also enjoy the feeling of belonging. It increases their participation in class, which in turn augments how much they get out of the class.

The best way to foster this feeling of belonging is to give the students the opportunity to introduce themselves and to get to know each other. There are several ways to accomplish this.

One way of helping the students to get to know each other is to divide them into small groups of two to four people. Give them four or five items of information that they are to find out about one other person in their group. They should find out the basics such as the person's name, what they do for a living or where they work, and why they are taking this course. Then have them find out something a little more personal such as where they took their last vacation and why they chose that place. Or perhaps they can ask about a favorite hobby, sport or something interesting that has happened to them at one time or another. After the allotted time is up, go around the room and let your students introduce each other to the class. This approach is often more comfortable for people than having each person introduce himself or herself.

As each person is introduced, you might welcome them to the class or just make a brief comment on something you learned about them that is a positive reinforcement for that person.

Some other ways to help your students feel as if they are part of the class is to occasionally break them into small groups to accomplish a given assignment. You can also buddy them with a partner, giving them each the responsibility for working with and helping each other as needed.

Presentation Mechanics

The presentation characteristics area is only one of two areas on which your presentation skills are scored. The second area is that of the mechanics of your presentation. There are fourteen presentation mechanics that are considered in your IPE score, including:

- Introduction of each section and the identification of the section objectives
- The use of signposts for each topic
- Establishment of each section's relevancy
- References to pages in various manuals
- Definition of new terms and acronyms
- Proper preparation
- Topic sequence that is logical
- Topic linking that aids student learning and retention
- Relevant and effective analogies
- Effective use of visual aids
- Effective use of questioning
- Promotion of class discussion
- Summarization of each topic discussed
- Summaries that do not include any new material

Section Introductions

You are not required by Novell to teach its materials in the exact order in which they are presented in the student course materials. You do, however, need to follow the basic outline for each section so that, at the minimum, you cover the information related to the section objectives. Sometimes you will cover all of that information in detail. Other times it may be necessary to cover some parts of the information very quickly, touching only on the main points. One of the things that you must do, however, is introduce each section and identify its objectives.

The Novell student manual lists objectives for the overall course near the beginning of the manual. Explaining the course objectives is a good way to start off the course itself. You must, however, at least begin each section by telling the students what they can expect to learn from the section.

How you introduce the objectives is up to you. For the sake of passing the IPE, however, it may be best to read and then briefly explain each objective.

You can also paraphrase each objective. If you choose to take this approach, be certain that you do not give the students the wrong impression of the objectives.

Signposting Topics

Signposting topics means showing transition from one topic to another. Listing topics on the white board and noting changes from one topic to another by checking them off as you go is usually sufficient to signpost topics, but you may use other more creative methods if you choose.

Establishing Relevancy

When you discuss section objectives, it is important for your adult students to understand why the concept or topic you are discussing is important to them. In order to be receptive to the information presented, your students need to know how they can apply it to their own situations.

Adults are mostly goal-oriented. The relevancy of the information that they are learning becomes very important to them. You must, therefore, make certain that you tell the students the purpose and value of each learning activity, whether it is attention to a lecture or a hands-on activity.

One of the best ways to make information relevant for your students is to understand their daily work requirements and experiences. Whenever possible, encourage the students to share their related experiences in class. Continually drawing on their own experiences, and sharing those experiences as examples with other students helps all of the students to better understand the relevancy of what they are learning.

If students seem hesitant to share their experiences with the other students, you can start a related conversation by asking relevant questions. If you are discussing the responsibilities of network administrators, for example, you can ask your students who network administrators are, or what they have observed to be the most important duty of a system administrator. Once your students see that others are sharing their experiences, and they see that your response to those students is positive, they are more inclined to share their experiences.

Relevancy can be established in other ways as well, such as by helping the student see the whole picture. Some ways in which you can help your students see the whole picture include:

- Explaining the concept behind the topic

- Showing them how the activity or information relates to their daily responsibilities

- Pointing out how the information they are learning now will make it easier for them to learn another important skill or item of information later on in the course

- Relating the skills they are learning now to job descriptions they may see posted in newspapers

Some of your classes are likely to contain students that are just now seeking a job in the networking field. Others may be looking to present their current employer with a reason to grant them a promotion or pay raise. You can help these people see the relevancy of the course and its topics by bringing advertisements for networking administration positions into the classroom. Post them or pass them around so that the students can see how the time and money they are now investing can pay off for them later.

You can also help your students see the relevancy of each topic by pointing out to them the relationship between what you are teaching them and their own personal goals. If you have each student tell why they are taking this particular course when they

191

first introduce themselves, you can later use that information to show the students the relevancy between what they are learning and what they had hoped to learn from the course.

Regardless of the ways you establish relevancy for your students, the fact that you establish it is very important. Most adults are goal-oriented individuals. If they did not come into your course with clear goals in mind, you may be able to help them see the relevancy of the course by showing them how its objectives and information can someday be of benefit to them, even if they themselves cannot immediately see the benefit.

Providing Page References

Providing page references is another method of orienting and directing your students. Page references also allow students to read additional information about a given topic, and help them to keep pace with the class.

If a student finds a particular topic that you are discussing worth additional study, page number references to the student manual as well as the Novell manual set helps the student in several ways:

- It allows the students to pay closer attention and make the shift to the next topic, because they know where they can later find more information

- If the student was temporarily distracted, page number references allow that student to quickly catch up with the rest of the class without disturbing other class members

- Students who are taking your course(s) because they want to pass the related CNA/CNE/ECNE test will appreciate knowing where they can turn for more information after the course is over

Many of Novell's courses, like their products, are complex and require much more time to thoroughly master than the course's two, three, or five days. Referencing different materials for later review helps the students learn more.

Students who consult page references are better prepared to deal with real situations when they occur. Network administrators who know how to use the reference materials to quickly find answers to their questions when needed, are less likely to waste time trying to solve problems. They are also less likely to be forced into calling Novell's service and support lines for help.

This approach also lets each student get more out of the course. Not only do the students leave the course feeling as though they have learned a great deal, but they also go away knowing how and where to get additional information when they need help.

Defining Terms and Acronyms

Most professions have their own sets of special terms and acronyms that speed communication among professionals in the field. Some fields require new terms and acronyms, because they touch on subjects or functions for which there are now well-defined terms. Computer science and networking are two of those fields.

Whenever you introduce your students to an unfamiliar term or acronym, you should tell the student what it means the first time that you use it. For example, the term *LAN* is a common term in networking circles. LAN means *local area network*. Now that both the term and its meaning have been introduced, you are better prepared to learn about networking, or local area networks. If you take this same approach with your students each time that you introduce a new term or acronym, they too will be better prepared to learn the rest of the material that you want to teach them. Just because a term is familiar to you, you should not assume that everyone in the class knows what it means.

Showing Proper Preparation

One of the most irritating things that can happen to you as an instructor is to walk into a classroom full of students and find yourself unprepared to conduct the class. Not only is it unpleasant for you, but it is equally irritating to the student.

As a student in college, I once had an instructor who showed me the importance of coming to class prepared.

This was the first college course that she had taught. She had minor problems with class preparedness throughout the year. Most of the students found it somewhat annoying. But the worst day was the last day of school.

According to the college's schedule, the class was supposed to take its final exam on this last day of school. The instructor had confused her dates. After the class settled down, she began a lecture she had prepared. After about five minutes, one student raised her hand and asked when we would be taking our final. The instructor looked somewhat annoyed by the question but answered it stating that the final exam would be next Tuesday evening. She then continued with her lecture.

Another student raised her hand and told the instructor that she believed that today was the last day of class, and that the students were all scheduled to take their final test today. The instructor and student argued until the student volunteered to go to the office and check with the administration. The instructor agreed and continued lecturing.

When the student returned, the instructor did not like what the student had to say. Tonight was the scheduled night of the final.

The instructor, angry at both the student and herself, discontinued the lecture. She was unprepared to give the students a final exam. She told the students that she would have to apply their midterm exam grades toward a final exam. Then she dismissed the class.

This teacher was not unprepared for the class she thought she was giving that night, but she was completely unprepared for the class she was supposed to be giving. As a result, the students lost their opportunity to truly prove their knowledge on a final exam, and possibly improve their course grade.

Everyone in this instructor's class lost that day, because the instructor was unprepared.

Proper preparation for a class involves several things. As you can see from the Author's Note, preparing for the correct class is one. A strong knowledge of the topic that you plan to discuss is another. Although these two preparations may be the most important, they are not the only preparations that an instructor must make. Instructors must also:

◆ Make certain that all of their presentation materials are available and ready to use

◆ Check the electronic equipment, such as overhead projectors or VCRs, to make certain that they are all in working order

◆ Bring a sufficient number of copies of handouts if they will be used

◆ Arrange the lecture area so that everything you need is readily available

◆ Be sure that you have enough dry-erase markers or chalk, and that the markers are still useful

Besides preparing your presentation, you need to take care of all of the little details. A lack of preparation in any one area can cost you time, student attention, and, in the IPE, can cost you several points.

Sequencing Topics

While you prepare your lecture, you should consider the best order in which to present the information. That is, you should consider the sequence of topics to be discussed.

195

Novell's student and instructor manuals have already been de-signed to present information in a reasonably logical order. You are not required, however, to follow that order if your experience indicates that a better presentation order exists.

You need to present the information to the students in an order that is sufficiently logical to allow them to build their knowledge as they go along.

Putting topics in logical sequence is much like constructing a house. You must build the basic framework before you put on the roof. Before you build the basic framework, however, you must construct a strong foundation. And before you lay a strong foun-dation, you must prepare the ground. The same is true with the way you present your NetWare lessons.

The first step in presenting a lesson is to prepare the ground. Most of the time you can accomplish this task by discussing the section objectives. Once you are certain that the students have grasped the objectives, or that you have prepared the ground, you can con-tinue on with the next logical step—that of laying the foundation.

You lay the foundation of the course by giving students any background information necessary to further build their knowl-edge of the topic you want to teach them. Background information may be as simple as defining a few acronyms and terms, or as complex as explaining network protocols.

Once the foundation is laid and you are certain that it is sufficient to hold the structure, you can begin building by giving the stu-dents the information that they need to know. Again, you need to supply that information in a logical order. You would not install an opening for a window into a wall that you had not yet con-structed. The logical flow of information to the students must likewise proceed in a rational and structured manner.

To accomplish this goal, you should start by teaching students the central ideas that unify everything, before you begin teaching them the details and information about any peripheral ideas.

For example, if you are teaching the students about different types of networking protocols, you must first teach them about protocols in general. After they know what a protocol is, and what protocols exist, you can teach them about the function and details of a single protocol.

For those instructors who know their material inside and out, it can be difficult to separate the important basic concepts from the little details. To an instructor who really loves the topics he or she teaches, many of the little details seem as important as the whole. Although that may sometimes be the case, your students need to be able to distinguish between what is important overall, and what are supplementary details.

As the instructor, one of your most important responsibilities is to help your students build their level of knowledge by developing an organized hierarchy of information. This allows the students to see the overall structure, and still recall the details as they need them.

After the structure has been built, you can complete it or top it off with its roof. In teaching, regardless of the topic, you top off the information by providing a summary of what you just taught.

Other instructors and writers have put this process into different terms. They tell you to tell the student what you are going to tell them, then to tell them what you told them you would tell them, and then to finally tell them what you told them.

This process builds a strong foundation for your students, gives them the information that they need to know, provides them with a review of what they learned, and prepares them to learn even more.

Linking Topics

A logical flow or sequence of topics must be matched with a linking of topics as well. If the structure has been properly developed, new ideas and information can be linked to the old, much as the walls of a house are linked or connected to the foundation.

In learning, as in building, everything must be linked together if the information is to be retained for any length of time.

Linking gives meaning to information that may otherwise be meaningless. The more well-established the current base of knowledge, the easier the linking and ultimately the retrieval of the new information is for the student.

Learning and storing information in our memories is not an isolated event. The more closely the information being stored is linked to other knowledge, the easier that information is to learn, retrieve, and to use.

One way of linking new information to existing knowledge is to relate it to something the students already know, even if what they already know does not seem to be normally related.

For example, you have been shown in the previous section how to link new and potentially unrelated information to existing knowledge through the use of an analogy. That section explained the use of sequencing in relation to building a house. Although most of you have never built a house, you have a basic understanding of its structure. You may have gained this understanding from seeing houses being built, from doing minor repairs to a house of your own, or just from living in a house. The point is that the basic structure of a house is familiar to many of you.

Even though the sequence for building a house is seemingly totally unrelated to sequencing topics when you teach, the use of that analogy allowed you to build a mental path by which you stored the information on sequencing topics, and by which you will later be able to retrieve that information. Your students need similar help when it comes to learning.

Ideally, you link new networking knowledge to existing networking knowledge. But when that basic knowledge is not yet there, or is insufficient for the topic that you need to teach, you can form the link to logical but unrelated topics.

You can also make links to related topics even when they are indirectly or only slightly related by discussing the new topic within a related context.

For example, you can link the topic of network security to a discussion of corrupted or compromised network systems. This approach may work best if your class is composed mostly of network administrators. But what if your class contains mostly authorized resellers?

In that case, you may be able to link the same topic, that of network security, to a discussion of situations in which NetWare's security can prevent illegal entry and access of network files.

If your class contains mostly network users, you might link the network security information to explanations of how to implement security so that users in one department can share a common database, while preventing users from other departments from gaining access to that database. As you can probably tell by now, linking can be related in several ways, including:

◆ Indirectly or directly to the topic you are discussing

◆ Depending on the current knowledge level of your students

◆ Drawing on your students' past experiences and their potential use for this new information

Learning and storing new information for future retrieval and use is not an isolated event. Whether or not you help your students to link the information, or they subconsciously form their own links, it is a necessary process of memory.

You can help your students learn the necessary information quicker, retain it longer, and retrieve it faster by also helping them form logical links, even when none seem to exist. This assistance requires a little more work on your part as an instructor, but it is part of your responsibility, and may even provide you with a sense of personal satisfaction.

Using Analogies

Webster's New Concise Dictionary by Modern Publishing describes analogy as being "agreement, resemblance or correspondence in relations between different objects." An analogy in teaching is the use of one thing to help define or explain another. In this chapter, you have seen several examples of analogies.

199

The previous description of the basics of building a house as it corresponded to logically sequencing topics that you teach was an example of an analogy. Analogies help students learn necessary information, even when that information seems confusing or unlearnable. Developing analogies, however, can be a very difficult task for the instructor.

One way in which you can develop analogies for your students is by focusing on the topic that you are teaching, and then thinking about anything that may be similar. Some of the thoughts that first come to mind may not seem very useful. Others will seem quite natural.

For example, you may need to teach your students how the accounting feature works in NetWare. If you have any background in accounting, you can develop an analogy that compares standard accounting to Novell's network accounting.

In standard accounting, you track the moneys, goods, and services that you receive, and the expenses that you accumulate and pay. In NetWare, you set up the system to track the services that each person uses, and then you can charge each person accordingly. In this process, network accounting is analogous to standard accounting.

As time goes on, your students also figure out their own analogies. If they are encouraged to share them with the class, you may later be able to use these analogies in teaching other students.

Using Effective Visual Aids

A visual aid is any tool that helps you convey your message, and which helps your student understand that message. With a visual aid description as broad as this one, you can use just about any visual aid that you can think of. Just keep in mind that the visual aid must help your students picture what you are trying to teach them at the same time that you are verbally conveying the information.

Studies have shown that over 75 percent of what we learn and remember comes from what we see. Only 13 percent comes from what we hear. Therefore, if you want to help your students have their best chance of remembering what you teach them, it is important that you use good, effective visual aids whenever possible.

Presentations that use visual aids also tend to be more persuasive. You have probably seen public television pledge drives in which they display a graph that shows how many pledge dollars they have received so far. The graph has a top dollar amount showing how many dollars they need to receive. As the pledge drive continues, the graph climbs closer and closer to the top. When the ringing phones slow down, the public television representatives use the graph to show you how desperately they now need YOUR pledge. This visual aid is used to help convince you to call and do your part.

Other visual aids are used to convince you to buy offered merchandise, or to send your money to some deserving non-profit organization.

Visual aids can be very persuasive in teaching networking as well. An instructor trying to emphasize the benefits of using Ethernet over Token Ring, for example, can use visual aids to demonstrate the differences between the two, or to show one of the topologies, such as Token Ring, in a less-favorable manner.

Author's Note

One of the college courses I taught required that I explain how Token Ring and Ethernet functioned. Ethernet topology was easily explained by drawing a basic diagram on the white board. Token Ring functionality is not as easily explained using a two-dimensional white board drawing. I wanted to show students how Token Ring functioned, using something more effective than a white board drawing.

So, to make the lesson more interesting, and to persuade the students that Token Ring might not be the best choice in some situations, I set up a special visual aid.

continues

201

After each student was seated, I handed one student a ball of yarn. The student was instructed to hold the end on the yarn and then toss the ball to someone else in the classroom. That student was then told to hold onto a piece of the yarn and then toss the ball of yarn on to someone else. Each student, in turn, was instructed to do the same thing.

After the ball of yarn had changed hands about a dozen times, the ball of yarn was returned to the first person. The first person was then instructed to send a large round bead up the yarn to the seventh person on the "yarn" network. The seventh person was instructed to send the bead, our yarn-network token, to the third person. The third person was instructed to send the bead-token to the eleventh person on the network.

As you can imagine, it did not take the students very long to figure out that a Token Ring network functions differently than an Ethernet network, and that in some situations, a Token Ring network can be more difficult to implement, and to use.

The point was made clearly and effectively through the use of this special, and fun, visual aid. And, as an added bonus, when these students later answered questions about Token Ring networks, no student who had been in attendance the day we activated our "yarn and bead" Token Ring network missed any Token Ring-related test questions.

In this example, the visual aid that was used effectively persuaded the students of the advantages of one topology over another.

You can also use visual aids to lend additional credibility to your presentation, or to make it appear more professional. The type of visual aid that you use can also affect your lesson's level of credibility as well as professionalism.

By using several different types of visual aids, you can teach students how to load necessary files in order for a network client to establish a connection with a network server. Certain visual aids can make your lesson appear more professional and more credible than if you had chosen a different visual aid. Using a computer and special projection equipment, you can walk through the process of loading these files on your computer while it displays on the overhead. You can also walk the students through the process by showing a series of screen shots as overheads. Which presentation do you think will seem more professional and more credible to your students?

Visual aids can also be used to help spur interaction among your students. For example, if you choose to have your students use the interview technique described earlier to help them get to know each other, you can add a simple visual aid to help them get started. If you list on the board the four or five questions that you want them to ask each other, they can use this visual aid to start and continue their conversations.

You can also use visual aids to help gain consensus among your students. For example, a lab activity geared toward teaching students how to design security into their network, requires that the students ultimately come to a consensus and choose the final design for their network. This lab activity then requires that they present their final solution by writing it out on a clear overhead, and presenting it to the class. The fact that they must write it out and present it, helps the various groups come to an agreement about their network design.

There are many different types of visual aids, some of them are more common or better known than others, and have already been mentioned here briefly.

Some of the older and more common types of visual aids include:

- White boards and chalkboards
- Transparencies (overheads)
- Flip charts
- Handouts

White Boards and Chalkboards

Of these types of visual aids, the chalkboard is probably the oldest and most widely used, although many chalkboards today have been replaced with white boards and erasable markers.

One of the advantages of using a white board is that it is flexible in its use. White boards can be used for lists of items, rough diagrams of ideas you are presenting, and to help you establish security for your students. Any variety of information, particularly if it is not permanent in nature can be displayed on a white board.

The white board also allows you to use colors in a vivid and effective way. Although red, black, blue, and green are the most common erasable marker colors, erasable markers are available in a wide variety of colors.

Together the white board and the variety of colored erasable markers can be used to:

◆ Highlight important points of information

◆ Welcome students to your classroom on the first day of the course

◆ Provide the phone number of your facility where your student's coworkers or boss can call to leave a message

◆ List the day's objectives, one section at a time

◆ Further explain or diagram a concept that the students are having trouble grasping

◆ Post any information that needs to be kept only for a short period of time

You can also use the white board to teach and compare different items of information. For example, if you want to teach your students the lists of NetWare 3.1x rights and file attributes, write lists on the white board to help your students remember them. However, because both of these lists contain some of the same letters, it is better for your students if you can more distinctly differentiate between the two.

One way to differentiate like items on the white board is to list the items using different colored pens. Although this provides the reader with some differentiation, the visual aid is still just about the same. When the students later try to recall the list of file attributes by picturing them as they appeared on the white board, they may find it difficult to distinguish between the file attributes list and the rights list.

You can, however, help the student remember the information more distinctly by giving it a special location on the white board, in addition to using a different color.

For example, if your students are about to do a lab activity that requires them to create users and assign them rights, listing the rights in a corner of the white board for quick reference will not only help them with the lab activity, but may also help them picture the list of rights in their minds when they are trying to recall the list from memory.

The combined use of color and location of the information on the white board can contribute to a student's ability to remember the information presented.

Many instructors consider the white board to be a versatile visual aid. One of the biggest disadvantages of white boards, however, is that they are so close at hand, and so easy to use, and so versatile that it is very easy to overuse them. Such overuse leads to the exclusion of other visual aids, and can actually be detrimental for the student if the white board is used when a different visual aid would have been more effective. In addition, usingwhite boards can slow you up, especially if you are pressed for time. It takes time to write the information on the board.

Transparencies

Transparencies, on the other hand, are not only a good substitute for the white board, but preferable in some instances. Transparencies are particularly useful when it is not practical to draw a diagram on a white board, particularly when a highly complex diagram is needed or preferred. In this case, a professionally prepared transparency would be more useful, more effective, and save valuable time.

When creating transparencies, you can take the time to show complex relationships that you cannot show as effectively if you are trying to quickly draw a diagram on a white board.

You can also use overhead transparencies to build an idea, another option which is far more difficult to achieve using a white board than it is by using transparencies. Because of the transparent or "see-through" nature of transparencies, they can be layered on top of each other on the projector, until they are three layers or so deep. Layering transparencies allows you to gradually show detail or increasing complexity.

For example, you can use a series of stacked overheads to teach your students about the NetWare directory structure, as shown in figure 5.1. Figure 5.1 displays five separate transparencies. Each transparency is numbered one through five to show you the order in which they are to be layered.

You can use these layered overheads by placing the first one on the overhead projector and explaining the concept associated with it. Next, you add the second overhead on top of the first one, explaining the concept associated with it. Then you place the third overhead on top of the second one, and so on, until you have what finally appears in number five—a complete picture that you built one visual (transparency) at a time.

Of course, you could use just one of the overheads—the last overhead as shown in figure 5.1. The student then has the entire structure to look at right away. You only have to create and use one overhead this way, but you lose the effect of the layering technique, and the momentary concentration on each individual piece of information.

You can recover some of that concentration and separation, however, by creating one overhead but using a different color for each of the different sections of the NetWare directory structure. Both techniques are effective and creative uses of overheads, but both present the lesson with a different emphasis.

Another way that you can use transparencies to effectively transmit important information is to write or draw directly on the transparency, either before or during your presentation of the related information.

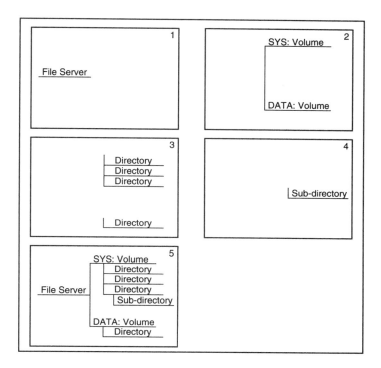

Figure 5.1

Increasing complexity displayed through the use of layered overheads.

The Novell instructor kits contain a set of transparencies for each particular course. You can enhance the value of these transparencies and personalize them for your presentation. You can circle the most important information presented on a transparency while you are displaying it, or you can add a brief note to encourage student retention. You can also use color to highlight important information.

For example, the transparencies that Novell provides in its instructor kits are prepared in black and white. You can use highlighting permanent markers to add color to these transparencies. By adding a little color you can enhance the entire transparency, or emphasize a particular portion of the information being presented on the transparency.

You can also use color to carry a theme or idea from one transparency to another. An example might be when you are discussing layers of the OSI model. You may have several different transparencies that show the gradual building of these layers. If you color each layer on each transparency with the same color of highlighting marker, it is easy for the student to follow the layers through the presentation.

In addition, you can use multiple colors on a transparency to highlight two separate but related points of information on a single transparency. For example, you can create a transparency that more clearly shows both the similarity and difference between the two pieces of information simultaneously, through the use of color. Figure 5.2 shows how this relationship can be shown by using only the colors of white and black.

Figure 5.2

Color variety to simultaneously show contrast and similarity.

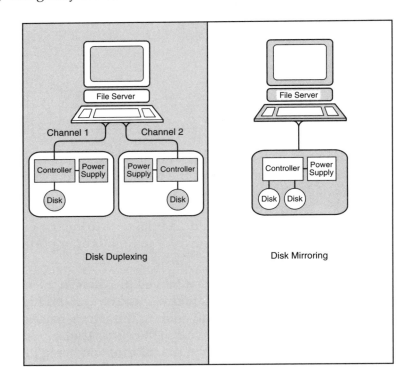

You can also add color simply for variety. A quick way to add color for this purpose is to keep a sheet or two of different colors of unused transparencies in your instructor kit. Then, to provide variety, use a colored sheet on top of or under the actual informative transparency. This adds color to the entire transparency, but does not highlight any particular portion of the transparency.

Keep in mind that some colors can have a negative effect on your students. For example, exposure to red colors have been shown to encourage anger and negative behavior in some individuals. The color blue often has the opposite effect of red.

This does not mean that you should never use red or that you should always use blue. It does imply, however, that you should carefully consider the colors that you do use, and the frequency with which you use them.

You should consider using transparencies when the information you want to present is:

◆ Complex in nature

◆ Easier to understand if shown as a visual

◆ Supplemented as an outline by details provided in your lecture

◆ Easily focused through the use of an overhead

◆ Likely to be referred to later when the transparency should be put back up on the overhead projector

One of the main advantages of using transparencies is that you can readily redisplay the information whenever it is needed. This is not as easy to do if you have drawn or written the information on a white board and subsequently erased it.

The main disadvantage of using transparencies is that they can become a substitute for creativity in your presentation. It is easy to prepare and present your entire course using only transparencies. Even varying the colors or layering your transparencies does not change the fact that you are constantly using them. You should, therefore, also include other visuals in your presentation.

Note The creative and varied use of visual aids is an important factor in your IPE presentation. You should use a minimum of four different visual aids when you take your IPE. If possible, use more than four visual aids. Do not, however, use so many visual aids that you distract from your presentation rather than enhance it.

Flip Charts

Flip charts can be generically described as oversized tablets of paper that stand on an oversized easel. They can contain plain paper, lined paper, graphic lined paper, and even decorative paper if you choose.

You can use one or more flip charts in your presentation, and you can place them anywhere in the room where you have easy access to them and where students can readily see them.

Flip charts can be used for many purposes, but are particularly effective when used to:

◆ Create lists of items or suggestions made by your students

◆ Present a list of section objectives to use when introducing the section

◆ Refer back to at the end of the session when you are summarizing the information covered in this section

◆ Let groups of students present their summary or other information that they were responsible for developing

◆ Write down information that can later be torn off and posted around the walls so that it is readily visible to all students

◆ Present information that is important to the topic at hand, and which you may need to refer back to later, but for which a more formal presentation is not really necessary

This last particular use of a flip chart is probably one of the best reasons for its use. This technique is particularly useful when you are conducting, for example, a discussion of the responsibilities of a NetWare network administrator.

You can use the flip chart to get the class rolling on a brainstorming session. Tell the students one responsibility of a NetWare network administrator. Write that responsibility, in slightly abbreviated form if necessary, on the flip chart. Then ask the class to tell you other responsibilities of a NetWare network administrator. As each responsibility is voiced, add it to the list on the flip chart. Later on, when class discussion or lecture relates to a particular NetWare network administrator's responsibility, go back to the flip chart and use it to reinforce your discussion.

Flip charts are also particularly useful when you want to neatly draw out or write up some information that you will need later on in the course, and which you do not want the students to see until that time.

For example, you can flip sheets back on the flip chart and list the day's section objectives. You can then cover this list back up by pulling the blank pages of the flip chart back down over the page(s) that you wrote out. You can prepare your flip charts hours, days, or even weeks before the class begins, while sitting at your kitchen table, with a ruler and pencil in hand. Flip charts which you have taken the time to neatly create in this manner can also be used on subsequent occasions when you teach this same course again.

Flip charts do have some disadvantages however. First of all, they are bulky and cumbersome to carry around. Most of them come with white paper so they are often not very colorful. You can add the color yourself, but that can add substantial time to your class preparation. They also wear out more quickly than do their stronger counterparts, transparencies.

Flip charts, along with the other visual aids discussed so far, have their use and their place in providing variety in your presentation.

Handouts

The potential variety of handouts is practically endless. Even if you never prepare separate handouts of your own, you can use some of the handouts provided in your NetWare course Instructor kits.

This section is concerned with handouts that you create and use to add variety and interest to your class.

When you think of handouts, the first thing that probably comes to your mind is mimeographed or Xeroxed copies of magazine articles and other items of information that your high school and college instructors use to give you; however, handouts can be prepared and presented in a variety of forms, and can be made to be both interesting and fun.

Author's Note

While attending a lunch-time presentation at a writing conference one year, I saw an interesting and fun example of a useful handout. It consisted of a piece of paper with several vertical lines. Each line started at the top edge and ended at a different location on the bottom edge.

Each line was numbered, though they did not seem at first glance to be numbered in any logical order. Each numbered line was accompanied by two lines of instructions. One line of instruction explained to you how and in which direction to fold the paper along its associated line. The other instruction explained one of the steps to follow in order to successfully complete a specific application program-related task.

If you followed the instructions in numerical order (after you were finished folding the paper and had completed each application-specific step), not only had you learned how to accomplish a particular task using the related application program, but you had also built a paper airplane from this handout.

Five minutes later, after all of the pretty blue paper airplanes had landed somewhere, the instructors left the stage to a round of applause. Much of the audience had increased their knowledge of the application program, and improved their digestion as well. (You know that old saying about laughter being the best medicine.)

Not all of your handouts need to be as creative as blue paper airplanes, or as ordinary as a photocopy of a related magazine article. Somewhere a happy medium exists that can make your handouts both effective and interesting. Just how effective and interesting your handouts are depends, at least in part, on why you are using them. Some reasons for using handouts include:

- ◆ Giving your students more in-depth information than otherwise available

- ◆ Providing variety in the way you present information to your students

- ◆ Allowing your students to have reference materials, such as special log-in instructions for lab work, that you do not want to make your students write down or memorize

- ◆ Giving them supplemental information that you have re-searched or developed yourself, and which you believe may be of future use to your students

The main advantage to using handouts is realized more by your students than by you as an instructor. If you use handouts for any of the previously described reasons, then your students have additional information at their fingertips, without having to spend their time and efforts on copying this information down. You may benefit as well, particularly if you do not have to take valuable class time to repeat information, or explain information that is important and useful, but which was not originally intended to take up much class time. In addition, you can make handouts from transparencies. As you present the transparencies, your students can make notes on the handouts.

The main drawback of handouts is the cost and time involved in preparing them. Therefore, consider using handouts only when they are truly worth the effort and expense, or when there simply is no better way to present the information.

Using a variety of visual aids is one of the most effective ways for you to help your students differentiate and remember important information. The four visual aids discussed so far are common and readily available to most instructors. There are, of course, other useful visual aids. However, these may not be as readily available. Some other visual aids include

◆ Video tapes

◆ Electronic computer screen overhead displays

◆ Software that lets you control what all students see on their own computer monitor

Video Tapes

You can find useful video tapes for almost any topic that you teach today, and networking is no exception. Some companies specialize in producing training tapes on video.

Many companies that use NetWare, or that have products which are compatible with or which run on a NetWare network, have produced videos related to their products.

One advantage to using videos is that they can show your students something that it would otherwise be impractical for you to show them yourself.

For example, you cannot show your students the process of creating electronic chips. Your classroom does not have the equipment to create them. In addition, they must be created in a sterile, dust-free environment, which your classroom is unlikely to be. Professionally prepared videos that show the process of creating computer chips are available. The only special equipment you need in order to show the video to your students is a VCR and a television set.

The biggest drawback to videos is that, if they are too long or too complex, they may put your students to sleep rather than teaching them what you wanted them to learn.

You can overcome this drawback by following a couple of recommendations. First, select video tapes carefully. Be certain that they tell the students what you want them to know.

If the video tapes you like are too lengthy, then show only pieces of each video to reinforce what you are teaching.

For this approach to be effective, you need to first preview the tape, prefereably on the classroom's video player. During the preview you should note the numbers on the video player that relate to the sections you want to show. Then, before you show the tape to your students, make certain that the video player that you show the tape on has the same settings as the video player on which you originally viewed the tape. Otherwise, the numbers may not match and you will waste class time trying to locate the proper section of tape.

One other step that will help you save class time is to set up the tape before the class starts, or during a break, so that it will begin playing at the location you have chosen. Again, you do not want to waste your class time fast-forwarding the tape to its actual starting point.

Electronic Displays

Special equipment is now available that lets you display the output of your computer's monitor onto an overhead display screen, by using the same overhead projector upon which you display your transparencies.

This equipment is quite useful when you cannot let the students access a computerized process for themselves, as you might

215

otherwise do in a laboratory session. If this is the case, the next best way to teach your students about a particular computerized process is to actually show it to them by means of this special equipment. This is, of course, one of the best reasons for using this type of equipment; otherwise it has two main drawbacks.

First, this type of equipment is expensive, therefore, not all classrooms will have this equipment installed or available. Second, the display is rarely perfect with this equipment. Sometimes the very top or very bottom of the screen display is cut off or too fuzzy for the students to read. In addition, the overall quality of the projection is often not nearly as good as looking directly at the screen itself.

Even so, this presentation equipment has its place and can be very useful. In addition, as the technology improves, so will the quality of the presentation.

Software that Controls the Student's Display

You can use special teaching software when you find it impractical to let all of the students run a particular piece of software themselves. This type of software lets you control what the students see on their networked computers. Once properly set up and after all students have logged on as instructed, each student sees repeated on his or her computer's monitor whatever you are doing and seeing on your computer's monitor.

This software is particularly useful for demonstrating single user-access software, such as installation software. It is also useful for demonstrating processes that require supervisor or administrative rights, and which might cause bindery corruption if several students attempted to simultaneously run the software.

The biggest advantage to the special software type of visual aid is that the presentation is as clear as each student's monitor allows.

The biggest disadvantage is that it does not allow the students to backup or go forward at their own pace. What they see is controlled strictly by what you do at the instructor's computer workstation.

There are other types of visual aids, and more are being developed every day. The visual aids that you use in teaching your classes are determined by your own personal preferences, and by the limitations of the classroom in which you teach.

When you choose your visual aids, select them for the benefits they provide your students. Ask yourself such questions as:

◆ Does the use of this particular visual aid add to the presentation?

◆ Will using this visual aid distract my students from learning?

◆ Can I effectively use this visual aid?

◆ Is there another visual aid that would be more useful or more effective?

As long as the visual aids add to your presentation, help your students learn what they need to know, and do not distract or disturb your students, then use the visual aids appropriately.

 Do you remember Murphy's laws? There is one which states that if anything can possibly go wrong, it will. This law must have been written with teaching in mind, because it seems that no matter how prepared you think you are, something always happens. For this reason, try to prepare not only for a great presentation, but prepare as well to successfully navigate around the problems which will inevitably crop up. Here are some basic suggestions to help you do just that:

◆ If you are working with electronic equipment, assume that it can and will break. Be prepared to finish your presentation with or without the use of spare electronic equipment.

continues

217

◆ If your presentation uses an overhead projector, figure that sometime when you are using it, the lightbulb will burn out. Correct this problem by carrying a spare and knowing how to replace it.

◆ Assume that someone will remove your erasable white board pens from their tray in your classroom. Bring an extra set. Do not forget to bring an eraser too. The person who borrowed your erasable pens will probably borrow the eraser as well.

◆ Assume that someday your car will break down on the way to class. (Of course, you just know that it is going to be when you are on the way to your IPE.) Keep a portable cellular phone in your car, prearrange with someone to look for you if you do not arrive at a prescribed time, or have another instructor be prepared to start your class for you if you do not check in with them by a given time.

In other words, be prepared no matter what the potential problem. If you teach for any length of time, you can almost guarantee that something will go wrong. It is not the fact that a problem occurs that matters, because we all have to deal with them. It is how you deal with it that makes all the difference.

Questioning Effectively

If you watch any of the currently popular television police or detective programs, or if you enjoy listening to the old radio detective programs, you have probably noticed that the detectives are all very good at questioning suspects. By the time an experienced detective is finished with a suspect, that suspect's signature is affixed to a signed confession.

Well, instructors are not intent on getting signed confessions from students, but rather on getting students to participate actively and effectively in class discussions. One of the best ways to do that is by using effective questioning techniques.

Well-designed questions can be used to:

◆ Start lively, interesting, and informative discussions among your students

◆ Motivate your students to think more intensely or more conscientiously about the topic being discussed

◆ Help you find and solve problems that students may be having in understanding a particular topic

◆ Encourage your students to feel comfortable about asking relevant questions themselves

◆ Guide your students ever closer to accomplishing the goals that they have set for themselves in relation to this course

The technique of effective questioning is more involved than just asking the students if anyone has any questions, or if there is anything that they did not understand and which they would like you to clarify.

 Note Most students do not respond when asked the types of questions posed in the previous paragraph, particularly if no one else is responding to these types of questions.

Few people like to admit that they did not quite understand what you told them. Nor do they want to be the individual that makes everyone else sit and listen while the instructor once again explains a topic to them.

Your ability to ask questions that get the response that you are looking for, depends upon your understanding of different types of questions, and your knowledge of how to ask the proper questions at the appropriate time. These different types of questions fall into one of two categories:

◆ Closed questions

◆ Open questions

Closed questions are questions which prompt responses such as yes, no, I do not know, or a simple statement of fact. The problem with closed questions is that they do not:

◆ Act as catalysts to start lively, interesting, and informative discussions among your students

◆ Motivate your students to think more about the topic being discussed

◆ Help you find and solve problems that students may be having in understanding the current topic

◆ Make your students more comfortable about asking relevant questions themselves

◆ Move your students closer to their goals

In fact, asking closed questions often does precisely the opposite of the effects listed previously.

Closed questions also put your students into a potentially embarrassing position. If the student has not understood the topic well enough to correctly answer the closed question, then the chances are pretty good that he or she will answer incorrectly and feel embarrassed. Even if the student does answer the question correctly, a closed question that is correctly answered does not tell you whether or not the student truly comprehends the meaning of the question or the topic to which it relates.

In addition, a closed question does not start your students thinking about the topic. It does not generate a good discussion of the topic. For these and other reasons, it is important for you to ask open instead of closed questions.

Learning to ask open questions is often the most difficult task for new instructors to overcome. Many of us have asked closed questions all of our life. But as instructors, we need to learn to ask open questions.

 Your score on the IPE depends in part on your ability to develop a certain skill at asking open questions. As you prepare for your IPE, you should think of open questions related to the topic that you are teaching, and then be certain that you use those open questions during your presentation.

Your IPE audience is composed of other IPE candidates, plus the IPE instructors who are conducting your evaluation. Although you are expected to ask at least one of each type of open question during your presentation, the audience is not really expected to answer. However, if you do not ask open questions, it will reduce your IPE score.

There are three types of open questions:

◆ Memory questions

◆ Comprehension questions

◆ Application questions

Memory Questions

You ask memory questions to determine if your students have learned sufficient factual information so that they can repeat all or some of it back to you. Memory questions are not intended to start stimulating class discussions on topics, but are used to find out what your students have learned.

Memory questions look for facts. You may recognize this type of question from school. You were answering memory questions when you provided the answers to such questions as:

- In what year did Christopher Columbus sail the ocean blue?
- What two elements are found in H_2O?
- When does the summer solstice occur?
- What does the term *disjointed* mean?

As an instructor you must now learn to ask memory questions.

From the previous examples you may be able to determine that memory questions fall into four primary types, depending on their function or purpose.

You can use memory questions to ask for the following facts:

- Who
- What
- When
- Meaning

Meaning refers to definitions, usually in relation to a term. For example, you are asking a meaning memory question when you ask your students what the term *networking* means.

Some who, what, when, and meaning memory questions that you may consider asking, depending on the topic you are covering in your class or IPE, are shown by type in table 5.1.

Table 5.1
Examples of Memory Questions

Type	Example
What	What are the primary responsibilities of a network administrator?
	Which network right(s) must you grant to a user in order for that user to perform the duties of the administrator when the administrator is on vacation?
	What is the largest size allowed for a single network volume?

Type	Example
When	When is the best time to perform a system backup on your network?
	When should you format your file server's hard disk?
	When is disk duplexing more appropriate than disk mirroring?
Meaning	What is a bindery?
	What does NCP stand for?
	What is a passive hub?
Who	Who should be given supervisor-equivalency?
	Who has rights to run BINDFIX on the file server?
	Who should you call if you have a problem and nothing you have done has corrected it?

Comprehension Questions

You ask a comprehension question when you expect your students to give you an answer that shows that they not only understand the information, but are able to make some use of or sense out of the basic idea behind the material.

There are four common types of comprehension questions:

◆ Translation

◆ Interpretation

◆ Extrapolation

◆ Comparison

Translation questions require that your students take what they have learned and reword or restate it so that it has more meaning to them.

The type of information that you give to your students to translate can be presented to them in any form: verbal, written, or graphic form. The translation that the student gives to you, however, must be in verbal form.

Some examples of translation questions include the following:

◆ Explain to me what you think is happening in this particular graphic.

◆ Tell me how this problem could best be resolved.

◆ Give me a reason why this particular approach is not as effective as the others that we discussed earlier.

Asking an interpretation question requires that your students be able to interpret something that they have learned, or reorder it so that the original idea or group of ideas is still properly conveyed.

Some examples of interpretation questions include:

◆ Tell me why you think one topology is better than the other.

◆ The other students who responded all think that this process should be done this way; tell me what you think.

◆ Discuss the difference between clean and dirty cache buffers.

Asking an extrapolation question requires that your student go beyond the presented information, and include inferences, implications, or consequences. This type of question requires that the students present subjective information based on what they have learned.

Some examples of extrapolation questions include:

◆ If the power were to go out just as you were starting a backup of your file server, what would you expect to see when the power was reinstated?

◆ If the network administrator goes on vacation and has not given anyone supervisor-equivalent, what do you think will happen when the administrator returns?

Comparison questions require the student compare or contrast two or more ideas or concepts.

Some examples of comparison questions include:

- ◆ What are the main differences between disk mirroring and disk duplexing?

- ◆ What do the NetWare 2 and the NetWare 3 operating systems have in common that is not also true for the NetWare 4 operating system?

Application Questions

Your students can take the information that they have been taught, and apply it to their own specific situations, or to situations which you create for testing purposes.

Many students take Novell courses to learn how to use or administer NetWare in their own work environment. All the conceptual information in the world is useless to these people if they cannot take it back and apply it to their own situations. It is important, therefore, that you ask occasional application questions to see if they are understanding the information well enough to be able to directly apply their knowledge to their work environment.

Application questions can take either of two approaches. For the first approach, you present a scenario and have the students explain what they would do, or show you how they would handle a particular aspect of of that situation.

You can also ask the student when this type of event might be likely to occur. This second approach to an application question asks the student to present the possible causes of a given situation. Knowing the possible causes of a given situation helps speed up the process of troubleshooting and resolving any problems that the situation may create. Table 5.2 provides examples of application questions that you might use while teaching Novell courses.

Table 5.2
Examples of Application Questions

Type	Examples
Situational	If you were asked to add a new user to your network, what steps would you follow to add the user and make certain they have sufficient network access?
	What is the first step you should take when your file server's uninterrupted power supply (UPS) indicates that power has been lost to the server?
	If a user forgets their password and tries repeatedly to log in using an incorrect password, thus activating intruder lockout on their account, what must you do to allow that user to regain access and set a new password?
Occurrence	What would cause the intruder lockout feature of NetWare to become active on a particular user account?
	If you check the MONITOR utility and notice that the Hot Fix area is almost full, what might be the reason?
	If a user who has not previously had any trouble logging in to the network comes in for the first time on a Sunday and cannot log in, what might be the cause of this user's inability to log in on a Sunday?

Answering a student's questions is as important as asking the right open-ended questions yourself. Both become easier with time and practice. There are even ways of turning student questions into questions that you can use to guide the entire class. Keep these hints in mind as you learn to ask and answer questions easily:

◆ Ask questions using only those terms that are familiar to your students

◆ Ask questions that let any student in the class respond

◆ Take questions that students ask you and give them back to the class to answer

◆ Be specific about the questions that you ask, making certain that you give hints in the question itself to lead the students in the right direction

◆ Use questions to direct the discussion towards your topic, not away from it.

◆ Encourage, support, and assist students who have the answer only partially right by responding positively to a portion of their answer

◆ Ask and answer questions using simple wording that does not distort the meaning of either the question or the answer

◆ Give students sufficient time to work out the answer to questions you give them that require thought

◆ If student answers are incorrect, be sure that the class understands the correct answer

Promoting Student Discussion

Actively participating students learn quicker and retain more than students who do not participate in class. There are several things that you can do to encourage class participation.

First, let the students know early in the course that you want them to participate. Tell them you will be asking questions to help stimulate discussion. Explain to them that you recognize that they are all professionals who have something valuable to share, and that you hope they will take the opportunity to share their knowledge and experience with the class.

As your students begin to participate in the class by answering questions, asking questions, or sharing information, make every effort to give them positive reinforcement.

When students start asking questions, tell them when you think their question is important or good. Let them know that you appreciate their participation.

When students answer questions, be very careful not to embarrass or ridicule either the student or the answer. Comments such as, "that is an interesting solution," "I had not considered it in that light," or "that is a possibility; does anyone have anything they would like to add," are all nonembarrassing ways of acknowledging the student's participation without giving the impression that the student's answer is correct.

You can also encourage participation by asking memory, comprehension, or application questions. After posing the questions, allow the students the opportunity to run with their discussion. Do not, however, let them run away from the topic at hand. If the topic begins to stray, bring them back on target. Try to find a point made by one or more students that you can use to swing the conversation back on the right track, or to stop it and lead on to the next topic.

All of these approaches to boost class participation are also methods of keeping control of your class. Your ability as an instructor to do both is graded when you take your IPE; therefore, practice and master these techniques. You are expected to display most or all of them during your IPE.

Summarizing Topics

As you reach the end of a lecture or discussion on a specific topic, it is important for you to summarize the information that the class has learned.

Giving a summary provides two major benefits. First, it reviews and reinforces the information that the students have been studying. Second, it signals a mental conclusion to one topic so that your students are prepared to go on to the next topic.

Summarizing the information that your students have just discussed as a class, is also an effective way of bringing the class back to the topic at hand if the conversation has strayed.

As the instructor, you can step into the conversation with statements that begin in one of the following ways:

◆ If I correctly understand what you have said, then...

◆ So, in general, the class believes that...

◆ There is obviously some difference of opinion here, but all of you have made valid points, including...

◆ Then, what we have narrowed it down to is...

With a little practice you will find ways of your own to bring your students back to the topic being discussed, and to subsequently summarize the information presented.

Introducing New Materials in the Summary

Do not let this section heading give you the impression that you should introduce new material in the topic summary. The opposite is true. You should never introduce new material when you are summarizing the topic, particularly when you are taking your IPE. You will lose points for introducing new material in your summary.

Deciding Where To Go from Here

Once you successfully pass your first IPE and receive your letter from CNI Administration, you can teach any of the courses for which you are certified. Your Novell CNI is only a beginning, however, not an end. Where do you go from here? You have several options.

You can teach courses for NAECs or NEAPs. You can also become a contract CNI and teach as an on-call instructor for any NAEC or NEAP that needs you.

If you prefer, you can also seek employment as a full-time CNI for private companies. Large fortune 500 corporations, for example, often hire their own in-house CNIs to teach certified Novell courses to their employees. By doing so, these companies enable large numbers of employees to get certified training using certified course materials for substantially less money than it would cost to send their employees to NAEC- or NEAP-sponsored courses.

You may also decide to apply for a position with Novell's NTI. NTI instructors often travel to different Novell locations to teach certified courses for both Novell and non-Novell students.

These are just a few of the options available to you after you have obtained your CNI. Reviewing the newspaper advertisements, networking with other CNIs, and continuing your Novell education may also open opportunities for you.

Summary

Novell's CNI certification is the most time-consuming and possibly the most technically-oriented of all of the certification programs. But it may also hold the most reward, particularly if you love to teach.

Because of what it takes to become a CNI, a love of teaching and technology are the two basic prerequisites that you need in order to become a successful CNI. This chapter has shown you some of the other skills and information that you need, as well, to become a CNI.

This chapter discussed important and related topics which included information on how to prepare to become a CNI, increase your chances of getting accepted into the CNI program, as well as information to help you understand (and to overcome any nervousness related to) the IPE, what IPE-relevant teaching skills you need to develop and how to develop them, and some options to consider once you obtain your CNI.

Chapter 6, "Choosing Your Certification Courses," provides you with details about Novell's available certification courses, many of which are applicable to the CNI certification, in addition to the CNA, CNE, and ECNE certifications.

Choosing Your Certification Courses

The courses you select for Novell certification can be applied to an additional certification.

For example, the ECNE program requires that you obtain a CNE before enrolling in the ECNE program. If you choose the NetWare 4.0 Operating System (OS) track for your CNE, those same courses can be applied as the OS track for your ECNE. However, if you choose to pursue NetWare 2.2 for your CNE OS track, those courses can only be applied as electives to your ECNE program. You must then choose another OS track for the ECNE program.

If time and funds are limited, it is particularly important to start out in the Novell certification programs by choosing your courses wisely. This chapter is intended to help you make the choices that may be best for you.

After reading this chapter, you will be able to do the following:

◆ Select the right courses for certification

◆ Understand the course descriptions and objectives for the seven main course tests

◆ Consider other available NetWare courses and their descriptions

Selecting the Right Courses for Certification

Selecting the right courses for your chosen certification should depend on three factors:

First, consider whether or not the courses you are choosing provide you with the information needed to successfully perform your work, when your present job and duties are NetWare related.

Novell has specified which tests you must pass to become certified, although some freedom of choice is provided, particularly in the area of the OS track and electives that you can choose. Therefore, the second factor involves the free choice that Novell allows within the certification program you are pursuing.

The third factor relates to the specific options available for the certification you want to obtain, particularly concerning the OS track.

Each of the four different certification programs have different requirements and course options. Before you can logically select from among the available course options, you need to know what those options include.

Course Options for CNAs

Certification as a NetWare Administrator is available for each of the four NetWare versions, including:

◆ NetWare 2.2

◆ NetWare 3.11

◆ NetWare 3.1x

◆ NetWare 4.x

Note In addition to these four versions, a CNA option for UnixWare is now available as well. The test number is 50-392, with test objectives based on course 680, UnixWare System Administration. You can apply the credits toward the operating system requirements for CNE certification. If you take the UnixWare OS track for your CNE, you do not have to pass test 50-134 (UnixWare System Administration) if you passed test 50-392. Also, test 50-392 will count towards CNE certification (if you are going to obtain your CNE as well as your CNA).

There are specific courses that set the test objectives for each of these certification tests. In order to pass the related certification test, you must either take the course or study the material that covers the test objectives.

Each certification course contains a list of course objectives. These are generally outlined at the beginning of each section of the course's student manual. Course objectives and test objectives are the same.

If you do not take the related course and/or purchase the course student manual, you can find out the objectives for each course by calling Novell's FaxBack system (1-800-NETWARE), and requesting a copy of the objectives for the course in which you are interested. To decide how to choose a course, first order the FaxBack catalog containing a list of all courses and course numbers. From this list, you can select the appropriate course objectives.

NetWare 2.2

Two courses apply to the NetWare 2.2 CNA program. These courses are:

◆ NetWare 2.2 System Manager (course number 501)

◆ NetWare 2.2 Advanced System Manager (course number 502)

235

Only one test is required to obtain the NetWare 2.2 CNA—test number 50-115. It covers both the NetWare 2.2 System Manager and the NetWare 2.2 Advanced System Manager course/test objectives.

 If you plan to pursue your CNE, test 50-115 cannot be applied for credit in the CNE program.

NetWare 3.11

Two courses apply to the NetWare 3.11 CNA program. These courses are:

◆ NetWare 3.11 System Manager (course number 505)

◆ NetWare 3.11 Advanced System Manager (course number 515)

Only one test is required to obtain the NetWare 3.11 CNA—test number 50-116. It covers both the NetWare 3.11 System Manager and the NetWare 3.11 Advanced System Manager course/test objectives.

 Test number 50-116 is being discontinued after June 30, 1994. Therefore, you should take the CNA 3.1x test number 50-390 instead. Until May 1, 1994, test 50-130, NetWare 3.1x Administration, can be used for CNA certification. After that date, it can only be counted for credit toward a CNE elective.

NetWare 3.1x

Only one test/course is required to obtain the NetWare 3.1x CNA certification—the NetWare 3.1x Administration course (test number 50-390).

236

This certification only requires you to take one test. However, there are two different tests—passing either one completes the certification testing requirement for the NetWare 3.1x CNA. The difference between the two tests depends on when you take it.

If you took the NetWare 3.1x CNA test on or before February 28, 1994, the test number was 50-130. After that date, the new test number is 50-390.

Note The NetWare 3.x and NetWare 4.x CNA tests can be used as CNE credits, regardless of whether you take either the 50-130 or 50-390 NetWare 3.1x test, or the 50-122 or 50-391 NetWare 4.x CNA test.

NetWare 4.x

The NetWare 4.1x CNA program also requires that you learn the objectives of only one course—the NetWare 4.0 Administration course (number 520).

The NetWare 4.x CNA certificate requires that you pass one of two tests. Before February 28, 1994, the required test is number 50-122. After that date, the required test number is 50-391.

Figure 6.1 shows the CNA certification options and the courses and tests required in order to obtain certification.

Course Options for CNEs

To earn the CNE from Novell, you must pass all required courses, in addition to some elective course tests, to total nineteen (19) credits.

Course requirements, and subsequently course options, fall into four categories for the CNE certification. These categories include the following:

◆ Prerequisite requirements (2 credits)

◆ Operating system requirements (5 credits)

237

◆ Core requirements (10 credits)

◆ CNE elective requirements (2 credits)

Figure 6.1

CNA Program
Options.

CNA Program Options		
CNA Program	Test Number	Course Objectives to Study
NetWare 4.x	50-122 (Through Feb.28, 1994) 50-391 (After Feb 28, 1994)	NetWare 4.0 Administration (Course number 520)
NetWare 3.1x	50-130 (Through Feb. 28, 1994) 50-390 (After Feb 28,1994)	NetWare 3.1x Administration (Course number 508)
NetWare 3.11	50-116	NetWare 3.11 System Manager (Course number 505) NetWare 3.11 Adv. Sys. Manager (Course number 515)
NetWare 2.2	50-115	NetWare 2.2 System Manager (Course number 501) NetWare 2.2 Adv. Sys. Manager (Course number 502)

Prerequisite Requirements

The CNE program requires

 that you pass the test for the DOS/Microcomputer Concepts course (number 1100-1). The test number is 50-15, carrying two credits.

 Note If you are planning on choosing UnixWare as your core operating system, you may substitute the UNIX OS Fundamentals for NetWare Users (course number 220) test (number 50-107) for the DOS/ Microcomputer Concepts test. This test is also worth two credits. However, credit for taking this test cannot be applied as elective credit in either the CNE or ECNE program.

Operating System Requirements

The CNE program requires that you pass two tests in one of the available NetWare operating system areas. The two tests for each

NetWare operating system total five (5) credits. The NetWare operating system options include the following:

♦ NetWare 4.0:

Test # 50-122—NetWare 4.0 Administration (3)

Test # 50-123—NetWare 4.0 Advanced Administration (2)

♦ NetWare 3.1x:

Test # 50-130—NetWare 3.1x Administration (3)

Test # 50-131—NetWare 3.1x Advanced Administration (2)

 Note Because Novell is changing NetWare 3 certification from NetWare 3.11 to NetWare 3.1x requirements for its CNE certification program, Novell will let you mix the tests for the NetWare 3.1x and NetWare 3.11 operating system requirements until May 1994.

For example, if you have already taken the NetWare 3.11 System Manager test, you can now take the NetWare 3.1x Advanced Administration test instead of the NetWare 3.11 Advanced System Manager test to meet the operating system requirements.

After April 1994, you must register for and take both of the NetWare 3.1x tests instead of the NetWare 3.11 tests. If you have taken and passed one or both of the NetWare 3.11 tests before May 12, 1994, you are given credit for them toward your CNE.

♦ NetWare 3.11:

Test # 50-91—NetWare 3.11 System Manager (3)

Test # 50-82—NetWare 3.11 Advanced System Manager (2)

NetWare 2.2 used to be an OS track option for the Novell CNE program. However, as of March 1, 1994 it was removed from the program. If you have already started in the CNE program and chose NetWare 2.2 as your OS track, you can complete your CNE with this track as long as you finish your certification requirements before June 30, 1994. After that time (or if you have not yet started your CNE program), you can only apply the credits for these tests as elective credits.

◆ NetWare 2.2:

Test # 50-20—NetWare 2.2 System Manager (3)

Test # 50-44—NetWare 2.2 Advanced System Manager (2)

 If you prefer, Novell offers a CNE in UnixWare. In addition to taking the UnixWare OS Fundamentals test (number 50-107, course number 220) instead of the DOS/Microcomputer test, you meet your operating system requirement by passing:

◆ The UnixWare System Administration test—number 50-134, course number 680

◆ The UnixWare Advanced System Administration test—number 50-135, course number 685

In addition, you can use the credits earned by taking the CNA UnixWare test (number 50-392) towards your CNE certification.

Core Requirements

NetWare requires that you take ten (10) credits of core requirements. The core requirements include three tests:

◆ Networking Technologies:

Test # 50-80—Networking Technologies (3)

 Note This course is a prerequisite to NetWare Service and Support.

◆ NetWare Service and Support:

Old Test # 50-46—NetWare Service and Support (5)

(or)

New Test # 50-118—NetWare Service and Support (5)

 Note Novell is replacing the NetWare Service and Support course (currently course number 701, test number 50-46) with an updated version of this course. The new course number is 801.

You can register for the old test (50-46) through October 17, 1994. You can take the test after that date as long as you take the test on or before December 5, 1994. After that date, you can only register for the new Service and Support course test—number 50-118.

The new Service and Support test also requires that you pass a related Installation and Configuration test, depending upon the NetWare Operating System you choose.

◆ Installation and Configuration (As part of the core requirements, you must also take one of the following courses as a prerequisite to the new NetWare Service and Support course):

Test # 50-132—NetWare 2.2/3.1x Installation and Configuration Workshop (2)

241

or

Test # 50-126—NetWare 4.0 Installation and Configuration Workshop (2)

Elective Credits

Novell also requires that you obtain two elective credits to complete your requirement of 19 total credits.

Some of the CNA tests, including the courses listed previously under the different requirements for a CNE, can be counted as electives *if they have not already been counted to meet requirements in each of the three required areas.*

For example, if you choose to take the CNA test for NetWare 3.1x, then decide to pass the NetWare 4.1 tests to meet your operating system requirement for your CNE, the CNA test that you took may count as an elective.

You can choose from the courses/tests in Appendix A to meet your elective requirements.

Course Options for ECNEs

Certification as an Enterprise Certified NetWare Engineer is dependent upon first obtaining your CNE. The CNE certificate is the core requirement for the ECNE program.

Once you have earned your CNE from Novell, you must pass all required and some additional elective course tests to total nineteen (19) credits. These credits are in addition to your CNE elective credits and are intended to greatly expand your knowledge of Novell products.

Course/test requirements, and subsequently course/test options, fall into three categories for the ECNE certification. These categories include the following:

◆ Core requirement—Valid CNE certification

Note You must presently hold a valid CNE in order to be eligible for the ECNE program. If you have been decertified, you must reestablish your CNE certification before you can begin the ECNE program.

◆ Operating System requirements (7 or 10 credits)
◆ ECNE elective requirements (9 or 12 credits)

Core Requirements

NetWare requires that you obtain your CNE before you can obtain your ECNE. This is the only core requirement for ECNE certification.

Some of the nineteen (19) credits that you earn in the process of obtaining your CNE may be eligible for credit toward your ECNE program.

For example, the CNE program requires that you pass two tests in one of the NetWare operating system areas. The two tests for each NetWare operating system total five credits. The NetWare operating system options include:

◆ NetWare 4.0
◆ NetWare 3.1x
◆ NetWare 3.11
◆ NetWare 2.2

Note UnixWare operating system courses are also applicable.

243

Of these CNE NetWare OS options, only two are valid options for the ECNE: NetWare 3.1x and NetWare 4.0.

Operating System Requirements

The ECNE program enables you to choose between two NetWare operating systems to fulfill your OS track requirements. These two OS options are NetWare 4.x or NetWare 3.1x, which include the following tests (followed by credit value):

- ◆ NetWare 4.x:

    Test # 50-122—NetWare 4.0 Administration (3)

    Test # 50-123—NetWare 4.0 Advanced Administration (2)

    Test # 50-130—NetWare 3.1x Administration (3)

    Test # 50-131—NetWare 3.1x Advanced Administration (2)

- ◆ NetWare 3.1x:

    Test # 50-130—NetWare 3.1x Administration (3)

    Test # 50-131—NetWare 3.1x Advanced Administration (2)

    Test # 50-122—NetWare 4.0 Administration (3)

    Test # 50-123—NetWare 4.0 Advanced Administration (2)

    Test # 50-124—NetWare 3.11 to 4.0 Update (2)

You may take tests # 50-122 and 50-123. If you choose in place of these to take test # 50-124, you will need three additional elective credits.

If you received your CNE in either of the other two NetWare operating systems, NetWare 2.2 or 3.11, those credits can be applied as elective credit. Then you must choose from one of the above listed operating systems options.

If you choose to make NetWare 4.0 your primary operating system track, you must also pass the NetWare 3.1x Administration and Advanced Administration tests.

If, however, you take the NetWare 3.11 System Manager and Advanced System Manager tests before the May 12, 1994 deadline, you can apply the NetWare 3.11 tests to the operating system requirements in place of the NetWare 3.1x Administration and Advanced Administration requirements.

In addition, if you take and pass the NetWare 3.11 OS Features Review course prior to May 12, 1994, you can apply this test as an alternative to the NetWare 3.11 System Manager and Advanced System Manager tests, or the NetWare 3.1x Administration and Advanced Administration tests.

If you choose the NetWare 3.11 OS Features Review course to complete the NetWare 4.0 OS track operating system requirements, you must take 12 additional elective credits. This replaces the 7 elective credits that you would need if you took two of the four NetWare 3.11 or NetWare 3.1x tests, one of which must be an Advanced OS test.

If you choose to make NetWare 3.1x your NetWare OS track, you must also pass either the NetWare 3.11 to 4.0 Update (test # 50-124), or both the NetWare 4.0 Administration (test # 50-122) and the NetWare 4.0 Advanced Administration (test # 50-123) tests, in addition to the NetWare 3.1x Administration and Advanced Administration tests.

You can only follow the NetWare 3.11 track, including the NetWare 3.11 System Manager and Advanced System Manager courses, and the

continues

NetWare 3.11 to 4.0 Update course, if you complete these tests before May 12, 1994, and complete your certification requirements before June 25, 1994.

In addition, if you choose the NetWare 3.11 System Manager and Advanced System Manager tests, plus the NetWare 3.11 to 4.0 Update, you need 12 additional elective credits instead of 7.

Elective Credits

Novell also requires that you obtain sufficient elective credits to complete your requirement of 19 total credits.

Some of the CNA tests, as well as the courses listed previously under the different requirements for a CNE, can be counted as electives *if they have not already been counted to meet requirements in each of the three required areas.*

For example, if you have already taken the CNA test for NetWare 3.1x, then passed the NetWare 4.1 tests to meet your operating system requirement for your CNE, the CNA test that you took may count as an elective.

You can choose from the courses/tests listed in Appendix A to meet your elective credits requirement.

Course Options for CNIs

As you probably know by now, the certification process for a Certified NetWare Instructor is substantially different from any of Novell's other certification programs. Some of the ways in which the CNI program differs from the other certification programs include:

◆ Novell does not require that CNI candidates obtain any of Novell's other certifications before seeking the CNI certification

◆ A CNI candidate does not have core course or elective course requirements to meet

◆ Novell does not require the CNI candidate to obtain any predefined number of credits in order to become certified

This does not mean that as a CNI candidate you have no requirements. On the contrary, as a CNI candidate you must have a minimum of one year's experience as an instructor, you must submit an application for the CNI program, and you must have your application approved before you can take any CNI-level tests.

Novell also recommends that you establish a relationship with a NAEC or NEAP before you apply for the CNI program. However, it is not a requirement as it once was.

Once you meet these three requirements, you have the prerequisites that you must fulfill. The prerequisite depends on the course which you choose for your IPE.

If you are going to take an IPE in the Core/Operating System Product Courses group, you must pass the following test as a prerequisite to enrolling in your chosen IPE:

◆ Test 50-15—CNI-level DOS/Microcomputer Concepts

You must obtain your CNI in the Core/Operating System Product group before you are allowed to take an IPE in either the Advanced Product or Development Product groups.

If you are going to take an IPE in the Advanced Product Courses group, you must pass the following tests as a prerequisite to enrolling in your chosen IPE:

◆ Test 50-15—CNI-level DOS/Microcomputer Concepts

   or

   50-950 CNI-level UNIX Systems Skills

◆ Test 50-47—NetWare 3.11 System Manager

   or

   50-230—NetWare 3.12 Administration

   or

   50-222—NetWare 4.0 Administration

◆ Test 50-81—Networking Technologies

If you are going to take an IPE in the Development Product Courses group, you must pass the following tests as a prerequisite to enrolling in your chosen IPE:

◆ Test 50-15—CNI-level DOS/Microcomputer Concepts

◆ Test 50-47—NetWare 3.11 System Manager

   or

   50-230—NetWare 3.12 Administration

   or

   50-222—NetWare 4.0 Administration

Once you have met your prerequisites, you are then required to accomplish three more tasks before you can register for your IPE:

◆ Attend the course that you plan on using for your IPE. It must be a Novell-authorized presentation of the course. Therefore, you must attend the course at a NAEC or NEAP.

◆ Submit a copy of your course certificate to Novell's CNI Administration (in the U.S. and Canada) or to your AEM (if you are outside the U.S. or Canada).

◆ Take and pass the CNI-level test for your target course (the course you are going to use for your IPE).

Once you have accomplished all of the preceding tasks, you can then register to take your IPE. If this is your first IPE, then you must choose an IPE from among the eligible Core/OS Product courses. Otherwise, you can choose your IPE from either the Advanced Product Courses group or the Development Product Courses group. You must choose your IPE course from the list of eligible IPE courses. There are three available IPE course groups.

Core/OS Product Group

The Core/OS Product group is divided into two sections: eligible IPE courses and additional courses. Once you pass an eligible IPE course, you can teach that course. You only need to pass one eligible IPE course for the Core/OS Product group to become a CNI. Then, to teach any of the other courses in this group, you must attend a certified version of the course and pass the related CNI-level test.

Eligible IPE Courses

Courses from which you can choose in order to take your IPE include the following (preceded by course number):

◆ 200—Networking Technologies

◆ 508—NetWare 3.12 Administration

◆ 518—NetWare 3.12 Advanced Administration

◆ 520—NetWare 4.0 Administration

◆ 525—NetWare 4.0 Advanced Administration

◆ 530—NetWare 4.0 Design and Implementation

◆ 535—Printing with NetWare

◆ 801—NetWare Service and Support

Additional Courses for Certification in the Core/OS Product Group

Additional courses from which you can choose but which do not make you eligible for the IPE include the following:

◆ 102—Introduction to Networking

◆ 501—NetWare 2.2 System Manager

◆ 502—NetWare 2.2 Advanced System Manager

◆ 802—NetWare 2.x/3.x Installation and Configuration Workshop

◆ 506—NetWare 3.11 OS Features Review

◆ 507—NetWare 3.11 to 3.12 Update Seminar

◆ 804—NetWare 4.0 Installation and Configuration Workshop

◆ 550—NetWare Navigator

 Note As Novell phases out some courses and adds others, this list is likely to change. For the most current list, you can call FaxBack at 1-800-233-3392 (inside the U.S. and Canada) or 1-801-429-5363 (outside the U.S. and Canada), or contact your Novell Technology Institute (NTI) manager or Area Education Manager (AEM).

Advanced Product Courses Group

The Advanced Product Courses group is also divided into two sections: eligible IPE courses and additional courses. As with the Core/OS Product Courses group, once you pass an eligible IPE course in the Advanced Product Courses group, you can teach that course. You only need to pass one eligible IPE course for the Advanced Product group to become a CNI with certification in that group. Then, to teach any of the other courses in this group, you must attend a certified version of the course and pass the related CNI-level test.

Eligible IPE Courses

Courses from which you can choose in order to take your IPE in the Advanced Product Courses group are divided into two categories: NetWare and UNIX.

If you choose the NetWare category, you must have passed the CNI DOS/Microcomputer Concepts test as a prerequisite.

Eligible NetWare courses include:

◆ 718—NetWare Connect

◆ 702—NetWare for SAA Installation and Troubleshooting

◆ 740—NetWare Internetworking Products

If you choose the UnixWare category, you must have passed the CNI UNIX System Skills prerequisite test.

Eligible UNIX courses include:

◆ 610—NetWare NFS

◆ 605—NetWare TCP/IP Transport

◆ 680—UnixWare System Administration

◆ 685—UnixWare Advanced System Administration

◆ 851—UnixWare Service and Support

Additional Courses for Certification in the Advanced Product Courses Group

Additional courses from which you can choose, but which do not make you eligible for the IPE, are also divided into two categories: NetWare and UNIX.

Eligible NetWare courses include:

◆ 205—Fundamentals of Internetwork Management and Design

◆ 615—NetWare for Macintosh Connectivity

◆ 750—NetWare Global MHS

Eligible UNIX courses include:

◆ 601—LAN WorkPlace for DOS Administration

◆ 611—NetWare FLeX/IP

◆ 625—NetWare NFS Gateway

◆ 220—UNIX OS Fundamentals for NetWare Users

◆ 618—UnixWare Installation and Configuration

Development Product Courses Group

The Development Product Courses Group is also divided into two sections: eligible IPE courses and additional courses. As with the other two groups, once you pass an eligible IPE course in this group, you can teach that course. Then, you only need to pass the test and attend a certified version of any other course in this category that you want to teach in order to be eligible to teach those courses. This is true whether or not the course is categorized as being eligible for the IPE or as being an additional course in this category.

Eligible IPE Courses

Courses from which you can choose in order to take your IPE in the Development Product Courses group include:

◆ 911—NetWare Database Administrator

◆ 941—NetWare Programming Directory Services

◆ 930—NetWare Programming NLM Development

◆ 945—NetWare Programming Protocol Support

- 905—Programming with Btrieve
- 912—Programming with NetWare SQL

Additional Courses for Certification in the Development Product Courses Group

Additional courses from which you can choose, but which are not IPE courses, include:

- 904—Btrieve: An Overview
- 940—NetWare Programming Basic Services
- 907—Xtrieve PLUS

Understanding the Course Descriptions and Objectives for Ten Common Certification Tests

Before you take even one NetWare certification test, you should review the objectives for that test to make certain that you know everything that the test may cover. Because there are several tests that you may have to pass, depending on the certification you seek, this section provides the course/test objectives for 10 of the most common certification tests.

The information covered in the following sections is available from Novell's FaxBack line. This section lists the course/test objectives for the following Novell certification tests, as listed on Novell's FaxBack system:

- DOS and Microcomputer Concepts for NetWare Users (Test # 50-15)
- NetWare 2.2 System Manager (Test # 50-20)
- NetWare 2.2 Advanced System Manager (Test # 50-44)
- NetWare 3.1x Administration (Test # 50-130)

253

- ◆ NetWare 3.1x Advanced Administration (Test # 50-131)
- ◆ NetWare 4.0 Administration (Test # 50-122)
- ◆ NetWare 3.11 to 4.0 Update (Test # 50-124)
- ◆ NetWare 4.0 Installation and Configuration (Test # 50-26)
- ◆ Networking Technologies (Test # 50-80)
- ◆ NetWare Service and Support (Test # 50-46)

DOS/Microcomputer Concepts for NetWare Users

The DOS/Microcomputer Concepts for NetWare Users course/ test covers various aspects of DOS such as commands, file and directory services, and so on. In addition, it covers information on microcomputers, particularly discussing the components of a microcomputer and how all of its parts work together.

Because the DOS/Microcomputer Concepts for NetWare Users test covers two distinct items, it contains two sets of objectives. Displayed first are the test objectives related to DOS, followed by the test objectives related to microcomputers.

DOS-Related Objectives:

1. Define DOS.
2. Describe the basic function of DOS.
3. Explain the use of the Control-Alt-Delete key combination.
4. Describe the computer boot process.
5. Explain the importance of the COMMAND.COM file.
6. Differentiate between internal and external DOS commands.
7. Explain the use of command line switches.
8. Demonstrate the proper use of the following DOS commands: DATE, TIME, VER, PROMPT, and CLS.

9. Explain the purpose of hard disks and floppy diskettes.

10. Explain the purpose of formatting a disk.

11. Match floppy disk size, density, and format capacity.

12. Explain the difference between a bootable and nonbootable disk.

13. Explain the purpose of a hard disk partition.

14. Explain the function of the FDISK command.

15. Demonstrate the proper use of the following DOS commands: FORMAT, VOL, and LABEL.

16. Explain the proper DOS file naming rules.

17. Define the DOS reserved and industry accepted DOS filename extensions.

18. Identify acceptable DOS filenames.

19. Explain the DOS wild card characters and how they are used.

20. Demonstrate the proper use of the following commands: COPY, XCOPY, DISKCOPY, TYPE, DEL, REN, and ATTRIB.

21. Explain the functions of the /s, /e, and /w switches of the XCOPY command.

22. Explain the DOS directory structure.

23. Explain the use of subdirectories.

24. Explain the DOS command search order.

25. Demonstrate the proper use of the following commands: CHDIR (CD), MKDIR (MD), and RMDIR (RD).

26. Demonstrate the use of the PATH command.

27. Demonstrate the proper use of the DIR command.

28. Explain the purpose of batch files.

29. Identify the key sequence that terminates a batch program during execution.

30. Explain the use of the following batch file commands: REM, ECHO, and PAUSE.

31. Create a batch file.

32. Explain the function of the CONFIG.SYS file.

33. Explain the purpose of CONFIG.SYS file commands: DEVICE, FILES, BUFFERS, and LASTDRIVE.

34. Explain the purpose of the AUTOEXEC.BAT file.

Microcomputer objectives:

1. List and describe the major hardware components of a microcomputer.

2. Describe the basic functions of a computer.

3. Describe the binary number system and explain how a microcomputer uses it to process data.

4. Describe the ASCII code.

5. List five types of microprocessor chips made by Intel Corporation.

6. Distinguish between real and protected modes of the 80286, 80386, and 80486 microprocessors.

7. Describe the difference between the 80386DX and 80386SX microprocessors.

8. Identify the general differences between the 80386 and the 80486 Intel microprocessor chips.

9. Describe the 68000 Motorola microprocessor chip family.

10. Explain how the data bus of the IBM AT has become the Industry Standard Architecture (ISA) bus.

11. Explain the basic characteristics of the ISA bus, the MCA bus, and the EISA bus.

12. Explain the basic bus characteristics of the Apple Macintosh.

13. Explain how interrupt, memory, and I/O address settings are made on expansion boards.

14. Explain why it is important to avoid interrupt, memory, and I/O address conflicts.

15. Describe the main function of RAM.

16. Explain the differences between dynamic memory and static memory.

17. Describe parity checking and its purpose.

18. Describe the purpose of ROM.

19. Explain the difference between extended memory and expanded memory.

20. Identify the capacities of both 5.25-inch disks and 3.5-inch floppy disks.

21. Describe the compatibilities of 5.25-inch disk drives and 3.5-inch disk drives.

22. Explain why a disk is formatted.

23. Explain the purpose of partitioning a hard disk.

24. Explain what is meant by the random-access time of a hard disk.

25. Describe the common types of video monitors available.

26. Define CGA.

27. Define EGA.

28. Define VGA.

29. Describe how the parallel port transmits data.

30. Describe how the serial port transmits data.

31. Explain what is meant by the baud rate.

32. Describe why parallel transmissions do not travel very far.

33. Describe how the settings on the system board are made.

34. Describe what a terminating resistor does.

35. List the purpose of the device drivers.

36. Describe the microcomputer initializing (boot) process.

257

NetWare 2.2: System Manager

The NetWare 2.2 System Manager course/test covers various aspects of working with NetWare 2.2, including such topics as creating users, setting up directories, making the system user-friendly with menus and login scripts, and implementing security, including system backup.

NetWare 2.2 System Manager test objectives:

1. List the responsibilities of a system manager.
2. Relate course topics to those responsibilities.
3. Fill in a NetWare log.
4. Use general system management resources provided by Novell.
5. Define a network.
6. List the hardware components of a network.
7. Choose the best option for expanding your network.
8. List the software components needed to access the network from the DOS environment.
9. Choose and load IPX and the shell.
10. Create a distributed processing environment.
11. Use various fault tolerance features of NetWare 2.2.
12. Diagram the levels of the NetWare directory structure.
13. Name the required volume, the four required directories, and their contents and location in the directory structure.
14. Diagram possible directory structures given an organization and its needs.
15. Create an organized and efficient directory structure.
16. Construct a directory path using the required syntax.
17. Work with DOS and NetWare commands related to directory structures and their contents.

18. Identify the default drive pointers in both the DOS and NetWare environments.

19. Use the MAP command to move through the directory structure.

20. Differentiate between drive mappings and search drive mappings.

21. Understand the effects of the DOS CD command on MAP.

22. List the levels of NetWare security.

23. Use command line utilities to apply NetWare's security to a basic directory structure.

24. Understand security features implemented on the system through "user types."

25. Understand the correlation between NetWare command line utilities and NetWare menu utilities.

26. Identify the workstation commands incorporated in these menus.

27. Recognize the specific tasks which can be accomplished within each menu utility.

28. Use the appropriate menu utility to create trustees, make trustee assignments, adjust all aspects of security, view directories and their contents, copy files, send messages, and manipulate drive pointers.

29. Describe the purpose of specific supervisor commands.

30. Identify the directory where supervisor commands are located and the limitations of other users to this directory.

31. Function within the special menu utilities reserved for supervisor use.

32. Recognize the function of console commands and where they are issued.

33. Identify the two printing services available.

34. Identify parameters for choosing the right service.

35. Create print queues.

36. Assign queues to printers.

37. Create spooler assignments.

38. Create a system AUTOEXEC.SYS file.

39. Print files by using CAPTURE, ENDCAP, and NPRINT.

40. Create, control, and monitor queues through PCONSOLE.

41. Determine application compatibility with NetWare.

42. Recognize the features necessary to enable multiuser access.

43. Determine the placement within a directory structure for easiest access and maintenance.

44. Perform the steps required by security to assure safe and reliable results.

45. Contrast the three login scripts used on the network.

46. Identify and use login script commands to create a system and user login script.

47. Debug problems in login script logic.

48. Identify vital mappings that must exist in the system login script.

49. Customize a user environment using menus.

50. Recognize the menu option file format and syntax.

51. Create custom menus.

52. Execute custom menus.

53. List the functions of the NBACKUP utility.

54. Identify the rules for running NBACKUP.

55. List the basic steps for backing up a file server.

56. Identify the basic steps for restoring backed-up data.

57. Use NBACKUP to protect your data.

58. Configure a network.

59. Control security.

60. Organize login scripts.

61. Create menus.

62. Understand and use most of the commands introduced in this course.

NetWare 2.2: Advanced System Manager

This test covers advanced NetWare 2.2 topics such as installation, network optimization, print server setup and configuration, memory management, and use of supervisor utilities.

NetWare 2.2 Advanced System Manager course/test objectives:

1. Choose the correct installation mode for your network environment.

2. Install NetWare 2.2 in the chosen mode.

3. Install the workstation software that best fits each user's needs.

4. Update workstation files from an earlier version of NetWare to be used on a NetWare 2.2 workstation.

5. Use multiple methods for creating and defining trustees.

6. Use multiple methods to restrict and/or control user access and use of your Novell network.

7. Use the FCONSOLE utility to master performance management techniques.

8. Expand your printing options and capabilities by installing and configuring a NetWare Print Server.

9. List the hardware requirements for a file server.

10. List the software requirements to install the operating system.

11. Understand the options available during operating system installation.

12. Choose the correct installation options for your network environment.

13. Install the NetWare 2.2 operating system in the chosen mode.

14. Understand the environment of the workstation.

15. Select the appropriate shell files for each workstation.

16. Use WSGEN to create the workstation files required for different environments.

17. Use WSUPDATE to update your shell and other files.

18. Define and create a router.

19. Create specialized configuration files for individual users' needs.

20. Restrict how many workstations can use the same login name at one time

21. Restrict users to specific workstations.

22. Control minimum password length.

23. Control how often the password must be changed.

24. Restrict the times when users can be logged in.

25. Restrict network disk storage by user.

26. Set parameters to help detect and deny intruder logins.

27. Use SYSCON to view the File Server Error Log.

28. Use NDIR to access network information on files and directories.

29. Use options of NDIR to find files with specific characteristics.

30. Establish resources for NetWare resource sharing.

31. Control and monitor use of file server resources.

32. Create charges to be assessed against users for use of those resources.

33. Use the ATOTAL command to track summaries of file server resource use.

34. Use the PAUDIT command to view details of resource use.

35. Use advanced utilities to set up users.

36. Recognize which utility is best suited for a particular situation.

37. Establish defaults that fit your own users' needs.

38. Write the minimum and maximum memory requirements for NetWare 2.2.

39. Explain what a File Service Process is.

40. Explain how DGroup memory affects the number of file service processes.

41. Change certain user-definable variables to possibly increase File Service Processes.

42. Use FCONSOLE to determine if there is enough memory in a file server to run efficiently.

43. Find other statistics in FCONSOLE to help manage memory and other functions of the network file server.

44. Determine if a network performance problem is indicated, given individual statistics from the Statistics Summary, Cache Statistics, and Disk Statistics screens.

45. Identify the possible course(s) of action to take when specific problems are indicated in the statistics screens.

46. Identify printing services and specifications.

47. Describe the purpose and functions of specific printing utilities.

48. Implement the appropriate steps in the NetWare 2.2e printing setup process.

49. Identify and use command-line utilities with the correct syntax for printing-related tasks.

50. Use PRINTDEF to create customized printer definitions, modes, and forms.

51. Use PRINTCON to create customized print jobs.

52. Print files using the jobs created in PRINTCON.

NetWare 3.1x Administration

This test covers such NetWare 3.1x topics as creating login scripts and menus, setting up network security services, creating users, developing a directory structure, and backing up your NetWare 3.1x system.

NetWare 3.1x Administration course/test objectives:

1. Describe the basic function and services of a network.

2. Identify the client types that are supported in NetWare 3.12.

3. Describe workstation communications with the network, and list the files required to connect a DOS workstation to the network.

4. Describe the function of the software necessary to connect a workstation to the network, including local operating systems, NetWare DOS Requester, communications protocols, and network board.

5. Connect a workstation to the network by loading the appropriate DOS workstation files.

6. Explain and perform the login procedure.

7. Identify, navigate, and perform similar basic functions using a DOS text utility, a command-line utility, and a graphical utility.

8. Activate and navigate Help for each type of utility.

9. Activate and navigate Novell ElectroText.

10. Explain the basic concepts of network file storage, including volume and directory structures.

11. Describe a volume and its technical specifications.

12. Describe a directory, including its main function, hierarchical structure, directory name, and directory path.

13. List the system-created directories on the SYS volume and describe their contents.

14. Access file systems by mapping network drives to volumes and directories.

15. Navigate volumes and directories by using network drives.

16. Access network applications by mapping search drives to application directories.

17. Display and modify the display of file system information on volumes, directories, and files.

18. Perform directory management tasks, such as creating, deleting, and renaming directories.

19. Perform file management tasks such as copying, moving, deleting, salvaging, and purging files.

20. Identify the levels and functions of network security.

21. Describe login security including user account restrictions, time restrictions, station restrictions, and intruder detection.

22. Set up network user accounts and apply account restrictions.

23. Set up group accounts and user account management.

24. Describe packet signature.

25. Describe NetWare 3.12 file system security, including the concepts of trustees, directory and file rights, inheritance, Inherited Rights Mask, and effective rights.

26. Make a trustee assignment and apply rights in SYSCON and FILER.

27. Calculate effective rights.

28. Describe directory and file attributes and their use in a file system security plan.

29. Implement a file system security plan using command line and menu utilities.

30. Describe the function of the CONFIG.SYS, AUTOEXEC.BAT, and NET.CFG configuration files.

31. Alter workstation configuration files such that they contain all pertinent information to automate the process of connecting to the network, loading the DOS Requester, and logging in to the network.

32. Perform a DOS and MS Windows client installation using the NetWare client installation software.

33. Describe the types of login scripts and how they coordinate at login.

34. Explain each login script command, propose standard procedures that are executed through login scripts, and plan a system of login scripts for user login.

35. Build and execute the plan using system and user login scripts.

36. Describe the components of a user menu system.

37. Describe NetWare 3.12 menu command language, and plan a simple user menu.

38. Build and execute a NetWare 3.12 menu.

39. Convert menu files from earlier versions of NetWare into the new menu utility.

40. Describe the function of a server, its interface, and its communication with the network.

41. Describe console commands and identify the function of commands commonly used by administrators.

42. Describe NLMs, explain how they are loaded, and identify their types.

43. Identify the purpose and function of the major NLMs, such as INSTALL, MONITOR, and UPS.

44. Describe remote console management, and list the steps necessary to set up a server for both SPX and asynchronous remote connections.

45. Use RCONSOLE.EXE to connect remotely to the server, and describe the purpose and function of the available options in RCONSOLE.

46. Implement console security features on the server by assigning a console password and placing the server in a secure location.

47. Describe the basic components of network printing and how they interrelate in processing a print job. Describe the general steps necessary for setting up the components.

48. Set up a network printing environment by creating and configuring a related and functional print queue, printer, and print server.

49. Set up network printing hardware by bringing up a print server on a dedicated workstation or NetWare server, and connecting a printer to the network through a NetWare server or a DOS workstation.

50. Send print jobs to network printers by redirecting print jobs with CAPTURE or NPRINT.

51. Perform basic network printing maintenance tasks such as viewing and modifying printing information in PCONSOLE.

52. Manage print jobs in the print queue by viewing their properties, pausing, rushing, delaying printing, and deleting jobs in the queue.

53. Describe how you use PRINTDEF and PRINTCON to customize print jobs.

54. Explain System Fault Tolerance (SFT) and describe how to implement it.

55. Describe SMS and strategies for implementing successful storage management.

56. Use SBACKUP, NetWare's utility for implementing SMS, to perform a simple backup and restore.

57. Describe NetWare Basic Message Handling Service (MHS).

58. Describe the steps required to install Basic MHS on a NetWare server.

59. Perform administrative tasks, such as adding a user and creating a distribution list using the Basic MHS Administration software.

60. Send, read, and file mail in First Mail.

61. Identify basic guidelines for selecting application software.

62. List basic steps to be completed when loading applications.

NetWare 3.1x Advanced Administration

This test covers advanced NetWare 3.1 administration responsibilities such as memory management, print customization, back up of your network, the use of multiple protocols on your network, and other topics such as remote management and NetWare Name Services.

NetWare 3.1x Advanced Administration course/test objectives:

1. Identify and describe the server components.

2. Perform a server startup procedure.

3. Identify and describe server configuration files.

4. Identify commands and options used to customize the appropriate server configuration file.

5. Select the appropriate utility and edit the server configuration files.

6. Create server batch files that perform specific tasks, such as remotely downing the server.

7. Describe the communication and name space protocols supported by a NetWare server.

8. Identify the default Ethernet frame type and match the appropriate frame type to the communication protocol supported.

9. Identify the ODI support architecture and related files that are used at a NetWare server.

10. Describe the services provided by the NetWare protocol suite, including IPX, SPX, RIP, SAP, NCP, and Packet Burst.

11. Display and explain routing information with the TRACK ON utility.

12. Install TCP/IP support on a server.

13. Identify the components and requirements involved in name space support.

14. Install OS/2 and Macintosh name space support.

15. Identify optional multiple protocol products used for file and print sharing.

16. Describe the tables, blocks, and buffers that are important to the workings of server memory.

17. Determine NetWare 3.12 server memory requirements for given cases.

18. Identify NetWare 3.12 memory pools and describe the features, content, resource use, and effect of each.

19. Use MONITOR to view server memory statistics.

20. Describe server console commands related to memory.

21. Identify components that affect server and network performance.

22. Identify the relationships and balances needed between server memory components to maintain optimum server performance.

269

23. Use MONITOR to verify server and network performance, and view resource and processor utilization.

24. List interactions between various SET parameters and the considerations for changing settings.

25. Select and implement the appropriate SET parameter needed to alter network performance based on a given case.

26. Describe how the LIP (Large Internetwork Packet) and Packet Burst protocol affect network performance.

27. Identify the performance implications associated with the NCP Packet Signature.

28. Identify the purpose and procedures of server maintenance utilities, such as BINDFIX, BINDREST, VREPAIR, and SBACKUP.

29. Analyze the data presented on the disk information screen of MONITOR to determine the health of the server's hard disks.

30. Repair the server bindery using BINDFIX and BINDREST.

31. Describe the reasons you would use VREPAIR.

32. Use VREPAIR to remove name space support from a volume.

33. Back up and restore a server bindery and trustee assignments using SBACKUP.

34. Load the components needed to perform a client backup using SBACKUP.

35. Describe the utilities used to set time and time zone support.

36. Describe the utility used to support read-only devices.

37. Perform printing maintenance tasks with PCONSOLE and PSC.

38. Compare the steps required to set permanent and temporary settings for print queues and notification lists.

39. Use PRINTCON to create default print job settings to be used by CAPTURE and PCONSOLE.

40. Print a document using print job configurations that have been created in PRINTCON.

41. Identify advanced printing setup and management design considerations.

42. Summarize the capabilities of the NetWare DOS Requester modules.

43. Modify the NET.CFG file to configure the ODI environment.

44. Customize the NET.CFG file with parameters that affect the NetWare DOS Requester.

45. Identify the options available to load the NetWare DOS Requester.

46. Describe the changes made to a client station during the client installation for Microsoft (MS) Windows.

47. Update existing client files using WSUPDATE and describe the procedures and login script commands used to automate the process.

48. Describe the procedures used to protect against virus intrusion.

49. Describe the method used to support diskless client stations, and identify the files used with the method.

NetWare 4.0 Administration

This test covers various aspects of administering a NetWare 4.0 network including connecting to the network, using network resources, managing Directory Service, planning and managing network file systems, implementing security, and planning and implementing the user environment, including printing.

NetWare 4.0 Administration course/test objectives:

1. List several responsibilities of a network administrator.

2. List major topics covered in this course and relate them to the responsibilities of a network administrator.

3. Locate course and section objectives in the student manual.

4. Identify student manual references to NetWare product documentation.

5. Describe the basic function and services of a network.

6. Describe workstation communications with the network, and list the files required to connect a DOS workstation to the network.

7. Describe the function of the software necessary to connect a workstation to the network, including local operating systems, DOS Requester, communications protocols, and LAN drivers.

8. Connect a workstation to the network by loading the appropriate DOS workstation files.

9. Explain and perform the login procedure.

10. Identify, navigate, and perform similar basic functions using a graphical utility, a DOS text utility, and a command line utility.

11. Activate and navigate Help for each type of utility.

12. Activate and navigate the online documentation.

13. Describe NetWare 4.0 Directory Service (NDS) and the NDS database.

14. Describe NDS objects, properties and values.

15. Describe the Directory tree.

16. Create, delete, rename, and move objects within the NDS database.

17. Enter and modify property values of objects.

18. Set up network user accounts.

19. Define NDS context.

20. Demonstrate correct NDS object naming.

21. Access NDS information from command prompt using NLIST and CX.

22. Search NDS information using NetWare Administrator.

23. Explain the basic concepts of network file storage, including volumes and directory structures.

24. Describe a volume, including volume definition, technical specifications, physical volume names, and volume object names.

25. Define a directory, including its main function, tree structure, name, and path.

26. List the system-created directories on the SYS volume and describe their contents.

27. State recommendations for designing a network directory structure.

28. Identify the strengths and weaknesses of sample directory structures.

29. Design a directory structure based on a given scenario.

30. Access file storage by mapping network drives to volumes and directories.

31. Navigate volumes and directories by using network drives.

32. Access network applications by mapping search drives to application directories.

33. Display and modify the display of file storage information on volumes, directories, and files.

34. Perform directory management tasks, such as creating, deleting, and renaming directories.

35. Perform file management tasks such as copying, moving, deleting, salvaging, and purging files.

36. Identify the levels and functions of network security.

37. Describe NetWare 4.0 file system security including the concepts of trustees, object and property rights, inheritance, inheritance rights filters, and effective rights.

38. Plan file system security using groups, users, directory rights, file rights, and inheritance rights filters.

39. Describe directory and file attributes and their use in a file system security plan.

40. Implement a file system security plan using DOS command line utilities, NetWare Administrator, and Filer.

41. Explain Directory Services access control, including the concepts of trustees, object and property rights, inheritance, inheritance rights filters, and effective rights. Calculate effective rights.

42. Plan an NDS access control security using groups, users, object rights, property rights, and inheritance rights filters.

43. Implement Directory Services access control by adding and removing a trustee, adding and removing object and property rights, and setting an IRF.

44. List, define, and set up user account login restrictions.

45. Describe console commands and identify the function of commands commonly used by administrators.

46. Describe NLMs, how they are loaded, and their types.

47. Identify the purpose and function of the major management NLMs, such as INSTALL, MONITOR, SERVER MANAGER, and UPS.

48. Identify the purpose and function of the major enhancement NLMs involved in the area of STREAMS capability, network management (NMAGENT), source routing, and remote booting.

49. Describe remote console management, list the steps to setting up a NetWare server for both SPX and async. remote

connections, use RCONSOLE.EXE to connect remotely to the server, and describe the purpose and function of the options in RCONSOLE.

50. Implement console security features on the server through assigning a console password and keeping the server in a secure location.

51. Describe the basic components of network printing, how they interrelate in processing a print job, and the general steps to their setup.

52. Create and configure the Directory Service network printing object, print queue, printer, and print server.

53. Perform basic network printing maintenance tasks such as viewing and modifying printing object properties. Add and remove queue users and operators, print server users and operators, and printer notification users; view printer and print server status.

54. Set up network printing hardware by bringing up a print server on a NetWare server and a DOS workstation, and connecting a printer to the network through a NetWare server and a DOS workstation.

55. Send print jobs to network printers using NETUSER and CAPTURE redirection, and NPRINT file-printing techniques.

56. Manage print jobs in the print queue by viewing their properties, pausing, rushing, and delaying printing, and deleting jobs in the queue.

57. Describe the printer customization abilities of PRINTDEF and PRINTCON.

58. Set up CONFIG.SYS, AUTOEXEC.BAT, and NET.CFG such that they contain all pertinent information to automate the process of connecting to the network, loading of the DOS Requester, and logging into the network.

59. Describe the types of login scripts and how they coordinate at login.

60. Explain a selected set of login script commands, propose standard procedures that are executed through login scripts, and plan a system of login scripts for user login.

61. Build and execute a user login script.

62. Describe the significance of a user menu system.

63. Describe the NetWare 4.0 menu command language and plan a simple user menu.

64. Build and execute a simple NetWare 4.0 menu.

65. Explain the three levels of System Fault Tolerance (SFT).

66. Describe SMS and strategies for implementing successful storage management.

67. Use SBACKUP, NetWare's utility for implementing SMS, to perform a simple backup and restore.

NetWare 3.11 to 4.0 Update

This test covers basic NetWare 4.0 services including Directory Services, Security, client and utility changes, print services, auditing, storage management services, console changes, installation, and upgrade.

NetWare 3.11 to 4.0 Update course/test objectives:

1. Identify the new functions and features of NetWare 4.0.

2. Identify the benefits of the new features.

3. Identify NetWare Directory Services (NDS) terms and concepts.

4. Describe the difference between NDS and the bindery.

5. Identify and manage NDS objects.

6. Identify the levels, classes, and context used in NDS naming.

7. Identify the new utilities for NDS.

8. Plan and create a directory tree consisting of organizational units, users, printers, volumes, and servers.

9. Describe and create NDS partitions.

10. Identify the levels and functions of network security and describe the differences between NetWare 3.11 and NetWare 4.0.

11. Define Authentication.

12. Explain NetWare Directory Services access control including the concepts of trustees, object and property rights, inheritance, inheritance rights filters, and effective rights.

13. Calculate NDS object and property effective rights.

14. Plan NDS access control security using groups, users, object rights, property rights, and inheritance rights filters.

15. Implement NetWare Directory Services access control by adding and removing a trustee, adding and removing object and property rights, and setting an IRF.

16. Identify the components of the 4.0 DOS client software and compare to the 3.11 shell.

17. Set up a 4.0 DOS client and use it to log into the network.

18. Alter client configuration files as required by NetWare 4.0.

19. Identify changes to login scripts.

20. Create menus using the new menuing system.

21. Specify the changes between 3.11 and 4.0 utilities.

22. Identify the new 4.0 client utilities.

23. Perform the steps necessary to view the client utilities in a different language.

24. Describe the differences in print server configuration between 3.11 and 4.0.

25. Install and configure a 4.0 print configuration.

26. Identify the new and modified print utilities.

27. Describe the difference between the Auditor and the Admin user.

28. Enable the auditing feature on a NetWare volume and an NDS container.

29. Assign auditing rights to a user account.

30. Apply auditing to files, directories, and NDS objects.

31. Create an auditing report.

32. List the steps to change the auditing configuration.

33. Identify the components of Storage Management Services (SMS).

34. Choose an appropriate strategy for implementing effective backup and restore operations.

35. Use SBACKUP, NetWare's utility for implementing SMS, to perform a simple backup and restore.

36. Describe the new console commands.

37. Load an NLM using memory protection.

38. Describe the file system enhancements for 4.0.

39. Install a language module.

40. Identify the new SET parameters for NDS.

41. Use SERVMAN to view and change the SET parameters.

42. Describe the steps to prepare to migrate to 4.0.

43. List the steps to install the NetWare 4.0 server software.

NetWare 4.0 Installation and Configuration

This test covers installation of NetWare 4.0 and configuration of the NetWare operating system to accommodate your defined network.

NetWare 4.0 Installation and Configuration course/test objectives:

1. Perform a basic NetWare 4.0 installation.

2. Modify the Server Context to include a Country container object.

3. Install two volumes on the server.

4. Install a new NDS database.

5. Install the NetWare DOS Requester.

6. Configure the network board driver for proper operation.

7. Install NetWare for Windows client software.

8. Modify and configure the AUTOEXEC.BAT file.

9. Modify and configure the CONFIG.SYS file.

10. Create a default NET.CFG file.

11. Log in to your NetWare 4.0 server.

12. Demonstrate the significance of workstation current context.

13. Use correct NDS object naming conventions, such as complete names, partial names, leading and trailing periods, and attribute types.

14. Set your workstation Name Context in NET.CFG.

15. Perform a custom NetWare 4.0 installation.

16. Perform installation maintenance options.

17. Reinstall the NetWare Directory Services Database.

18. Build an NDS tree structure.

19. Manage NetWare Directory Services objects and their properties.

20. Manage how objects relate to other objects.

21. Understand and implement object rights and Access Control List.

22. Understand and implement effective rights.

23. Understand the implications of assigning the Supervisor object right to the Server object.

24. Understand inheritance.

25. Understand and implement the Inherited Rights Filter.

26. Understand how to use the PUBLIC trustee access.

27. Understand how to use the [Root] object.

28. Understand how to make a manager.

29. Create, set up, and manage printing objects using NetWare Administrator, the NetWare GUI utility.

30. Add and manage advanced printing functionality using the NetWare Administrator.

31. Create and set up a default network printing environment for one parallel printer using the Quick Setup Option in PCONSOLE.

32. Load print server software and set up remote printing.

33. Manage printers and print queues using printing utilities.

34. Install the device emulator and prepare for a backup and restore session.

35. Perform a backup session with a network server and workstation using SBACKUP.

36. Restore backed-up files to a correct directory on the network server and workstation.

37. Examine backup and restore session log and error files.

38. Use the SERVMAN.NLM utility to observe and change the console SET parameters.

39. Run DSREPAIR on a network server. Examine the DSREPAIR error log file.

40. Enable and manage file compression on a volume.

41. Load an NLM in a protected domain in ring 3.

42. Upgrade an existing NetWare 3.11 server to a NetWare 4.0 server using the across-the-wire technique.

43. Upgrade a NetWare 3.11 server to a 4.0 server in its own tree.

44. Upgrade a NetWare 3.11 server to a 4.0 server in another tree.

45. Install and implement NDS in a multisite network.

46. Manage partitioning and replicating across network servers.

Networking Technologies

This text covers basic concepts of data communications and networking. It provides such information as a brief overview of the history of networking, information on the OSI reference model, data translation and transmission, networking structures, and communication protocol implementation at different layers.

Networking Technologies course/test objectives:

1. Describe computer network development.

2. Identify the seven layers of the OSI Reference Model and the key responsibilities of each layer.

3. Recognize the interrelationship of the OSI model, protocols, and standards.

4. Identify the major standards organizations and their responsibilities.

5. Differentiate between analog and digital data.

6. Differentiate between analog and digital signals and how they are measured.

7. Identify the major coding techniques and their key characteristics for analog and digital signals.

8. Identify common message codes and reasons for using codes for message transmission.

9. Identify the key characteristics of baseband and broadband transmissions.

10. Define multiplexing and identify reasons for multiplexing.

11. Identify key characteristics of frequency-division and time-division multiplexing.

12. Define modem and identify reasons for using a modem.

13. Define codec and identify reasons for using a codec.

14. Identify a variety of media types and their key characteristics, including cost, ease of installation, speed/capacity, and resistance to interference.

15. Identify transmission modes and their advantages and disadvantages.

16. Identify asynchronous and synchronous communication, their key characteristics, and their advantages and disadvantages.

17. Identify common network topologies, their key characteristics, and when each might be used.

18. Identify the basic channel access methods, their key characteristics, and their advantages and disadvantages.

19. Identify the characteristics of circuit switching, message switching, and packet switching.

20. Identify the functions and capabilities of repeaters, bridges, routers, and gateways, along with the OSI model layers each involves.

21. Evaluate the advantages and disadvantages of repeaters, bridges, routers, and gateways.

22. Identify the components of the public switched telephone network and how they impact data communications.

23. Identify the standard networking services provided by ISDN.

24. Identify the interface standardized by the RS-232 standard.

25. Draw, label, or sequence the flow of the RS-232 handshaking signals.

26. Identify and discuss other important Physical layer interfaces.

27. Identify the principal organizations that promulgate or champion SDLC (Synchronous Data Link Control), HDLC (High-level Data Link Control), and LAPB (Link Access Procedure Balanced) protocols and the target environment of each protocol.

28. Identify the key characteristics of SDLC, HDLC, and LAPB.

29. Identify the major services provided by SDLC, HDLC, and LAPB.

30. Identify/label the fields of an SDLC frame and their functions.

31. Identify key characteristics of the IEEE 802 series standards.

32. Identify and briefly describe some of the lesser-known IEEE 802 specifications.

33. Identify key characteristics of the 802.2 standard and its relationship to the remaining 802 series standards.

34. Identify the characteristics of and major services provided by IEEE 802.3.

35. Identify the frame format and field functions of IEEE 802.3.

36. Identify major differences between IEEE 802.3 and Ethernet.

37. Identify the characteristics of and major services provided by IEEE 802.5.

38. Identify IEEE 802.5 frame fields and discuss their functions.

39. Identify the principal organizations that promulgate or champion ARCnet.

40. Identify the key characteristics of and major services provided by ARCnet.

41. Identify the frame format and field functions of an ARCnet frame.

42. Identify the principal organization that champions LocalTalk.

43. Identify the characteristics of and major services provided by LocalTalk.

44. Identify the frame format and field functions of a LocalTalk frame.

45. Identify the principal organizations that promulgate and/or champion FDDI protocols and their target environment.

46. Identify the major services provided by FDDI.

47. Identify the characteristics of FDDI.

48. Identify/label the fields of an FDDI frame and their functions.

49. Identify the principal organizations that promulgate and/or champion the Internet protocols and their target environment(s).

50. Identify the services provided by the major Internet protocols.

51. Identify the characteristics of the major Internet protocols.

52. Identify/label the fields and field functions of IP and TCP packets.

53. Identify the principal organizations that promulgate and/or champion NetWare protocols and interfaces.

54. Identify the major services provided by NetWare and related technologies.

55. Identify/label the fields and functions of NetWare IPX and SPX packets.

56. Identify the principal organizations that promulgate or champion the OSI protocols and their target environment.

57. Identify the major services provided by OSI.

58. Identify the characteristics of OSI.

59. Characterize the major services SNA provides.

60. Discuss the basics of SNA hierarchical terminal-to-host connectivity, which includes Network Addressable Units (SSCP, PU, and LU), mainframe-based networking, sessions, and network management.

61. Contrast SNA hierarchical networking with SNA peer-to-peer networking.

62. Identify the principal organizations that promulgate and/or champion DNA and its target environments.

63. Identify the major services provided by DNA.

64. Identify the characteristics of DNA.

65. Identify the principal organizations that promulgate or champion the AppleTalk protocols and their target environment.

66. Identify the major services provided by AppleTalk.

67. Identify the characteristics of AppleTalk.

68. Identify the trends that will shape the future of networking.

NetWare Service and Support

This test covers the maintenance and troubleshooting of NetWare networks. The older version of this course also covers installation of NetWare 2.x and NetWare 3.x products.

NetWare Service and Support course/test objectives:

1. Identify course goals and objectives.

2. Identify reference manuals you can use in addition to course material.

3. Identify the components in a NetWare network.

4. Describe how network components work together.

5. Describe how NetWare 2.x architecture differs from NetWare 3.x.

6. Explain the difference between a multiple-server network and internetworked networks.

7. Describe how to use NetWare's network addresses.

8. Make hardware settings on common network boards.

9. Select non-conflicting configurations for network boards.

10. Install network cables according to the cabling rules.

11. Recognize and correctly use cable linking devices.

12. Install and configure disk coprocessor boards.

13. Install disk mirroring in a NetWare network.

14. Describe disk/controller addressing and terminating.

15. Configure and install DOS workstation files for NetWare.

16. Install NetWare 2.2.

17. Install NetWare 3.11.

18. Install a NetWare router.

19. Install SFT NetWare 2.15.

20. Upgrade a NetWare 2.x file server to NetWare 2.2.

21. Upgrade a NetWare 2.x file server to NetWare 3.11.

22. Upgrade a NetWare 3.x file server to NetWare 3.11.

23. Describe the purpose of troubleshooting.

24. Describe the steps in the troubleshooting process.

25. Effectively use the pre-site checklist.

26. Effectively use isolating questions to narrow the range of possible problem causes.

27. Describe the functions of network diagnostic utilities.

28. Run selected diagnostic utilities.

29. Describe the functions of NetWare software repair utilities.

30. Run selected NetWare repair utilities.

31. Describe the services and tools available to troubleshooters.

32. Access NetWire to aid in troubleshooting.

33. Use the Network Support Encyclopedia to aid in trouble-shooting.

34. Identify possible network problems from given symptoms.

35. Given a network that is not functioning, be able to diagnose the problem and correct it.

 Instead of the newer course objectives, the older NetWare Service and Support course/test objectives are listed here, for three reasons.

First, as of the writing of this book, the newer NetWare Service and Support course/test objectives were not yet available on FaxBack.

Second, this older version of the test is still valid until the newer course is made available and Novell requires that you pass the newer Service and Support test.

Third, it contains some objectives that are relevant to the new NetWare 2.2/3.1x Installation and Configuration course/test, but whose course objectives were also not available through FaxBack at the time this book was written.

To ensure that you are reviewing the latest course/test objectives for these courses, call the FaxBack number and obtain the latest copy.

Considering Other Available NetWare Tests and Their Descriptions

Other courses/tests in addition to the 10 courses/tests just discussed are also offered by Novell. You can become certified by taking a variety of different tests, depending on the particular certification that you are pursuing.

If you are planning on obtaining your CNI, then you can become certified to teach almost every course that Novell offers.

Some of the other courses/tests offered by Novell are discussed in this section.

Fundamentals of Internetwork and Management Design

This test determines whether or not you understand the fundamentals of designing and implementing a complex internetwork and how to manage it. It covers internetworking technologies and other basic LAN information such as:

- Understanding the OSI model
- Considering internetwork design
- Managing internetworks
- Using repeaters, bridges, routers, and gateways
- Designing LANs
- Understanding Wide Area Networks (WANs) and Municipal Area Networks (MANs)

UNIX OS Fundamentals for NetWare Users

This test is the first requirement for you if you want to certify with UnixWare as your chosen operating system. It covers basic operating system information such as:

◆ Understanding the history of UNIX

◆ Accessing the UNIX operating system

◆ Using common UNIX commands

◆ Working with the file system

◆ Using the UNIX shell

◆ Providing security

◆ Understanding user processes

NetWare 4.0 Advanced Administration

This test covers skills and other knowledge that an experienced NetWare 4.0 user is expected to have mastered in the process of administering a NetWare 4.0 network. It covers advanced NetWare 4.0 networking information such as:

◆ Planning, administering, and distributing the Directory Services Tree

◆ Improving network security

◆ Managing network client services

◆ Optimizing performance

◆ Auditing the network

◆ Managing printing

◆ Backing up the network

NetWare Dial-in/Dial-out Connectivity

This test covers both the *NetWare Access Server* (NAS) and *NetWare Asynchronous Communication Services* (NACS). These two NetWare products provide asynchronous connectivity with NetWare LANs. NAS provides dial-in services, and NACS provides dial-out services. This test covers such topics as:

◆ Understanding basic concepts

◆ Using the physical and functional elements of NAS and NACS

◆ Installing, monitoring, and troubleshooting Access Servers

◆ Installing and troubleshooting NACS

LAN Workplace for DOS 4.1 Administration

This test challenges your knowledge of the installation, configuration, and use of four LAN Workplace products. It covers such topics as:

◆ Administering LAN Workplace

◆ Installing a LAN Workplace workstation

◆ Customizing, Monitoring, and Administering LAN Workplace

NetWare TCP/IP Transport

This test determines your knowledge of Novell's NetWare TCP/IP software. It covers such topics as:

◆ Understanding the basics of TCP/IP

◆ Installing, configuring, and managing TCP/IP on NetWare 3.1x

◆ Troubleshooting a TCP/IP-based server

NetWare NFS

This test reviews your level of knowledge of Novell's NetWare NFS software. It covers such topics as:

◆ Understanding the basics of UNIX

◆ Understanding the basics of NFS

◆ Installing and configuring NFS

◆ Using NFS Name Space

◆ Establishing print services and print gateways

◆ Managing NFS

◆ Understanding file and record locking

◆ Using XCONSOLE

◆ Using FTP

LANalyzer for Windows

This test covers the information contained in the LANalyzer for Windows self-paced workbook. It tests your knowledge of such topics as:

◆ Monitoring and troubleshooting Ethernet networks

◆ Monitoring and troubleshooting Token Ring networks

◆ Analyzing the performance of a network

◆ Identifying network problems with servers and routers

◆ Troubleshooting protocols in the upper layer

The tests described in this section are tests which you can choose to fulfill various certification requirements including core OS and elective requirements. There are other tests from which you can choose in addition to those discussed in this section. For more information on other available tests, refer to Appendix A. In addition, you can call Novell's FaxBack line and request course/test objectives for any of the courses listed in this chapter, as well as in Appendix A.

Summary

The courses you select for one Novell certification can have an effect on the courses that you later choose if you decide to pursue an additional certification. This chapter has shown you what courses are available for the different Novell certification programs.

Using the information in this chapter should help you plot the least time-consuming and least expensive path to certification for you, regardless of the certification program(s) in which you are interested.

This entire book is aimed at helping you understand, choose, and succeed at the Novell certification program(s) that you want to follow. It is intended to give you the information you need about each program, along with showing you where to go and who to contact for more information about any of the Novell certification programs.

You can use this book as an introduction to Novell's programs or as a step-by-step guide, depending on which approach best suits you.

As an introductory guide, this book helps you choose courses to take from NAECs or NEAPs, shows you how you can study to pass the tests without taking any courses, and helps you plot the best combination of self-study and instructor-led courses.

If you choose to complete your certification using only self-study materials, New Riders Publishing has a line of self-study books that enable you to learn what you need to know to obtain various Novell certifications. This book is designed as a companion to the New Riders Publishing series of training guides and as a guide to Novell certification.

It is this author's hope that your efforts toward Novell certification will be quick, easy, satisfying, and very successful.

Glossary of Terms and Acronyms

A

Administrator: An individual responsible for the overall functionality of a network.

Application software: A collection of programs that enable you to perform a specific task such as word processing.

Attribute: A condition associated with a file or directory. For example, the ability to read but not make any changes to a file is a file attribute (read-only).

B

BIOS: Basic Input/Output System. Basic method of handling electronic inputs and outputs.

Buffer: Memory set aside to temporarily store information being read from or written to the hard disk.

C

Cabling: The physical (wire) connection between personal computers.

Cache buffer: A temporary storage space for data being read from or written to a storage device such as a fixed disk.

Caching: Storing frequently accessed information in an area of RAM where it can be more quickly retrieved or temporarily held until stored back on the disk.

Centralized server: A server that provides services and storage space to all network users.

Certification: The process of obtaining written recognition from Novell, Inc. that indicates you have met the minimum requirements and level of networking knowledge.

Client: A PC used as a workstation to access any Novell NetWare, UnixWare server, or NetWare Directory Services Tree.

Client-server: A PC used both as a workstation and a server (it has Personal NetWare's SERVER.EXE loaded).

CNA: Certified NetWare Administrator. One of Novell's certifications that indicates an individual has met the minimum requirements to administer a specific NetWare network.

CNE: Certified NetWare Engineer. One of Novell's official certification programs that indicates an individual has met the minimum requirements to administer and troubleshoot a Novell LAN.

CNEPA: Certified NetWare Engineer Professional Association. A group of networking professionals—specifically Novell network administrators, students, and other interested personnel.

CNI: Certified NetWare Instructor. An individual who has been certified by Novell as competent to teach official Novell certified courses.

Command: An instruction to the processor. Usually referred to as a DOS command, because the instruction comes from DOS (the disk operating system).

CONFIG.SYS: A startup file used primarily to define and enhance your workstation's environment. It is executed each time you boot your workstation. It contains commands that perform a variety of tasks such as setting up your system for keyboard and country information.

Configuration file: A file that is accessed during startup of the PC so that details about non-standard hardware and software requirements can be obtained and utilized.

Connection: A physical or virtual attachment to a computer.

Conventional memory: The first 640 KB of workstation memory.

D

Database: A file containing multiple records, each of which contains the same type of data.

Default: The configuration or path used when a different configuration or path is not specified.

Device driver: The software program that enables the workstation to communicate with the installed NIB.

Disk: A piece of hardware on which data, program files, and other software can be stored.

Disk cache: See *cache buffer*.

Distributed Object Database: A group of files that contain related information about various aspects of the network such as users and their rights. Also referred to as a *DOD*.

DOS: Disk Operating System. A set of files responsible for performing various activities on the computer, including testing and making available the computer's memory and programs.

Down: To close a server so that its files are no longer open and access to the server is unavailable.

DRI: Digital Research Incorporated. A company purchased by Novell whose PC-based operating systems are now sold by Novell under the names of DR DOS 6 and Novell DOS 7.

Drive mapping: Establishing a path to a specific directory structure represented by a letter of the alphabet (a drive letter).

Driver: A piece of software that initializes a piece of computer equipment (such as a local area network interface card/board) so that communication between the computer and the equipment is possible.

E

ECNE: Enterprise Certified NetWare Engineer. Novell's certification that indicates an individual has sufficient knowledge to adminster, troubleshoot, and install one or more of Novell's networks, particularly a Novell NetWare 3.1x or 4.x network.

E-mail: Electronic mail. The ability to send messages between users on a network, using the capabilities of the network instead of the postal system.

Expanded memory: On a DOS-based computer, the memory above 640 KB that has been configured to the LIM (Lotus Intel Microsoft) specification.

Extended memory: Memory above 1 MB on computers with 80286, 80386, or 80486 Intel microprocessors.

F

FAT: File allocation table. The electronic map that specifies the location of data on a hard disk.

File server: A computer on a network that has the Novell NetWare SERVER.EXE and associated files loaded so that processing, programs, files, and equipment can be shared among network users.

G

GAN: Global Area Network. Refers to a world-wide network.

GUI: Graphical User Interface. Refers to the graphical design of the computer screens that the users see.

H

Hardware: All of the equipment, including the PC itself, printers, modems, and so on.

High memory: The first 64 KB of extended memory. That is, the first 64 KB of memory above 1 MB on computers with 80286, 80386, or 80486 Intel microprocessors.

Hub: An electronic box into which a cable for each PC is connected. A hub performs many functions, including boosting the network signal and routing network data packets.

I

IPX: Internetwork Packet eXchange. The protocol defined by Novell for exchange of information between systems.

L

LAN: Local Area Network. A group of PCs connected by a cabling system. A LAN requires at least one computer to act as a file server for the others. There are two main types of LANs: *client-server* and *peer-server*.

LANDA: Local Area Network Dealers Association.

Log in: To connect to a workgroup or server and identify yourself as a legal user.

Login name: The specific code name that you use to identify yourself as a legal user of the resources on a workgroup or server.

Log out: To close your connection to, and therefore the resources of, a workgroup or server.

M

MAU: Medium Access Unit.

Memory: A place in computers where information to be retrieved, processed, or stored is temporarily located.

Memory manager: Software designed to reduce RAM cram and give you more memory to run DOS programs.

MIB: Management Information Base.

Microprocessor: An electronic chip that enables a PC to perform logical and mathematical functions. A microprocessor is also often referred to as a *CPU* or *central processing unit.*

Modem: A device that enables communication between PCs across a telephone line.

MS-DOS: Microsoft Disk Operating System. (See also *DOS.*)

N

NET.CFG: A startup file that defines specific needs of your computer and its software.

NetWare: Novell's network operating system for Intel-based PCs.

NetWare aware: Refers to programs that understand and utilize the ability of Novell's NetWare software to share network resources.

Network: A group of computers and peripheral equipment connected for the purpose of sharing available resources.

Network aware: Programs that understand and utilize networking software and available network resources.

Network interface board: (NIB) An adapter card that fits into one of the slots inside each PC and, through the use of a connecting cable, provides the means of communication between PCs.

Network user: An individual who has been defined to the network as a legal and valid user of network resources.

NIB: Network Interface Board. (See also *network interface board*.)

NIC: Network Interface Card. (See also *network interface board*.)

NID: Network Interface Device. (See also *network interface board*.)

NIM: Network Interface Module. (See also *network interface board*.)

Node: A point on the network cable where devices such as workstations and printers are physically connected.

Non-dedicated server: A PC with Novell's NetWare 2.2 loaded that can be used as either a client or a file server.

NOS: Network Operating System.

O

Operating system: Software responsible for ensuring cooperation and functionality among the various pieces of a computer, or a network (if it is a networking operating system).

OSI: Open System Interconnection. The name of a model used for creating standards for communication among computers.

P

Packet: Data to be sent across a network's cabling system that has been encapsulated in information that defines such things as where the data is to be sent, who is sending the data, what protocol is being used, and so on.

Parallel port: An output receptacle on a PC to which a cable is connected so that communication can occur between the computer and another device, usually a printer.

Password: A series of characters used to identify whether or not a specific user name is being entered, for login purposes, by the person who is authorized to use that login name.

PC: Personal Computer. A collection of equipment that allows retrieval, processing, and storage of information.

Peer-server: A PC that shares its resources with other computers on the network.

Peer-to-peer network: A network in which any computer can share its resources with any other computer on the network.

Port: A physical connection on the computer that allows some type of cable connection.

POST: Power On Self Test. A test of the physical connection between a PC's components that is conducted by the PC each time the power is turned on to the PC.

Print queue: A place in the memory of a computer (usually a server) set aside to temporarily store files that are to be sent to a printer.

Protocol: An agreed upon method of exchanging information between two systems.

Public domain: Something in the public domain legally belongs to the public to use as they please.

Q

Queue: See *print queue*.

R

RAM: Random Access Memory. Computer memory for temporary storage and processing of files and information.

Remote: Attached other than directly, such as through a modem. Usually refers to a PC (client) accessing a network.

Rights: A user's defined permission to access and use network resources.

Root: The lowest level in a directory structure.

Route: A defined network path, expressed using network node addresses.

Router: Software that manages how information is exchanged between network cabling systems. Routers connect cabling systems that use different types of transmission media, as well as different types of addressing systems.

RS-232: An interface for communication between computers, printers, and modems. It is the standard for parallel printer cables.

S

SCSI: Small Computer System Interface.

Security: The method of implementing and enforcing use of the network and its resources by only those who are authorized to use it.

Server: A computer with special software loaded (SERVER.EXE and associated files) that enables it to share data, processing capability, storage, and peripheral equipment with workstations that are connected to it.

Session: A temporary connection between two network nodes. This connection is logical (through the network cables) rather than physical (direct connection of a cable from one PC/file server to another).

Shareware: Software that may legally be copied and passed on to other people without violating copyright laws. Most shareware assumes a try-before-you-buy stance, meaning that if you like and continue to use the software, you are expected to pay a fee to the creator. Paying the fee often registers the software and may entitle you to printed copies of the documentation and to software upgrades.

Shielded twisted pair: Cabling that is surrounded by a special metallic or foil shield. This type of cable is generally used for telephone connections.

SMS: Storage Management Services. SMS is a big NetWare feature that provides the necessary files to back up your Personal NetWare computer from another network computer.

Socket: An address in memory used for the exchange of information.

Soft copy: A computerized file copy of information, or a paper copy.

Software: The operating system, applications, and other programs that run on your computers.

STARTNET.BAT: A Personal NetWare batch file designed to automatically load the client files, among other tasks.

Supervisor: A user identification, as well as a pre-defined set of user access rights.

Syntax: Exact word or series of characters entered in a specific order.

System administrator: See *administrator*.

T

TCP/IP: Transmission Control Protocol/Internet Protocol. A method of communication between devices on network nodes that was developed originally by the U.S. Department of Defense. TCP/IP connection is becoming a common standard of communication among networks.

Topology: The way in which the PCs on your network are connected (physically cabled).

Traffic: The packets of information being sent over the network cabling system.

TSR: Terminate and Stay Resident. Refers to a software program that loads into memory and stays there virtually unnoticed until you need to run it.

Twisted pair: One or more sets of two insulated wires that are twisted together to create one type of network cabling.

U

Upper memory: The memory between 640 KB and 1 MB on a DOS-based computer.

User: An individual who accesses and uses the resources on a network.

User ID: The name that is recognized by the computer or network as a valid and legal individual with permission to access and use network resources.

Utility: A set of software programs geared towards performing a specific set of tasks.

V

VLM: Virtual Loadable Module. A set of logically grouped features that run as an executable program.

W

WAN: Wide Area Network. A network that covers a physically/geographically large area.

Workgroup: A set of clients and servers that have a special relationship of program, data, and hardware sharing.

Workstation: A computer used to access network or workgroup resources. (See also *client*.)

Choosing Courses/Tests

Table A.1 provides a list of courses/tests that can be used to fulfill the CNE and ECNE Elective Credits requirement.

Note A course with the letter "C" following the course number indicates that it is a CBT course, not an instructor-led course.

Table A.1
CNE/ECNE Elective Course/Test Options

Test # (Credits)	Course #	Course Name
50-20 (3)	501	NetWare 2.2 System Manager
50-44 (2)	502	NetWare 2.2 Advanced System Manager
50-45 (2)	506	NetWare 3.11: OS Features Review (This test is only available until May 12, 1994)
50-85 (3)	720	NetWare for SAA Installation and Troubleshooting
50-86 (2)	605	NetWare TCP/IP Transport

continues

Table A.1, Continued
CNE/ECNE Elective Course/Test Options

Test # (Credits)	Course #	Course Name
50-87 (2)	610	NetWare NFS
50-93 (2)	615	NetWare for Macintosh Connectivity
50-100 (1)	None	Product Information (See the Note imediately following this table for more information.)
50-102 (1)	675	UnixWare Personal Edition Installation and Configuration
50-103 (1)	676	UnixWare Application Server Installation and Configuration
50-104 (2)	601	LAN WorkPlace for DOS 4.1 Administration (If you have taken and passed test 50-95, this test cannot be counted as elective credit)
50-105 (1)	1125	LANalyzer for Windows
50-106 (2)	205	Fundamentals of Internetwork and Management Design
50-108 (2)	750	NetWare Global MHS
50-112 (2)	715	NetWare Dial-in/Dial-out Connectivity
50-117 (2)	740	NetWare Internetworking Products (This test cannot be counted as elective credit if you took and passed test number 40-109.)

Test # (Credits)	Course #	Course Name
50-119 (1)	625	NetWare NFS Gateway
50-124 (2)	526	NetWare 3.11 to 4.0 Update (Not available for elective credit if you chose the NetWare 4.0 track to meet your OS requirements.)
50-126 (2)	804	NetWare 4.0 Installation and Configuration Workshop
50-127 (1)	904	Btrieve: An Overview
50-129 (2)	905	Programming with Btrieve 2.0
50-133 (2)	678	UnixWare Installation and Configuration
50-137 (2)	535	Printing with NetWare
50-138 (2)	550	NetWare Navigator
50-205 (2)	730C	NetWare Expert for NMS

 Note The Product Information test does not have a separate course. To study for this test you must study the NetWare Buyer's Guide. A Product Information study guide providing information about preparing for this test, including objectives for the test, is available from Novell's FaxBack system. Request FaxBack document number 1600.

In addition, if you have taken either test 50-18 or 50-19, you cannot apply test number 50-100, as only one of these three tests can be applied toward your CNE.

307

Important Addresses and Numbers

This appendix provides a list of useful telephone numbers, fax numbers, and addresses for quick reference.

Telephone Numbers

CNI Administration	801-429-5445
	800-638-9273
CNA Administration	801-429-5508
	800-638-9273
CNE Administration	801-429-7556
	800-638-9273
ECNE Adminstration	801-429-7556
	800-638-9273
IPE Registration/Information	801-429-5508
	800-233-3382
Drake Training and Technologies	612-921-4173
	800-723-3926

| U.S. Novell Technology Institutes (NTIs) | Call FaxBack for a list |
| CNI Regional Novell Contacts | 801-429-5508 800-332-3382 Or contact your local Novell office |

Fax Numbers

FaxBack	801-429-5363 800-233-3382
CNI Administration	801-429-3900
U.S. Novell Technology Institutes (NTIs)	Call FaxBack for a list
CNI Regional Novell Contacts	801-429-5508 800-332-3382 Or contact your local Novell office

Addresses

CNA Administration
122 East 1700 South
Provo, Utah 84606

CNE Administraton
122 East 1700 South
Provo, Utah 84606

ECNE Administration
122 East 1700 South
Provo, Utah 84606

CNI Administration
122 East 1700 South
Provo, Utah 84606

Drake Training & Technologies
8800 Queen Avenue South
Bloomington, Minnesota 55431 USA

U.S. Novell Technology Institutes
(Call FaxBack for a current list)

European Training Centre
Novell House
London Road
Bracknell
Barkshire RG12 2UY
United Kingdom

Regional Novell Contacts for all programs
(Call FaxBack or call the program's administrator)

INDEX

A

accepted CNI program applications, 175

active study techniques for CBTs and tutorials, 104

adaptive testing, 130-131
marking and returning to questions, 138

additional courses
Advanced Product Courses group, 251-252
CNI certification, 42
Core/OS Product Courses group, 250
Development Product Courses group, 253

address changes (CNE certification), 27

addresses, 310

adjunct college faculty (CNI certification), 161-162

Administration test (CNE certification), 57

administrator, 293

adult education courses (CNI certification), 156-160

Advanced Administration test (CNE certification), 57

Advanced Product Courses group (CNI certification), 39, 250-252

Advanced System Manager test (CNE certification), 57

advantages of course taking, 112-113

AEM (Area Education Manager), 40, 165
test administration, 124

AEM list, obtaining (CNI certification), 166

After Market Products division
purchasing CBTs, 97

analogies (IPE presentation mechanics), 199-200

annual renewal (CNI certification), 75

answering typical test questions, 134-139
CNE assessment test, 129

application, 164-168
process (CNI certification), 174-176
questions (IPE preparation), 225-226
software, 293

applying to CNI programs, 163-170

assistance with CNI program application, 166

attending
courses desired to be taught (CNI certification), 174
presentation skills courses (CNI certification), 155

attitude (CNI certification), 61, 173

attribute, 293

audio tapes (CNA certification), 53

autonomy (IPE presentation characteristic), 186
available courses for NetWare certification, 108-111

B

belonging (IPE presentation characteristic), 188
beta-testing for validating test questions, 135
BIOS (Basic Input/Output System), 293
buffer, 293

C

cabling, 294
cache buffer, 294
caching, 294
calling Novell for information, 114-116
CBT (Computer Based Training)
    benefits, 93
    cost, 94
    courses, 108
    features, 94
    installing NetWare 4.x CBT sampler, 94-95
    location, 97-98
    Microsoft Windows, 93
    minimum requirements, 93
    models, 96
    NetWare certification, 92-104
    pricing models, 96
    purchasing through After Market Products, 97
    samplers, 94, 115
        running samplers, 95
    server license versions, 97
    single-user versions, 97
    starting, 98
    techniques and tips, 103-104
centralized server, 294

certification, 294
    benefits
        CNA, 16
        CNE, 23-25
        CNI, 36
        ECNE, 32
    CNE, 20-23
    CNI options, 38-40
    getting testing information, 115
    programs
        Novell NetWare, 13-49
        obtaining information, 115
    requirements
        CNA, 18
        CNE, 25-27
        CNI, 36-37
        ECNE, 33-34
    selecting courses, 233-292
changing addresses (CNE certification), 27
class belonging (IPE presentation characteristic), 188
classroom management (CNI prerequisites), 61, 172
client, 294
client-server, 294
closed questions (IPE preparation), 220
CNA (Certified NetWare Administrator), 294
    certification
        benefits, 16
        compared to CNE certification, 21
        cost of testing, 19
        course options, 234-237
        failing tests, 63
        identification for testing, 20
        NetWare 2.2 courses, 235-236
        NetWare 3.11 courses, 236
        NetWare 3.1x courses, 236-237
        NetWare 4.x courses, 237
        prerequisites, 52-55
        process, 62-64
        requirements, 18
        scheduling a test, 19
        selecting an operating system, 16-17

self-study options, 53
skills, 16-18
starting, 18-20
tests, 62
program, 14-20
test list, 126-128
CNA-level testing (Novell Certification Assessment disk), 99
CNE & ECNE Programs Novell Support Certification (booklet), 29
CNE (Certified NetWare Engineer), 294
assessment test, 126-129
assessment test disk (practice tests), 126
certification, 20-23
address changes, 27
Administration tests, 57
as core requirement for ECNE certification, 243-244
benefits, 23-25
community college certification programs, 21
compared to CNA certification, 21
continuing education, 26
core requirements, 240-242
cost of testing, 28
course options, 237-242
credit requirements, 23
ECNE prerequisite, 68
electives, 65, 242
elective course/test options, 305-307
identification, 29
Installation and Configuration test, 57
legal guidelines, 29
NetWare 2.2 courses, 240
NetWare 3.11 courses, 239
NetWare 3.1x courses, 239
NetWare 4.0 courses, 239
NetWare Service and Support test, 57
Networking Technologies test, 57
obtaining a certification agreement copy, 26
operating system requirements, 239-240

prerequisites, 55-57, 238
process, 64-68
requirements, 25-27
scheduling tests, 28
selecting an operating system, 56
skills, 25
starting, 27-30
System Manager tests, 57
testing, 28, 64-65
time limit, 28
program, 20-30
enrollment, 55-57, 66
CNE certification assessment disk, 126
CNE/ECNE/CNI test list, 126-128
CNEPA (Certified NetWare Engineer Professional Association), 46, 294
CNI Agreement (application), 169-170
acceptance or denial, 175
CNI (Certified NetWare Instructor), 294
certification, 35, 153-231
additional courses, 42
adult education courses, 156-160
advanced product courses, 39
Advanced Product Courses group, 250-252
annual recertification fee, 76
annual renewal, 75
application, 164-168
application process, 174-176
benefits, 36
certified course requirement, 106
CNI Agreement (application), 169-170
core operating system product, 38
Core/OS Product group, 249-250
course options, 246-249
development product courses, 39
Development Product Courses group, 252-253
differences from other programs, 246-247
getting experience, 156-162
interviews, 173
IPE class, 37, 176-180

IPE Instructor kit (application),
   168-169
minimum length of teaching
   experience, 156
obtaining a current course list, 40
options, 38-40
part-time college teaching, 161-162
preparations, 154-170
prerequisites, 172-173, 247
prerequisites compared to other
   programs, 153
presentation skills course, 155
private training, 162
process, 74-76
purchasing instructor kits, 75
requirements, 36-37, 173-174, 247
selecting IPE courses, 249
skills, 36
starting, 37-42
steps to completion, 40-42
teaching experience, 155
tutoring adults, 160-161
  program, 35-42
    IPE class prerequisites, 60, 74
    prerequisites, 59-61
    tests, 74-75
  Welcome Aboard kit, 176
CNI Program Description and
  Application, 163
CNI-level DOS/Microcomputer
  Concepts test (CNI certification), 247
CNI-level UNIX Systems Skills test
  (CNI certification), 248
college credit for NEAP courses, 107
command, 294
communication (CNI prerequisites), 60
communication of technical subjects
  (CNI prerequisites), 172
community college certification (CNE
  certification), 21
comparison questions (comprehension
  questions), 225
competency tests (CNI certification
  requirements), 174

completing
  CNI certification, 40-42
  CNI program application, 163-170
comprehension questions (open
  questions)
  IPE preparation, 223-225
  types, 223
confidence (IPE presentation character-
  istic), 181
CONFIG.SYS file, 295
configuration file, 295
connection, 295
contact person (with sponsor) for CNI
  application, 166
contacting international training sites
  (CNI certification), 168
continuing education
  CNE certification, 26
  CNI certification, 42
  ECNE certification, 72
contract CNIs (CNI program
  application), 165
conventional memory, 295
core requirements
  CNE certification, 240-242
  ECNE certification, 243-244
Core/Operating System Product
  Courses group, 249-250
  CNI certification prerequisites, 247
cost
  CBTs, 94
  CNA certification, 19
  CNE assessment tests, 125
  CNE certification, 28
  courses, 111-112
  tests, 124
courses
  advantages of taking, 112-113
  CBT-based, 108
  CNA certification, 234-237
  CNE certification, 237-242
  CNI certification, 246-249
  costs, 111-112
  descriptions and objectives, 253-287
  DOS/Microcomputer Concepts for
    NetWare Users, 254-257

ECNE certification, 242-246
Fundamentals of Internetwork and Management Design, 288
getting your money's worth, 113-114
instructor-led, 109-111
LAN Workplace for DOS 4.1 Administration, 290
LANalyzer for Windows, 291
materials (CBTs and tutorials), 104
NetWare 2.2 Advanced System Manager, 261-264
NetWare 2.2 System Manager, 258-261
NetWare 3.11 to 4.0 Update, 276-278
NetWare 3.1x Administration, 264-268
NetWare 3.1x Advanced Administration, 268-271
NetWare 4.0 Administration, 271-276
NetWare 4.0 Advanced Administration, 289
NetWare 4.0 Installation and Configuration, 278-281
NetWare certification, 108-111
NetWare Dial-in/Dial-out Connectivity, 290
NetWare NFS, 291
NetWare Service and Support, 285-288
NetWare TCP/IP Transport, 290
Networking Technologies, 281-285
objectives
    obtaining (self-study), 84
    testing, 136
options (CNE/ECNE), 305-307
selecting, 105-114, 233-292
tours (CBTs and tutorials), 98
UNIX OS Fundamentals for NetWare Users, 289
workbook-based, 109
CPU (central processing unit)
see microprocessor
creating test questions, 140-150
benefits, 142-143
details, 147
invalid answers, 149
key words, 148
memorizing list information, 149
objectives, 146
red manuals, 141
relating key words, 146
reviewing and preparing, 150-151
several correct answers, 147
student manuals, 141
third-party books, 142
credit
CNE certification, 23
NEAP courses, 107

D

database, 295
DATC (Drake Authorized Testing Center), 22
enrolling in NetWare certification programs, 54-55
testing process, 122
date (CNI program application), 165
decertification (ECNE program), 72
dedicated mode, 15
default, 295
defining terms and acronyms (IPE presentation mechanics), 193
denied CNI program applications, 175
descriptions of NetWare courses, 253-287
designing effective questions, 218-227
details in creating test questions, 147
developing
course ideas (adult education), 159
IPE-relevant teaching skills, 180-229
Development Product Courses group (CNI certification), 39-40, 248, 252-253
device driver, 295
discussion, promoting for IPE preparation, 227-228
disk, 295
disk cache
see cache buffer
DOD (distributed object database), 295

DOS (Disk Operating System), 18, 295
    CNA prerequisites, 54
    CNI prerequisites, 59
DOS/Microcomputer Concepts for NetWare Users course/test, 238, 254-257
down, 295
Drake Training and Technologies
    scheduling a CNA certification test, 19
dress (IPE presentation characteristic), 182-183
DRI (Digital Research Incorporated), 295
drive mapping, 296
driver, 296
dry runs (IPE), 179

E

e-mail, 296
ECNE (Enterprise Certified NetWare Engineer) certification, 30-35, 296
    benefits, 32
    CNE certification prerequisite, 68
    continuing education, 72
    core requirement (CNE certification), 243-244
    course options, 242-246
    decertification, 72
    electives, 69, 246, 305-307
    NetWare 2 only as elective, 58, 69
    NetWare 3 or NetWare 4 as possible tracks, 68
    NetWare 3.1x courses, 244
    NetWare 4.x courses, 244
    operating system requirements, 244-246
    pre-registration, 34
    prerequisites, 58
    process, 68-74
    requirements, 33-34
    skills, 32-33
    starting, 34-35
    tests, 70-71
    time limit, 34

effective questioning, 218-227
electives
    CNE program, 65, 242, 305-307
    ECNE program, 69, 246, 305-307
electronic displays (visual aids), 215-216
electronic test scoring, 123
eligible IPE courses
    Advanced Product Courses group (CNI certification), 251
    Core/OS Product Courses group (CNI certification), 249
    Development Product Courses group (CNI certification), 252-253
employment opportunities, 44-47
enhancing transparencies, 207
enrolling
    CNE program, 55-57, 66
    NetWare certification programs, 54
enthusiasm (IPE presentation characteristic), 184-185
establishing relevancy (IPE presentation mechanics), 190-192
Ethernet network compared to Token Ring network, 201-202
expanded memory, 296
experience as CNI requirement, 156-162
extended memory, 296
extrapolation questions (comprehension questions), 224
eye contact (IPE presentation characteristic), 183

F

failing tests, 123
    CNA program, 63
    IPE, 179
FAT (file allocation table), 296
fax numbers, 310
FaxBack
    catalog information, 117-118
    course descriptions and objectives, 253

obtaining AEM list, 166
placing orders, 116
requesting Novell documents, 116-119
faxing to receive CNI program application, 163
file server, 296
filler words and distractions (IPE presentation characteristic), 183-184
flip charts (visual aids), 210-211
form testing, 131-133
Fundamentals of Internetwork and Management Design course/test, 288

G

gaining networking experience, 47-49
GAN (global area network), 297
gestures and language (IPE presentation characteristic), 185-186
getting
experience (CNI certification), 156-162
Novell course information, 114-119
test taking information, 151-152
glossary, 293-304
guessing during self-study, 87
GUI (graphical user interface), 297

H

handouts (visual aids), 212-214
hands-on experience (CNI prerequisites), 59
hands-on study
NAECs (Novell Authorized Education Centers), 82
NEAP, 82
NetWare certification, 80-92
NLIST example, 88-91
NLIST options, 91
test taking, 88-92
hardware, 297
help with CNI program application, 166

high memory, 297
hints
course success, 113-114
IPE, 179-180
testing, 133-134
hub, 297

I

identification
CNA certification testing, 20
CNE certification, 29
important addresses and numbers, 309-311
Installation and Configuration test (CNE certification), 57
Installation and Configuration Workshop test (CNE certification), 242-243
installing the NetWare 4.x CBT sampler, 94-95
instructor experience (CNI certification), 156-162
instructor kits (CNI certification), 75
instructor-led courses, 109-111
international training sites (CNI certification), 168
interpretation questions (comprehension questions), 224
interviews (CNI certification), 173
introducing new materials in a summary, 229
invalid answers (creating test questions), 149
IPE (Instructor Performance Evaluation)
attendance and completion (CNI certification requirements), 174
autonomy (presentation characteristic), 186
class belonging (presentation characteristic), 188
classes (CNI program prerequisites), 60, 74
CNI certification, 176-180

confidence (presentation characteristic), 181

course numbers and names (CNI program application), 164

defining terms and acronyms (presentation mechanics), 193

developing relevant teaching skills, 180-229

dress (presentation characteristic), 182-183

duration, 177

enthusiasm (presentation characteristic), 184-185

establishing relevancy (presentation mechanics), 190-192

eye contact (presentation characteristic), 183

failure, 179

fee, 37, 124

filler words and distractions (presentation characteristic), 183-184

gestures and language (presentation characteristic), 185-186

hints and tips, 179-180

introducing new materials in a summary, 229

linking topics (presentation mechanics), 197-199

materials available, 177

pace (presentation characteristic), 184

payment information (CNI program application), 165

presentation characteristics, 176, 180-188

presentation mechanics, 176, 188-229

product type (CNE program application), 164

promoting student discussion, 227-228

providing page references (presenta-tion mechanics), 192-193

recording, 178

registration, 42

score notification, 179

scoring, 178-179

section introductions (presentation mechanics), 189-190

security (presentation characteristic), 186-187

selecting courses (CNI certification), 249

sequencing topics (presentation mechanics), 195-197

setting up, 178

showing proper preparation (presentation mechanics), 193-195

signposting topics (presentation mechanics), 190

summarizing topics in teaching preparation, 229

target course, 179

technical proficiency skill, 176-177

timing yourself on dry runs, 179

using analogies (presentation mechanics), 199-200

using effective visual aids (presentation mechanics), 200-218

voice modulation (presentation characteristic), 181-182

IPE Instructor Kit (application), 168-169

IPX (internetwork packet exchange), 297

J–K

job options after CNI certification, 230

key words (creating test questions), 146, 148

L

LAN (local area network), 15, 297

LAN Workplace for DOS 4.1 Adminis-tration course/test, 290

LANalyzer for Windows course/test, 291

LANDA (Local Area Network Dealers Association), 297

layering transparencies, 206

legal guidelines for CNE certification, 29

linking topics (IPE presentation mechanics), 197-199

locating CBTs and NetWare 4 tutorial, 97

log in, 297

log out, 298

login name, 298

long-term memory in self-study (NetWare certification), 85

M

managing classrooms (CNI prerequisites), 61

manuals in creating test questions, 141

marking and returning to adaptive test questions, 138

materials available (IPE), 177

MAU (medium access unit), 298

memorizing list information in creating test questions, 149

memory, 298

memory manager, 298

memory questions (open questions), 221-223

menus (CNE/ECNE/CNI test), 127

MIB (management information base), 298

microcomputer concepts
    CNA certification prerequisites, 54
    CNI certification prerequisites, 59, 172
    DOS/Microcomputer Concepts for NetWare Users course/test, 256-257

microprocessor, 298

Microsoft Windows (CBTs), 93

minimum experience (CNI prerequisites), 172

models (CBTs), 96

modem, 298

modulation of voice (IPE presentation characteristic), 181-182

MS-DOS (Microsoft Disk Operating System), 298
    see also DOS

multiple answers for questions, 137

N

NAEC (Novell Authorized Education Center), 45
    courses
        compared to NEAP courses, 105-108
        NetWare certification, 106-107
    hands-on study, 82
    lists, 115

NEAP (Novell Education Academic Partner), 45
    courses
        college credit, 107
        compared to NAEC courses, 105-108
        NetWare certification, 107-108
    earning college credit, 22
    hands-on study, 82
    lists, 115

NET.CFG file, 298

NetWare, 298

NetWare 2 (Novell operating system)
    as ECNE program elective only, 58, 69
    CNA certification, 15

NetWare 2.2
    CNA certification courses, 235-236
    CNE certification courses, 240

NetWare 2.2 Advanced System Manager course/test, 261-264
    CNA certification, 235

NetWare 2.2 System Manager course/ test, 258-261
    CNA certification, 235

NetWare 3 (Novell operating system)
    CNA certification, 15
    ECNE program track, 68

NetWare 3.11
    CNA certification courses, 234, 236
    CNE certification courses, 239

NetWare 3.11 Advanced System Manager
CNA certification, 236
main screen options (CBTs and tutorials), 99
NetWare 3.11 System Manager
CNA certification, 236
test (CNI certification), 248
NetWare 3.11 to 4.0 Update course/test, 276-278
NetWare 3.12 Administration test (CNI certification), 248
NetWare 3.1x
as primary OS track (ECNE certification), 245
courses
CNA certification, 234, 236-237
CNE certification, 239
ECNE certification, 244
NetWare 3.1x Administration course/test, 264-268
CNA certification, 236
NetWare 3.1x Advanced Administration course/test, 268-271
NetWare 4 (Novell operating system)
CBT minimum requirements, 93
CNA certification, 15
see also NetWare Directory Services
ECNE program track, 68
tutorial, 96-98
NetWare 4.0
as primary OS track (ECNE certification), 245
courses (CNE certification), 239
NetWare 4.0 Administration course/test, 271-276
CNA certification, 237
CNI certification, 248
NetWare 4.0 Advanced Administration course/test, 289
NetWare 4.0 Installation and Configuration course/test, 278-281

NetWare 4.x
CBT sampler, installing, 94-95
courses
CNA certification, 234, 237
ECNE certification, 244
NetWare aware, 298
NetWare certification
CBTs and tutorials, 92-104
courses, 108-111
descriptions and objectives, 253
hands-on learning, 81-83
preparations, 51-77
prerequisites, 51-61
programs, 13-49
processes, 61-76
selecting courses, 105-114
self-study, 83-88
testing, 121-152
training, 79-120
NetWare Dial-in/Dial-out Connectivity course/test, 290
NetWare Directory Services, 4, 15
NetWare NFS course/test, 291
NetWare Service and Support course/test, 285-287
CNE certification, 57, 241
NetWare TCP/IP Transport course/test, 290
network, 298
network aware, 299
network user, 299
networking
gaining experience, 47-49
trade publications, 44-45
Networking Technologies course/test, 281-285
CNE certification, 57, 241
CNI certification, 248
NIB (network interface board), 299
NIC (network interface card)
see NIB
NID (network interface device)
see NIB
NIM (network interface module)
see NIB

NLIST (hands-on study)
example, 88
options, 91
node, 299
non-dedicated mode, 15
non-dedicated server, 299
nonadaptive testing, answering questions, 139
noncertified courses (NetWare certification), 105-106
NOS (Network Operating System), 299
note taking (self-study), 87
notification of score (IPE), 179
Novell
employment opportunities after certification, 44-47
getting information, 114-119
NetWare certification programs, 13-49
tutorials, 96
Novell Certification Assessment disk, 99-103
CBT and tutorial techniques, 104
CNA-level testing, 99
viewing reports, 103
Novell CNI Administration, obtaining an AEM list, 166
NSE (Network Support Encyclopedia), 23
NTI (Novell Technology Institute), 40
finding or contacting, 167
IPE test, 125
NTS (Novell Technical Support), 23

O

objectives
creating test questions, 146
DOS/Microcomputer Concepts for NetWare Users course/test, 254-257
NetWare 2.2 Advanced System Manager course/test, 261-264

NetWare 2.2 System Manager course/test, 258-261
NetWare 3.11 to 4.0 Update course/test, 276-278
NetWare 3.1x Administration course/test, 264-268
NetWare 3.1x Advanced Administration course/test, 268-271
NetWare 4.0 Administration course/test, 272-276
NetWare 4.0 Installation and Configuration course/test, 278-281
NetWare certification courses, 253-287
NetWare Service and Support course/test, 285-287, 289-292
Networking Technologies course/test, 281-285
relating to questions, 136-137
testing, 88, 134
obtaining
AEM list (CNI certification), 166
CBT samplers, 94, 115
certification program information, 115
certification testing information, 115
CNE certification agreement copy, 26
CNE certification assessment disk, 126
CNI application, 163
course/test objectives for self-study, 84
current course list (CNI certification), 40
instructor experience (CNI certification), 156-162
NAEC or NEAP lists, 115
Novell Certification Assessment disk, 99
regional information, 115-116, 167
self-study products, 115
test taking information, 151-152, 167
occurrence application questions, 226
open questions (IPE preparation), 221-227

OS (operating system)
  CNE certification requirements, 239-240
  ECNE certification requirements, 244-246
  selecting for CNA certification, 16
  selecting for CNE certification, 56
OSI (open system interconnection), 299

P

pace (IPE presentation characteristic), 184
packet, 299
page references (IPE presentation mechanics), 192-193
parallel port, 300
part-time college teaching (CNI certification), 161-162
password, 300
PC (personal computer), 300
peer-server, 300
peer-to-peer network, 300
Personal NetWare, 48
placing FaxBack orders, 116
PO (Purchase Order) as CNI application payment, 165
port, 300
POST (Power On Self Test), 300
practice tests (CNE assessment test disk), 126
pre-registration (ECNE certification), 34
preparations
  CNI certification, 154-170
  NetWare certification, 51-77
  presentations, 177
  test questions, 134-135, 150-151
prerequisites
  CNA program, 52-55
  CNE program, 55-57, 238
  CNI experience, 172-173
  CNI program, 59-61, 247
  ECNE program, 58
  NetWare certification, 51-61

presentation characteristics (skill area)
  CNI certification, 155, 176, 180-188
presentation mechanics (skill area)
  CNI certification, 155, 176, 188-229
presentation preparation, 177
presentation skills
  CNI certification prerequisites, 172
  CNI program prerequisites, 59
presentation skills course (CNI certification), 155
pretesting, 139-151
previewing video tapes, 215
price
  CBTs, 94, 96
  CNA certification test, 19
  CNE certification test, 28
  courses, 111-112
  tests, 124
print queue, 300
private training (CNI certification), 162
processes
  CNA certification, 62-64
  CNE certification, 64-68
  CNI certification, 74-76
  ECNE certification, 68-74
  NetWare certification testing, 122-125
promoting discussion (IPE preparation), 227-228
proper preparation (IPE presentation mechanics), 193-195
proposing course ideas (adult education), 159
protocol, 300
providing page references (IPE presentation mechanics), 192-193
public domain, 300
purchasing
  CBTs through After Market Products, 97
  instructor kits (CNI certification), 75

Q–R

questioning effectively, 218-227
questions
    relating to objectives, 136-137
queue
    see print queue

RAM (random access memory), 301
recertification fee (CNI certification),
    76
recording (IPE), 178
red manuals (creating test questions),
    141
references for CNI program
    application, 166
referencing page numbers (IPE
    presentation mechanics), 192-193
regional information, 115-116
registering
    CNE certification testing, 28
    IPE (for CNI certification), 42
    tests, 125
registration information
    (CNI certification), 167
related tests (CBTs and tutorials), 104
relating key words when creating test
    questions, 146
relevancy (IPE presentation
    mechanics), 190-192
relevant teaching skill development
    (IPE), 180-229
remote, 301
renewing CNI certification, 75
reordering study materials, 86
repetition (self-study), 87
reports
    CNE assessment test, 129
    Novell Certification Assessment
        disk, 103
requesting documents with FaxBack,
    116-119
requirements
    CNA certification, 18
    CNI certification, 173-174
    DATC enrollment, 54-55
    testing, 122

resume (CNI program application), 166
retaking adaptive tests, 131
reviewing
    by creating test questions, 150-151
    test questions, 133
rights, 301
root, 301
route, 301
router, 301
RS-232 interface, 301
running a CBT sampler, 95

S

samplers (CBTs), 94, 115
scheduling
    CNA certification tests, 19
    CNE certification tests, 28
scoring an IPE, 178-179
SCSI (small computer system inter-
    face), 301
section introductions (IPE presentation
    mechanics), 189-190
security, 301
    (IPE presentation characteristic),
        186-187
selecting
    certification courses, 105-114, 233-292
    DATC for testing, 122
    IPE courses (CNI certification), 249
    operating systems
        CNA certification, 16
        CNE certification, 56
    tests (Novell Certification
        Assessment disk), 99
    visual aids, 217
self-study
    course/test objectives, 84
    guessing ahead, 87
    long-term memory, 85
    NetWare certification, 80-92
    note taking, 87
    options for CNA certification, 53
    products, 115
    reordering study materials, 86

repetition, 87
study techniques, 84
sequencing topics (IPE presentation mechanics), 195-197
server, 301
server license versions (CBTs), 97
session, 301
set up (IPE), 178
several correct answers (creating test questions), 147
shareware, 302
shielded twisted pair, 302
showing proper preparation (IPE presentation mechanics), 193-195
signature (CNI program application), 165
signposting topics (IPE presentation mechanics), 190
single-user versions (CBTs), 97
sites for testing, 124-125
situational application questions, 226
skills
CNA certification, 16-18
CNE certification, 25
CNI certification, 36
ECNE certification, 32-33
SMS (storage management services), 302
socket, 302
soft copy, 302
software, 302
controlling student displays (visual aids), 216-217
sponsor (NAEC/NEAP) on CNI application, 166
standard testing
see form testing
starting
CBTs and tutorials, 98
CNA certification, 18-20
CNE assessment test, 126
CNE certification, 27-30
CNI certification, 37-42
ECNE certification, 34-35
STARTNET.BAT file, 302

student manuals (creating test questions), 141
study techniques
NetWare certification, 84
writing out questions, 151
submitting a CNI program application, 163-170
substitute teaching (CNI certification), 158
summarizing topics
introducing new materials in IPE preparation, 229
supervisor, 302
syntax, 302
system administrator
see administrator
System Manager test (CNE certification), 57

T

taking notes (self-study), 87
taking tests
getting information, 151-152
hands-on learning, 88-92
NetWare certification, 121-152
target course (IPE), 179
TCP/IP (Transmission Control Protocol/Internet Protocol), 302
teaching assistantships (CNI certification), 157
teaching experience minimum (CNI certification), 155-156
technical communication (CNI prerequisites), 60, 172
technical proficiency skill (IPE), 176-177
techniques for CBTs and tutorials, 103-104
telephone numbers, 309-310
testing
adaptive testing, 130-131
answering typical questions, 134-139
CNA certification, 19
CNE assessment test, 126-129

CNE certification, 28
CNE options, 305-307
cost, 124
course objectives, 136
creating sample questions, 140-150
DATC selection, 122
ECNE options, 305-307
failure, 123
   CNA program, 63
form testing, 131-133
getting test-taking information,
  151-152, 167
hands-on learning, 88-92
hints and tips, 133-134
marking and returning to test
  questions, 138
multiple answers on typical
  questions, 137
NetWare certification, 121-152
Novell Certification Assessment
  disk, 99
objectives, 88, 134
preparation of questions, 134-135
pretesting, 139-151
registering, 125
relating objectives and questions,
  136-137
required information, 122
reviewing answered questions, 133
sites, 124-125
typical test questions, 137-139
validating questions, 135-136
tests
  CNA program, 62
  CNE program, 64-65
  CNI program, 74-75
  DOS/Microcomputer Concepts for
    NetWare Users, 254-257
  ECNE program, 70-71
  Fundamentals of Internetwork and
    Management Design, 288
  LAN Workplace for DOS 4.1
    Administration, 290
  LANalyzer for Windows, 291
  Netware 2.2 Advanced System
    Manager, 261-264

  NetWare 2.2 System Manager,
    258-261
  NetWare 3.11 to 4.0 Update, 276-278
  NetWare 3.1x Administration,
    264-268
  NetWare 3.1x Advanced Administra-
    tion, 268-271
  NetWare 4.0 Administration, 271-276
  NetWare 4.0 Advanced Administra-
    tion, 289
  NetWare 4.0 Installation and
    Configuration, 278-281
  NetWare Dial-in/Dial-out
    Connectivity, 290
  NetWare NFS, 291
  NetWare Service and Support,
    285-288
  NetWare TCP/IP Transport, 290
  Networking Technologies, 281-285
  UNIX OS Fundamentals for NetWare
    Users, 289
  types, 125-134
third-party books
  CBT and tutorial techniques, 104
  creating test questions, 142
timing yourself on dry runs (IPE), 179
tips
  course success, 113-114
  IPE, 179-180
  testing, 133-134
**Token Ring network compared to
  Ethernet network, 201-202**
**topic linking (IPE presentation
  mechanics), 197-199**
**topic sequencing (IPE presentation
  mechanics), 195-197**
topics summary (IPE preparation), 229
topology, 303
trade publications, 44-45
traffic, 30
**translation questions (comprehension
  questions), 224**
transparencies (visual aids), 205-210
  advantages, 209
  color, 206

disadvantages, 209
layering, 206
multiple colors, 208
writing upon, 206
TSR (terminate and stay resident), 303
tutorials, 96
location, 97-98
NetWare certification, 92-104
starting, 98
techniques and tips, 103-104
tutoring adults (CNI certification),
160-161
twisted pair (cable), 303
types of tests, 125-134
typical test questions, 134-139

U

uncertified courses
(NetWare certification), 105-106
UNIX OS Fundamentals for NetWare
Users course/test, 289
UnixWare (Novell operating system)
CNA certification, 15, 235
UnixWare Advanced System
Administration test (CNE certifica-
tion), 240
UnixWare OS Fundamentals test (CNE
certification), 240
UnixWare System Administration test
(CNE certification), 240
upper memory, 303
user, 303
user ID, 303
using
analogies (IPE presentation
mechanics), 199-200
effective visual aids (IPE
presentation mechanics), 200-218
utility, 303

V

validating test questions, 135-136
video tapes
advantages, 214
CNA certification, 53
disadvantages, 215
previewing, 215
visual aids (IPE presentation
mechanics), 214-215
viewing reports (Novell Certification
Assessment disk), 103
visual aids (IPE presentation
mechanics), 200-218
VLM (virtual loadable module), 303
voice modulation (IPE presentation
characteristic), 181-182
volunteer teaching assistantships (CNI
certification), 157

W–Z

WAN (wide area network), 303
Welcome Aboard kits (CNI), 176
white boards (visual aids), 204-205
Windows (CBTs), 93
workbook-based courses, 109
workbooks, prices, 112
workgroup, 304
workstation, 304
see also client
writing test questions while studying,
151

New Riders' Guide to NetWare Certification
REGISTRATION CARD

Fill out this card to receive information about future NetWare books and other New Riders titles!

Name _____ **Title** _____

Company _____

Address _____

City/State/ZIP _____

I bought this book because: _____

_____

I purchased this book from:

☐ A bookstore (Name _____)

☐ A software or electronics store (Name _____)

☐ A mail order (Name of Catalog _____)

I purchase this many computer books each year:

☐ 1–5   ☐ 6 or more

I currently use these applications: _____

_____

_____

_____

I found these chapters to be the most informative: _____

_____

I found these chapters to be the least informative: _____

_____

Additional comments: _____

_____

☐ I would like to see my name in print! You may use my name and quote me in future New Riders products and promotions. My daytime phone number is:_____

New Riders Publishing 201 West 103rd Street • Indianapolis, Indiana 46290 USA

Fold Here

PLACE
STAMP
HERE

New Riders Publishing
201 West 103rd Street
Indianapolis, Indiana 46290
USA

WANT MORE INFORMATION?

CHECK OUT THESE RELATED TITLES:

	QTY	PRICE	TOTAL
Inside Novell NetWare, Special Edition. This #1 selling tutorial/reference is perfect for beginning system administrators. Each network management task is thoroughly explained and potential trouble spots are noted. The book also includes a disk with an extremely easy to use workstation menu program, an MHS capable E-Mail program, and workgroup management tools. ISBN: 1-56205-096-6.	_____	$34.95	_____
NetWare 4: New Business Strategies. The ultimate guide to planning, installing, and managing a NetWare 4.0 network. This book explains how best to implement the new features of NetWare 4.0 and how to upgrade to NetWare 4.0 as easily and efficiently as possible. ISBN: 1-56205-159-8.	_____	$27.95	_____
Downsizing to NetWare. Get the real story on downsizing with *Downsizing to NetWare*. This book identifies applications that are suitable for use on LANs and shows how to implement downsizing projects. This book lists the strengths and weaknesses of NetWare—making it perfect for managers and system administrators. ISBN: 1-56205-071-0.	_____	$39.95	_____
LAN Operating Systems. Learn how to connect the most popular LAN operating systems. All major LAN operating systems are covered, including: NetWare 3.11, Appleshare 3.0, Banyan VINES 5.0, UNIX, LAN Manger 2.1, and popular peer-to-peer networks. The following client operating systems are covered as well: MS-DOS, Windows, OS/2, Macintosh System 7, and UNIX. This book clears up the confusion associated with managing large networks with diverse client workstations and multiple LAN operating systems. ISBN: 1-56205-054-0.	_____	$39.95	_____

Name _____

Company _____

Address _____

City _____ State ____ ZIP _____

Phone _____ Fax _____

☐ Check Enclosed ☐ VISA ☐ MasterCard

Card #_____Exp. Date _____

Signature _____

Prices are subject to change. Call for availability and pricing information on latest editions.

Subtotal _____

Shipping _____

$4.00 for the first book and $1.75 for each additional book.

Total _____
Indiana residents add 5% sales tax.

New Riders Publishing 201 West 103rd Street • Indianapolis, Indiana 46290 USA

Orders/Customer Service: 1-800-428-5331
Fax: 1-800-448-3804

Fold Here

PLACE
STAMP
HERE

New Riders Publishing
201 West 103rd Street
Indianapolis, Indiana 46290
USA

Become a CNE with Help from a Pro!

The NetWare Training Guides are specifically designed and authored to help you prepare for the **Certified NetWare Engineer** exam.

NetWare Training Guide: Managing NetWare Systems

This book clarifies the CNE testing process and provides hints on the best ways to prepare for the CNE examinations. *NetWare Training Guide: Managing NetWare Systems* covers the following sections of the CNE exams:

● NetWare 2.2 System Manager

● NetWare 2.2 Advanced System Manager

● NetWare 3.*x* System Manager

● NetWare 3.*x* Advanced System Manager

ISBN: 1-56205-069-9, **$69.95 USA**

NetWare Training Guide: Networking Technology

This book covers more advanced topics and prepares you for the tough hardware and service/support exams. The following course materials are covered:

● MS-DOS

● Microcomputer Concepts

● Service and Support

● Networking Technologies

ISBN: 1-56205-145-8, **$69.95 USA**

OPERATING SYSTEMS

INSIDE MS-DOS 6.2, 2E

NEW RIDERS PUBLISHING

A complete tutorial and reference!

MS-DOS 6.2

ISBN: 1-56205-289-6

$34.95 USA

DOS FOR NON-NERDS

MICHAEL GROH

Understanding this popular operating system is easy with this humorous, step-by-step tutorial.

Through DOS 6.0

ISBN: 1-56205-151-2

$18.95 USA

INSIDE SCO UNIX

STEVE GLINES, PETER SPICER, BEN HUNSBERGER, & KAREN WHITE

Everything users need to know to use the UNIX operating system for everyday tasks.

SCO Xenix 286, SCO Xenix 386, SCO UNIX/System V 386

ISBN: 1-56205-028-1

$29.95 USA

INSIDE SOLARIS SunOS

KARLA SAARI KITALONG, STEVEN R. LEE, & PAUL MARZIN

Comprehensive tutorial and reference to SunOS!

SunOS, Sun's version of UNIX for the SPARC workstation, version 2.0

ISBN: 1-56205-032-X

$29.95 USA

WINDOWS TITLES

ULTIMATE WINDOWS 3.1
FORREST HOULETTE

The most up-to-date reference for
Windows available!

Covers 3.1 and related products

ISBN: 1-56205-125-3

$39.95 USA

INSIDE WINDOWS NT
JOHN STODDARD

A complete tutorial and reference to
organize and manage multiple tasks
and multiple programs in Windows.

Windows NT

ISBN: 1-56205-124-5

$39.95 USA

WINDOWS FOR NON-NERDS
JIM BOYCE

This helpful tutorial for Windows
provides novice users with what they
need to know to gain computer
proficiency...and confidence!

Windows 3.1

ISBN: 1-56205-152-0

$18.95 USA

INTEGRATING WINDOWS APPLICATIONS
ELLEN DANA NAGLER, FORREST HOULETTE,
MICHAEL GROH, RICHARD WAGNER, &
VALDA HILLEY

This book is a no-nonsense, practical
approach for intermediate- and
advanced-level Windows users!

Windows 3.1

ISBN: 1-56205-083-4

$34.95 USA

To Order, Call 1-800-428-5331

GRAPHICS TITLES

INSIDE CORELDRAW! 4.0, SPECIAL EDITION

DANIEL GRAY

An updated version of the #1 best-selling tutorial on CorelDRAW!

CorelDRAW! 4.0

ISBN: 1-56205-164-4

$34.95 USA

CORELDRAW! SPECIAL EFFECTS

NEW RIDERS PUBLISHING GROUP-BRICKLEY

An inside look at award-winning techniques from professional CorelDRAW! designers!

CorelDRAW! 4.0

ISBN: 1-56205-123-7

$39.95 USA

CORELDRAW! NOW!

RICHARD FELDMAN

The hands-on tutorial for users who want practical information now!

CorelDRAW! 4.0

ISBN: 1-56205-131-8

$21.95 USA

INSIDE CORELDRAW! FOURTH EDITION

DANIEL GRAY

The popular tutorial approach to learning CorelDRAW!...with complete coverage of version 3.0!

CorelDRAW! 3.0

ISBN: 1-56205-106-7

$24.95 USA